A Psychodynamic Understanding of Modern Medicine

placing the person at the center of care

Edited by

MAUREEN O'REILLY-LANDRY PhD
Assistant Clinical Professor of Medical Psychology (in Psychiatry),
Columbia University College of Physicians and Surgeons,
New York, USA

Foreword by

MYRON L WEISFELDT MD
William Osler Professor of Medicine
Chair, Department of Medicine
Johns Hopkins University School of Medicine
Baltimore, MD, USA

Radcliffe Publishing
London • New York

Radcliffe Publishing Ltd
33–41 Dallington Street
London
EC1V 0BB
United Kingdom

www.radcliffepublishing.com

British Library Cataloguing in Publication Data

A catalogue record for this book is available from the British Library.

ISBN-13: 978 184619 519 8

The paper used for the text pages of this book is FSC® certified. FSC (The Forest Stewardship Council®) is an international network to promote responsible management of the world's forests.

Typeset by Phoenix Photosetting, Chatham, Kent, UK
Printed and bound by TJI Digital, Padstow, Cornwall, UK

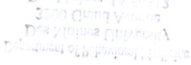

Contents

Foreword

The last time the modern physician had the luxury to contemplate patient motivation was likely in medical school. Like most physicians today, I have often thought that some of the most age-old and esteemed skills of doctoring have been lost to today's fast-paced world of medicine. Thirty-five years ago, when I was an intern caring for patients who had survived a major heart attack (now called an acute ST elevation myocardial infarction or STEMI), I would spend hours at their bedside for weeks at a time. In those days, STEMI survivors stayed in the hospital for six weeks but aside from monitoring them for arrhythmias, we didn't have many therapies to improve their outlook. Most of my patients were male, in their 50s, in the prime of life, with children and a wife who depended on their support. I had to tell patients they were facing a catastrophic illness – 20% would die in the hospital, another 20% would die within a year. That obviously generated a huge amount of fear and stress, both for my patients and for me. But seeing these patients and their families every day, I felt I could understand their obvious fears and unspoken feelings, and the effect of the illness on their families. I believe my support and suggestions were valuable to the patients and families.

Now we have much better treatments. Within 90 minutes of appearing in the emergency department, patients are whisked into the cath lab where we perform an angioplasty to get rid of the clot that caused the heart attack. Ninety-eight percent will leave the hospital alive, usually in two or three days, and 96% of those will survive at least one year. I would not want to trade these treatments for the ones we had 35 years ago. In fact, I am proud of my role in establishing the value of some of these treatments in my own clinical research and in helping to guide their adoption during the time I led the American Heart Association as President. Today, aside from occasional 15-minute office visits, physicians do not see their patients very much. They do not have time to contemplate the hidden issues that may be preventing patients from taking their pills, for example, or to address their fears aroused by internet-based information on the risks of another heart attack, heart failure or sudden death. Instead, we've become much more comfortable talking about their laboratory and imaging results. We expound on the latest clinical trial that treated thousands of similar patients. The discussion is occasionally salted with demographic correlates of success or failure, side-effects or adverse outcomes, and then it is on to the next patient. But being a good clinician is more complicated than simply making the right diagnosis or writing the correct prescription. Our comfort and support, our listening and understanding are just as vital in the therapeutic relationship and to the patient's wellbeing.

In *A Psychodynamic Understanding of Modern Medicine*, Maureen O'Reilly-Landry has put together a remarkable volume that will help physicians to step back and consider the illness through the eyes of their patients and establish a better therapeutic alliance. Do not let the word 'psychodynamic' put you off. This is not a book filled with psychoanalytic ideas and jargon unfamiliar to practicing physicians, nurses or technicians. The authors are all experts in psychoanalytic theory but they are also clinicians who are involved in the day-to-day care of patients with complex and chronic medical illnesses. Again and again, the authors depict the conditions and circumstances in which psychological insight and a care strategy are challenging and important. From the teenager on kidney dialysis who rejects her nurses' attempts to help her insert her needles, to the successful young lawyer who has to scale back her career ambitions in the face of lupus, to the patient who simply misses his appointment, clinicians will recognize their own patients in the examples that are poignantly discussed in each chapter. I read the book in days, not my usual weeks, as I became fascinated by the diversity of conditions, insights and approaches to these serious everyday problems. And for the lay person who picks up this eminently readable book, they will recognize themselves, their families, and their medical caregivers, to good effect.

Much to the credit of the many authors and authorities who provide chapters, the presentation in this compendium is often 'case-based learning.' As most physicians are aware, much more is retained about a condition or strategy when there is a real patient presented. At Medical Grand Rounds at Johns Hopkins, discussions of current patients, or even interviews with real patients, instill in physicians the gravity and context of the clinical problem. In my view this book succeeds, like Grand Rounds at Hopkins, in making a deep impression on physicians.

There is an important message conveyed in each chapter: that much of what goes on in the patient–clinician relationship is hidden beneath the surface. Attention to these concealed feelings – not just the patients' but also our own – can only improve our patients' lives and the quality of their care. The book is also a reminder to busy clinicians that they need not go it alone when dealing with the interpersonal and psychological dimensions of their patients. There are trained mental health professionals who understand the stresses of the modern medical environment, and can be employed in medical settings to assist patients and practitioners.

Those of us still involved with medical students and trainees know that these interpersonal issues frequently cross the minds of the youngest members of our profession. But unfortunately, as teachers, most of us are relatively ill equipped to guide them. This volume fills that void and can help every health care provider to understand how they can build effective therapeutic partnerships with their patients.

Myron L Weisfeldt MD
William Osler Professor of Medicine
Chair, Department of Medicine
Physician-in-Chief, Johns Hopkins Hospital
Johns Hopkins University School of Medicine
Baltimore, MD

Preface

In this book, modern psychoanalysts analyze modern medicine. These skilled observers turn their well-trained eyes to the interpersonal and psychological dimensions of medical care in its current context of specialization and advanced science and technology. Trained in psychoanalysis or psychodynamic theory, all authors work in medical settings where they either treat or study medical patients and practitioners. They are essentially medical anthropologists – participant-observers who are themselves embedded in the culture they are studying. As psychoanalysts, they are able to peek beneath the surface to glimpse the unconscious and covert psychological processes that occur commonly, and frequently present problems, in the current system of medical care.

Authors range from those with national and international reputations, to the ordinary but wise and experienced clinical practitioners who gently probe their subjects in order to better understand health care phenomena at their deepest levels. Their insights are rooted in psychodynamic theories such as classical, relational or interpersonal psychoanalysis, or integrated with attachment theory or neuroscience. Each chapter assists the reader to understand the complex process of interacting subjectivities in which well-meaning yet anxious people on both sides of the medical relationship are doing the best they can to cope with situations that nonetheless threaten to overwhelm them. The book examines the psychological impact of the rapid advancement in the practice of medicine and the effect these changes have on patients, families, and medical practitioners themselves. These psychoanalysts examine the human side of a discipline that has been able to harness science to save people and enhance the quality of their lives while it has also moved away from the practice of medicine as simply a humane art.

The idea for the book arose from my work as team psychologist on a chronic dialysis unit, where I discovered I was able to use my psychoanalytic training to better understand the dialysis patients and their families, as well as their interactions with the doctors, nurses, and other medical clinicians as, together, they faced issues of life, death, and disease. I presented a paper at conferences about the experiences of patients and staff when a patient on a dialysis unit dies. A second paper focused on the real and fantasied relationships that can arise in the context of organ failure, such as between organ donor and recipient, and between human being and life-sustaining machinery. Both papers appear in this volume. At these conferences, I discovered that other psychoanalysts were having similar experiences in medical settings, where their knowledge of subjectivity, psychological defenses and unconscious processes enabled them to arrive at insights that were lost to those who attend only to measurable surface behaviors. Clearly, there was a place for the voices and insights of the psychoanalyst.

Psychoanalysis and modern medicine, at first glance, appear to exert opposing forces – psychoanalysis with a regressive pull to the past and modern medicine, thorough science and technology, pushing to the future. Yet many psychoanalysts and psychodynamically trained clinicians work in medical settings or with ill people, where they make valuable contributions. I believe the chapters in this book demonstrate the clinical usefulness of attending to the subjective, interpersonal, symbolic and unconscious aspects of modern medical care.

This book is designed to provide a useful and insightful resource for readers seeking to better understand the psychological and interpersonal issues pertinent to giving and receiving medical care. It has special relevance to health psychologists, consultation liaison psychiatrists, and medical social workers, all of whom intervene in medical situations at the level of the psychological and the interpersonal. Medical practitioners such as physicians, nurses and technicians in any medical setting should benefit from the insights put forth in the book. The book is, in its own way, an example of medical anthropology and as such, should benefit those with interest or expertise in this area of inquiry. The book would be useful as a supplemental textbook in graduate courses in clinical psychology, health psychology, psychiatry and other residency programs, nursing and social work programs, as well as in psychoanalytic training programs. Further, patients, caregivers and all other professionals who interface with the field of clinical medicine will find the insights interesting and useful to read.

Modern medicine has accrued great knowledge and developed powerful tools to better enable our healers to heal us. But it has also placed strain on all participants in the medical encounter – clinician, patient and caregiver. This book is a collection of chapters, each of which views an aspect of modern medical care through a psychoanalytic lens. Each chapter provides a means to understand this psychological strain and makes suggestions for managing it.

Chapter 1 examines the impact of the interpersonal and the psychological on the field of medicine as it is practiced in the 21st century, and discusses why psychoanalytic ideas can be usefully applied in this arena. Chapter 2 provides a brief introduction to some important psychodynamic concepts as they appear in the book. Chapters 3–8 examine the subjective experience, both conscious and unconscious, of medical patients, and the personal meaning of having an illness or being under medical care. Chapters 9–13 discuss important aspects of the relationship between patient and medical provider and the psychological influence patient and provider have on one another. Chapters 14–16 look at the novel relationships that have arisen from the integration of technology and medicine, along with the concomitant capacity of people to donate or lend their bodies and body parts to others. Chapters 17–20 examine the many ways in which families are affected when a member becomes ill, and the impact of caregiver and medical personnel on each other's psyches.

Many people and entities have been instrumental to the development of this book. First are the chapter authors, who were chosen for their deep knowledge of psychodynamic theories combined with expertise in some aspect of modern medical care. Editing this book has enabled me to bring together clinicians and researchers from disparate professional cultures and areas of specialization (psychology, psychiatry, medicine, pediatrics, family practice, dentistry), with the goal of helping to reunite the art of medical practice with its science. Google enabled me to discover and assemble this diverse group of authors. If not for the internet, how could a psychologist on the Upper West Side of Manhattan ever know about a psychoanalytically trained dentist in Dundee, Scotland? The Psychoanalytic Society of the Postdoctoral Program in Psychotherapy and Psychoanalysis awarded me a Scholar's Grant for this project. This was valuable as much for the monetary support as for the fact that once I received it, there was no turning back – now I had to finish the book. Thanks also go to Gillian Nineham and Jessica Morofke at Radcliffe Publishing: Gillian, who saw fit to decide to publish this book, and especially to Jessica, who was always available to troubleshoot any number of issues and problems along the way to completion.

Mike Sloma first brought to my attention the many psychological challenges experienced by dialysis patients and families, and provided me with my first opportunity to work with this wonderful group of patients and families. The Consultation-Liaison Service at Columbia University warmly welcomed me to their fold and invited me to their Journal Club where I learned, among many things, something about how psychiatrists think. This experience inspired the idea for this book. The staffs at the Columbia University/Davita and the St John's Episcopal Hospital dialysis centers deserve recognition for their sensitivity to the psychological needs of medical patients. With this book, I acknowledge and honor the patients and families at these centers for their strength in dealing with the new twist to their lives that dialysis has wrought, and to all the patients in this book whose stories are told. I am grateful to the Columbia University Seminar on Death for the opportunity to present the book proposal in its early stages.

The following people helped by reading or discussing aspects of the book at various stages along the way: Fran Anderson, Lew Aron, Susan Conova, Don Kornfeld, Don Landry, Jeff Lieberman, Ellen Luborsky, Jay Meltzer, Juan Oliver, Anne O'Reilly, Janet Plotkin-Bornstein and Pat Vitacco. Above all, I want to convey my greatest love and appreciation to my husband, Don, and my children, Chris and Michael, for supporting and tolerating my intense engagement with this project. Don has been involved from the beginning. He was my first liaison to the medical world and he also spent many hours discussing and reading drafts of the book, from proposal to final manuscript. But above all, he is the model of the caring and dedicated physician, husband, father and human being. Watching him in these various roles has been a source of inspiration for me, for this book, and for the way I try to conduct my life. It is to my wonderful family that I dedicate this book.

A note about confidentiality: various methods have been used to protect patients' identities. In most cases, identifying information was significantly changed or omitted, so that the patient will not be recognizable. Some authors blended together two or more people so that, while the story is essentially true, the specific patient does not actually exist. In the very small number of instances in which the identity could not be completely protected, the patient granted permission for his or her still partially disguised story to be used.

About the editor

Maureen O'Reilly-Landry, PhD, is Assistant Clinical Professor of Medical Psychology (in Psychiatry) at the Columbia University College of Physicians and Surgeons in New York City, where she is part of the Psychiatry Consultation-Liaison service and works with medical patients on chronic dialysis and their families and caregivers.

Dr O'Reilly-Landry received her PhD in Clinical Psychology from New York University. Her Psychology Internship and Fellowship were spent at Cambridge Hospital/Harvard Medical School, in Cambridge, MA and she graduated *summa cum laude* in Psychology and Social Relations from Harvard-Radcliffe College. She has taught and supervised Psychological Assessment and Testing in various doctoral psychology programs. She is a graduate of the New York University Postdoctoral Program in Psychotherapy and Psychoanalysis, where she also completed an Advanced Specialization in Couple and Family Therapy.

She maintains a general private practice in New York City where she sees individuals and couples, including many patients and caregivers coping with the stress and trauma of having a medical condition, as well as medical professionals. She also does psychological assessments, psychoeducational evaluations and parent guidance. She lives in New York City with her husband and two sons.

Contributors

Pauline Boss PhD
Professor Emeritus, Department of Family Social Science, University of Minnesota, Saint Paul, MN, Private Practice in Family Therapy

Diane Ehrensaft PhD
Reproductive Technology Study/Research Group, Psychoanalytic Institute of Northern California, Oakland, CA, Private Practice, Oakland, CA

Peter Fonagy PhD FBA
Freud Memorial Professor of Psychoanalysis and Head of Department, Research Department of Clinical, Educational and Health Psychology, University College, London, Chief Executive, Anna Freud Centre, London

John R. Freedy MD PhD
Director, Behavioral Science Curriculum, Trident/MUSC Family Medicine Residency, Associate Professor of Family Medicine, Medical University of South Carolina (MUSC), Charleston, SC, Council, American Balint Society

Ruth Freeman BDS PhD MMedSc
Professor of Dental Public Health Research, Director of the Oral Health and Health Research Programme, Clinical and Population Sciences and Education, University of Dundee, Dundee, Scotland

Suzanne Garfinkle MD MSc
Fellow, Child and Adolescent Psychiatry, Mount Sinai School of Medicine, New York, Private Practice, New York

Jon J. Hunter BSc MD FRCPC
Associate Professor, University of Toronto Department of Psychiatry, Head, Consultation-Liaison Service, Mount Sinai Hospital, Toronto

Tamara McClintock Greenberg PsyD MS
Associate Clinical Professor of Psychiatry, University of California, San Francisco, CA, Private Practice, San Francisco, CA

Richard Kradin MD MS (Chemical Physics) DTM&H (London)
Departments of Medicine and Pathology, Massachusetts General Hospital Center for Psychoanalytical Studies, Boston, MA, Analyst, C.G. Jung Institute, Boston, MA, Associate Professor, Harvard Medical School, Boston, MA

Susan Kraemer PhD
Clinical Instructor in Psychology, Psychiatry and Pediatrics, Columbia University College of Physicians and Surgeons, Faculty: Parent-Infant Psychotherapy Training Program, Columbia University Center for Psychoanalytic Training and Research, New York, Private Practice, New York

Albert Lichtenstein PhD LMFT
Director of Behavioral Science, Guthrie Family Medicine Residency, Guthrie Clinic/Robert Packer Hospital, Sayre, PA, President-Elect, American Balint Society

Ruth H. Livingston PhD
Director, Living with Medical Conditions Study Group and Referral Service, William Alanson White Institute, New York, Private Practice, New York

Ellen B. Luborsky PhD
Independent Writer/Consultant in Early Childhood, Private Practice, New York

Norka T. Malberg DPsych
Anna Freud Centre, London, Private Practice, New Haven, CT

Robert G. Maunder MD FRCPC
Associate Professor, University of Toronto Department of Psychiatry, Psychiatrist, Mount Sinai Hospital, Toronto, Canada

Philip R. Muskin MD
Professor of Clinical Psychiatry, Columbia University College of Physicians and Surgeons, Chief of Service: Consultation-Liaison Psychiatry, New York-Presbyterian Hospital, Columbia Campus, Faculty: Columbia University Psychoanalytic Center, New York, Private Practice, New York

Donald E. Nease Jr MD
Associate Director, Practice Based Research, Associate Clinical Professor Department of Family Medicine, University of Colorado-Denver, Colorado Health Outcomes, Denver, CO

Maureen O'Reilly-Landry PhD
Assistant Clinical Professor of Medical Psychology (in Psychiatry), Columbia University College of Physicians and Surgeons, New York, Private Practice, New York

Janet Plotkin-Bornstein PhD
Private Practice, New York

Shara Sand PsyD
Assistant Professor of Psychology, LaGuardia Community College, The City University of New York, New York, Private Practice, New York

C. Paul Scott MD DLFAPA
Clinical Professor of Psychiatry, University of Pittsburgh School of Medicine, Pittsburgh, PA, Private Practice, Pittsburgh, PA

Peter A. Shapiro MD
Professor of Clinical Psychiatry, Columbia University College of Physicians and Surgeons; Director, Fellowship Training Program in Psychosomatic Medicine, New York-Presbyterian Hospital Columbia University Medical Center, New York

Anne Skomorowsky MD
Assistant Professor of Clinical Psychiatry, Columbia University College of Physicians and Surgeons, Barbara Jonas Psychiatric Hospitalist, New York-Presbyterian Hospital, New York

Zina Steinberg EdD
Assistant Clinical Professor of Medical Psychology (in Psychiatry and Pediatrics), Faculty: Parent-Infant Program, Columbia Center for Psychoanalytic Training and Research, Columbia University College of Physicians and Surgeons, New York, Private Practice, New York

Jeffrey L. Sternlieb PhD
Psychologist, Lehigh Valley Hospital FPRP, Allentown, PA, Clinical Assistant Professor, Pennsylvania State University College of Medicine, President, Metaworks, Inc., Wyomissing, PA, President, American Balint Society

Patricia B. Vitacco PsyD
Private Practice, New York

List of abbreviations

ART	assisted reproductive technology
CCRT	core conflictual relationship theme method
DSM	*Diagnostic and Statistical Manual of Mental Disorders*
ECT	electroconvulsive therapy
ER	emergency room
ESRD	end-stage renal disease
FEV_1	forced expiratory volume in 1 second
GLBTQ	gay, lesbian, bisexual, transgender or queer
ICU	intensive care unit
IVF	*in vitro* fertilization
MS	multiple sclerosis
NICU	neonatal intensive care unit
NSAID	non-steroidal anti-inflammatory drug
OCD	obsessive compulsive disorder
PDM	*Psychodynamic Diagnostic Manual*
PTSD	post-traumatic stress disorder

SECTION I
Introduction

CHAPTER 1

The Interpersonal and Psychological Dimensions of Modern Medicine

Maureen O'Reilly-Landry

For centuries, the effective doctor was a trusted authority figure, empathic and wise. The primary role of the early physician was to comfort and console. Healing, such as it was, lay more in the relationship to the patient than in the application of the science, as there was until recently very little good medical science to apply. New therapies posed grave risks in an age prior to the protection of a Food and Drug Administration, accepted standards for evidence-based medical treatment, and mandates for informed consent. Yet so potent were the relational aspects of care that the physician could be revered despite the likes of leeches and blood letting, among other well-intentioned but ultimately destructive primitive medical modalities and practices.

The modern explosion in biomedical science and technology changed everything. The tools currently available to medical practitioners have vastly improved their power to truly heal and have minimized the likelihood of inflicting serious harm. But incorporation of advanced science and technology into medical practice came at a price: the diminution of the once revered interpersonal aspects of care. In privileging science, a lesser emphasis came to be placed on understanding a patient's psychology and relational context, to the detriment of medical practice.

In this chapter, I will address two questions. First, why study the interpersonal and psychological dimensions of modern medicine? Second, how can insights derived from psychoanalysis be applied to modern medical practice?

WHY STUDY THE INTERPERSONAL AND PSYCHOLOGICAL DIMENSIONS OF MODERN MEDICINE?

As the body of knowledge in a field increases, so do division and fragmentation. Nowhere is this more obvious than in the practice of medicine, wherein the volume of medical information has long surpassed the hope of any single practitioner to master it. Thus arose the need for specialists. Doctors may narrow their focus to one particular organ system, a single disease entity or a specific medical procedure. Nurses are required to have specialized training for a high-tech setting, such as an intensive care unit. Social workers may specialize in counseling and social services for specific medical populations, such as those on chronic dialysis. While underpinning great improvements in health and survival, the necessary result of such specialization has been a fragmentation in the care itself. Medical specialists risk losing contact with the whole patient and may regard themselves as treating a body part rather than a person, which may in turn be manifest in the self-experience of the patient, e.g. 'I take my kidneys to the kidney doctor and my eyes to the eye doctor.' In the 21st century, mind and body have never appeared so separate, while being so intricately intertwined.

In addition to multiple doctors, the modern patient also encounters an overwhelming array of nurses, nurse's aides, physician's assistants, medical technicians, pharmacists, psychologists, social workers, occupational therapists, physical therapists, patient care co-ordinators, secretaries, patient advocates, hospital volunteers and home health aides, all having direct contact with the patient. And the complexity encompasses institutions and enterprises that include managed care organizations, hospital administrations, insurance companies, medical ethics boards, medical researchers, pharmaceutical companies, charities and philanthropic donors, the Department of Health, the United States Congress and the Office of the President of the United States, all with influence over the type of medical care a patient will receive.

Modern medicine has ushered in a new type of relationship, one without precedent, but upon which a patient's life or quality of life may depend: the relationship to those who donate their bodies or body parts, including blood donors, organ donors, and surrogate mothers. And as a consequence of advanced technology, patients now develop very close and highly dependent relationships with inanimate objects. While there have always been medicines, there are now electric wheelchairs, prostheses, incubators, dialyzers, respirators, ventricular assist devices and extracorporeal membrane oxygenators, all of which evoke strong reactions from the patients who use them. With cosmetic surgery, even people who are not sick become willing recipients of medical care and develop a relationship with the medical profession.

And patients are not sick in a vacuum. There are the spouses and partners, parents, children, siblings and caregivers, who are always affected when a family member becomes ill. Finally, and rarely mentioned, are the relational connections of family and friends of medical professionals, whose lives may also be deeply affected by medical practice.

Thus, advances in biomedical science and technology are having a far-ranging effect on our relationships and our individual psychologies. They have brought medical personnel and institutions into our relational matrix more than ever before, while at the same time, an ever-increasing need for caregivers for the chronically ill medicalizes many of our most intimate relationships. Clearly, the interpersonal and psychological dimensions of medical practice demand our attention as never before

In 2004, the Institute of Medicine recognized the importance of the psychological and interpersonal dimensions in the practice of medicine and deemed the following to be the top five topics for reform of the medical school curriculum:

➤ mind–body interactions in health and disease
➤ patient behavior
➤ physician role and behavior
➤ physician–patient interactions
➤ social and cultural issues in health care.[1]

This book addresses each of these topics, with particular emphasis on patient behavior, physician role and behavior, and physician–patient interactions, with specific attention paid to the interpersonal, subjective and unconscious dimensions of behavior in a wide variety of medical settings. Behavioral scientists and clinicians can play an important role in this enterprise.[2]

Modern medicine, though powerful, is effective only when the patient actually makes proper use of it. The failure of patients to follow medical recommendations is a source of great concern for medical professionals and has inspired an extensive literature. Patients frequently avoid going to the doctor despite obvious need, refuse recommended procedures, and neglect to follow prescribed diets or to take prescribed medications. With some serious medical conditions, a great deal of effort must be expended just to stay alive, but patients are not always disposed to make this investment. Conversely, some patients look to fulfill some of their own psychological and relational needs by overusing medical resources.[3]

Medical non-compliance for organ transplant recipients is estimated at 20–50%[4] and such non-adherence to medical protocol not uncommonly leads to organ rejection for kidney transplant patients.[5,6] Shapiro *et al*[7] found that in a pretransplant interview, psychiatrists were able to identify in advance those patients who were less likely to follow their medical regimen and were therefore more likely to die as a result of this non-adherence. Nurses, because of their often close and frequent contact with patients, can play a major role in patient adherence. Cameron suggests that nurses and other clinicians take a history of a patient's compliance in order to better understand the factors that contribute to this lack of self-care.[8] Van Hecke *et al*, for example, found that it was often poor communication or patient misunderstanding about expectations, rather than lack of motivation, that resulted in non-adherence in patients with leg ulcers.[9]

A visit with a medical professional, particularly regarding a serious illness, can be fraught with anxiety for both patient and clinician. A problem not often appreciated is that such anxiety may impair a patient's ability to think clearly and reduces the capacity to take in, process, and recall important information. This often leads to the doctor or nurse believing that she has communicated information that the patient claims never to have heard.

It is common to have complex responses to illness, whether one's own illness or that of others.[10-12] The particular reaction will depend on the personal meaning the illness has for the person reacting to it and varies from person to person. When medical clinicians can be aware of such reactions in their patients, they can help to understand perplexing patient behavior and to intervene effectively. Moerman has named this multifaceted dimension of medical care 'the meaning response.'[13] Charon proposes that the capacity of physicians to elicit and grasp a patient's personal story of meaning, rather than a mere chronology of his symptoms, makes for a much more effective doctor.[14,15] This type of 'narrative medicine' is becoming more difficult to practice. Modern physicians are under pressure from insurance companies and from the health organizations that employ them to see more patients in less time, leaving little opportunity to listen for and elicit the meaning behind their patients' stories. Reimbursement is far greater for the performance of a procedure than for a doctor–patient interaction that involves talking, even when the talking has the greatest importance, such as an effort to understand why the patient is not taking her life-sustaining medication or to find out from a relative whether an 80-year-old man who lives alone is remembering to turn off the stove. Such interventions are no less life-altering for the patient than a procedure, and they can only be accomplished through a process of asking and listening.

Although its value has long been recognized and is now being supported by research, over time the relational aspect of medical care has become devalued. In general, caregiving and relationship-based activities, most often conducted by women, are held in lower esteem and pay less than non-caregiving professions and disciplines. Possibly a similar trend is being reflected in the strong privileging of the more stereotypically masculine, technological aspects of modern medical care over its relational dimension.

While illness and suffering can have personal significance for a patient, the act of healing has meaning as well. The medical efficacy of placebos highlights the extent to which meaning in the practice of medicine is a powerful force unto itself. There is a whole psychology to the mere act of taking medication.[16] Inert blue pills, for example, are more sedating than pink ones, two placebo pills work better than one, and a placebo delivered intravenously has a more powerful effect than when it is in pill form.[17,18] Further, people are more likely to take medication when it is in capsules, rather than tablets.[19] Clearly, the formal characteristics of medical treatment can powerfully affect a patient's medical behavior and outcome.

Not only patients but doctors, nurses, other medical clinicians and family caregivers have their own personal reactions to illness. Those who chose a profession related to medicine may have done so precisely because of the power it bestows to heal the sick and the suffering. On the other hand, family caregivers often find their role thrust upon them, demanded by life circumstances, and so may have a very different reaction to caring for a sick person. That which a clinician regards as professional fulfillment may be experienced by a family member as chronic stress. An illness that is chronic and debilitating can have a profound effect on family dynamics.[20] Family members must cope with the changes the illness causes in their loved one, and potentially with changes in their roles and in their relationship to the ill family member. Stressed caregivers not only have increased depression and anxiety[21] but also poorer physical health and greater susceptibility to infection[22-24] and even slower wound healing[25] than caregivers who report less stress. Further, caregivers who are both depressed and demonstrate a lack of respectful behavior may be at risk for elder abuse and neglect.[26] Thus, high caregiver stress can lead to depression which, under the right circumstances, may lead to harmful behavior. Attention to caregiver wellbeing is therefore essential to the safety and wellbeing of the vulnerable patient.

The impact of the doctor himself on the healing process has long been recognized[27] and later scientific studies have confirmed the importance of the physician–patient relationship and communication on health outcomes.[28] Drawing on research suggesting that positive relationships have a positive effect on immune function and overall health, Adler suggests that positive social engagement in a relationship as significant as that of doctor and patient can be a health-enhancing experience, even apart from the specific content of what gets discussed or what gets done during the office visit.[29] A patient's own personal history may affect the manner in which she presents to medical professionals or interacts with medical institutions, which may in turn affect the quality of care she receives.[30] It is of course not a one-way street. Medical clinicians can also be deeply affected by their work with patients, including their own mistakes and failures, and must develop ways to cope with these feelings. Kenworthy and Kirkham, for example, have written about profound grief in midwives, who frequently encounter the deaths of babies in the course of their work, and must contend with their own grief as well as that of the mothers for whom they are caring.[31]

Problems can arise at a number of levels when doctor and patient interact – or when they fail to do so. The clinician's behavior can carry a great deal of meaning for a patient, and even simple demonstrations of respect and concern can go a long way in building the bond between them. Kahn refers to this as 'etiquette-based medicine.'[32] The physician's mere act of sitting down at the hospital bedside, rather than remaining standing, for example, results in patient perceptions that the doctor is more compassionate and that she has spent more time with the patient.[33] Further, both practitioner and patient develop defenses against anxieties related to sickness, death or failure to heal, and may respond by blaming or distancing themselves from one another. Overt disagreements may occur, but problems can also arise as a result of unrecognized clashes of meaning between doctor and patient.

For example, what makes a medical intervention effective, and who decides whether or not it has worked? In the *New England Journal of Medicine*, Wechsler *et al* reported a study in which asthma patients showed improved airflow (measured by forced expiratory volume in 1 second (FEV_1)) when treated with an albuterol inhaler.[34] No such improvement in FEV_1 occurred with placebo or sham acupuncture or when patients received no treatment at all. However, patients reported the same degree of subjective improvement whether they received albuterol, placebo or sham acupuncture. The study authors declared the patients' self-reports of improvement to be potentially unreliable insofar as they did not correspond to their FEV_1 status. But an editorial in the same journal issue criticized this dismissal of the patients' subjective reports,[35] pointing out that it was the subjective distress of wheezing and feelings of suffocation, not lowered FEV_1 levels, which brought the patients to the doctor in the first place. If the patient felt better even though his FEV_1 levels had not improved, whose definition of 'improved' should be considered to be accurate or true?

Meltzer points out that the doctor has great influence over whether a patient has a sense of being sickly or well, particularly in the case of chronic ambulatory illnesses.[36] An asymptomatic and only mildly hypertensive person, for example, may walk into the doctor's office feeling healthy but leave feeling ill because of a doctor's overzealous, unilateral decision to medicate a symptom that does not yet require medication. Meltzer advocates a more empowering stance that emphasizes physician–patient interaction, rather than a more traditional one-sided authoritarian approach in which a patient must comply with the doctor's orders.

Members of some medical disciplines are typically more action oriented and less reflective by nature, qualities that may well make them effective at their jobs.[37] But when this action orientation leads to a devaluing of the relational aspect of medical care, both physician and patient are deprived of the benefit of a satisfying doctor–patient relationship. Lack of introspection may also increase the potential for burnout on the part of the physician or feelings of abandonment on the part of the patient, especially during moments of high vulnerability, such as when facing the possibility of death.[38] Anxiety about sickness and death can be high for both patient and medical clinician and result in any number of defensive reactions, including the avoidance of difficult topics.

This stymied communication may then contribute to a sense of alienation that neither doctor nor patient desires.

HOW CAN INSIGHTS DERIVED FROM PSYCHOANALYSIS BE APPLIED TO MEDICAL PRACTICE IN THE 21ST CENTURY?

Originally trained as a neurologist, Sigmund Freud sought insights into the functions of the mind but, lacking modern brain-imaging techniques, he devised another means of figuring out what goes on inside a person's head. He turned to the subjective, internal psychological state of mind as his unit of study. Seeking to understand the human psyche at this deeper, hidden level, he pointed out the myriad ways people have of not knowing or feeling what they are too afraid to know or to feel.[39] An interpersonal psychoanalyst, Harry Stack Sullivan, described the phenomenon of 'selective inattention,' in which important aspects of our interpersonal interactions are actively excluded from conscious awareness because of the anxiety they might elicit.[40] Thus, it became clear that a good deal of psychological life occurs outside our awareness, and the notion of the unconscious rendered comprehensible some behavior previously seen as enigmatic or irrational. Freud was an investigator who put forth many ideas, so of course, some of them were wrong and some had only limited applicability, but enough were so profoundly informative that they became woven into the fabric of our thinking, no longer even credited to him. How often do we hear someone say, for example, 'You are being defensive' or 'I did that unconsciously'?

The development of psychoanalytic thought did not end with Freud and Freudian psychoanalysis spawned a number of theoretical progeny. (See Chapter 2 for a brief introduction to some useful psychoanalytic concepts.) Some later theories extended psychodynamic thinking to previously unstudied clinical populations, while others integrated psychoanalytic concepts with other perspectives. Psychodynamically oriented practitioners and researchers have developed the *Psychodynamic Diagnostic Manual* (PDM), a compilation of psychiatric disorders.[41] The PDM is based on an integration of psychodynamic theory with research from cognitive psychology, neuroscience and attachment theory, and provides a useful complement to the standard psychiatric diagnostic manual (*Diagnostic and Statistical Manual* – DSM).[42] Today, various commonly practiced psychodynamic psychotherapies are derivatives of psychoanalysis, including some short-term therapies.

Natural scientists have historically eschewed psychoanalytic ideas, perhaps because they have been difficult to study in the laboratory. But some neuroscientists, most notably Eric Kandel, the first fully trained psychiatrist to win the Nobel Prize, have maintained a broader perspective and aspects of neuroscience are adding a great deal to our understanding of how the mind works at the level of brain functioning.[43] New medical and technological innovations have provided a foundation for the emerging field of neuropsychoanalysis, making it possible to begin to understand what is happening in the nervous system during psychological trauma,[44] psychiatric disorders[45] and unconscious experiences.[46]

At the same time that psychodynamic theories were developing, other distinctly different psychological theories also arose, most prominently behaviorism. In an effort to attain objectivity and increased scientific rigor, the behaviorist approach emphasized measurement of observable behavior as the object of study, actively rejecting many aspects of psychology that are at the core of psychoanalysis. In discarding all insights derived from psychoanalytic ideas, much has been lost, including the ability to understand complex phenomena as they occur in the world of everyday life, in their natural state outside the well-controlled environment of the laboratory.

To the extent that psychoanalysis attempts to address subjects that are complex, ill defined and subjective, it does pose a difficult subject for research but studies have increasingly demonstrated the usefulness of psychoanalytically based approaches to psychotherapy.[47] Long-term psychodynamically oriented therapy is an effective treatment for psychological and psychiatric problems that are more complex, including personality disorders.[48,49] Further, therapeutic changes brought about through psychodynamically oriented psychotherapy are longer lasting than other empirically supported forms of treatment and the benefits increase with time.[50] A possible interpretation of this finding is that deeper internal change is more enduring than changes that are symptom focused and more superficial. Luborsky and Luborsky have delineated some specific psychoanalytically based concepts and interventions that have demonstrated clinical utility.[51]

Psychoanalysis is not only a therapeutic modality but also a valuable conceptual tool for understanding how people operate psychologically. As a 'depth psychology,' it attempts to understand the self and others at a level beyond surface behaviors. Relational and interpersonal psychoanalytic perspectives are particularly useful when attempting to understand a person's response to another. Concepts derived from these perspectives are frequently used in organizational psychology and have been used to analyze problems in health care utilization.[52] According to these relational theories, human beings have a primary and fundamental need to be in a relationship with others,[53] and the quality of our early relationships influences our later behavior, including our medical behavior. There is an extensive body of work demonstrating that insecurity in interpersonal attachments leads to higher risk of disease and difficult patient–provider relationships.[54,55] There is evidence that the number of adverse childhood events, including abuse and neglect, is correlated with a higher incidence of physical illness in adulthood.[56] Vaillant followed Harvard undergraduates from their college years until old age and demonstrated that the types of psychological defense mechanisms these men utilized while in college were related to their later physical and mental health, happiness and longevity.[57,58]

Having a serious illness allows many opportunities for self-destructive behavior, frequently through non-adherence to the prescribed medical regimen. An approach based on what is known about unconscious mental processes enables clinicians to address the many ways in which a patient might express unacknowledged wishes and conflicts through medical behavior, for example, by forgetting to take medication or attend doctor's appointments.

As a clinical practice, psychoanalysis, like clinical medicine, is idiographic; it seeks to understand the singular, unique individual person or interpersonal phenomenon. The basic sciences, whether natural or social, are nomothetic, seeking general laws and principles for how things work. They are reductionistic by design and intentionally remove the variables of interest from their real-world context in order to better characterize them. In contrast, clinical sciences and activities, while relying on what has been learned from nomothetic and reductionist approaches, require additional real-world data because these provide the context and specificity essential to understand fully the individual or interpersonal interaction. It has been suggested that research focusing on the single case study is perhaps a more suitable method of investigation for idiographic questions.[59] Therein lie the stories of personal meaning captured by narrative medicine, which has been likened to psychoanalysis.[60]

To the degree that it addresses the complexity and uniqueness of *in vivo* situations, an effective clinical approach utilizes, but then goes beyond, what has been empirically validated in the laboratory or the randomized controlled trial. Ideally, the goal would be to construct the 'medical narrative,' an integration of evidence-based and narrative medicine.[61] Clinical judgment, an often spontaneous integration of previously acquired factual information, observation, pathophysiology, clinical experience and, I would add, theory of mind, is necessary to most effectively elucidate a real-life problem or situation. As an illustration, consider a measurable example of useful clinical judgment of a basic type. Known as the 'surprise question,' it is a one-item measure in which dialysis nurses were asked 'Would you be surprised if this patient were to die within the year?' The chances of dying within one year were 3.5 times higher for patients in the 'no' group than in the 'yes' group.[62] This study has been replicated for cancer patients.[63] The surprise question in combination with certain actuarial data surpassed other measures in predicting mortality in the dialysis population,[64] reinforcing the conviction that undefined clinical judgment is a most valuable resource in patient care.

The ability to exercise judgment in social situations is a critical human ability. A vast literature from the field of social-cognitive development accumulated over the last four or five decades documents the way children come to acquire knowledge and make judgments about themselves and their physical and social environments. The capacity to make complex assessments about the physical environment is present from a very early age. Twelve-month-old infants, for example, are able to automatically integrate observation with abstract knowledge to make accurate predictions about unfamiliar, complex situations in their physical environment.[65] The authors of this study contend that the capacity to usefully integrate information from various sources in complex, real-life situations constitutes the essence of human intelligence. On the negative side, there is also now evidence from experimental psychology that many of our judgments of others are influenced by unconscious stereotyping and that these attitudes can over-ride more consciously held beliefs.[66] It also seems that our negative social judgments are often expressed through unconscious 'microaggressions,' which are subtle hostilities, condescension and failures of empathy, which may be either conscious or unconscious.[67] A physician's emotional state, for example, can affect her judgment and decision making with respect to determination of a patient's mental capacity for decision making.[68]

A perspective derived from knowledge of relational psychodynamics and attention to the mutual psychological interaction (intersubjectivity) and unconscious phenomena can be usefully adopted at many levels of medical care, both clinical and academic. First, researchers can continue to address issues of medical behavior with an eye toward understanding phenomena at a deeper level. Chapters by Maunder and Hunter, and by Kradin on attachment styles in the present volume are excellent examples of ways in which interpersonal relationships affect medical practice in multifaceted ways, and can be readily studied. Martin suggests an additional narrative-based approach to research.[69] Second, medical clinicians, especially physicians and nurses, can be educated about research regarding the interpersonal and psychological dimensions of medical care, including aspects of subjectivity and unconscious phenomena as they affect patients' medical behavior and the clinician–patient relationship. Third, mental health specialists working in medical settings, e.g. consultation liaison psychiatrists, health psychologists and medical social workers, can be similarly but more extensively trained in psychodynamic theory and research, so that they can be of assistance to patients and to other medical practitioners in their interactions with patients. Fourth, private practitioners, chiefs of service in medical, surgical and intensive care units, hospices, nursing homes, etc., can give thoughtful consideration to the best ways to include the expertise of appropriately trained mental health professionals into the care of medical and surgical patients. Different models exist for this and are reflected in the various chapters in the current book. The consultation model is one in which a psychiatrist or psychologist is called upon when there is a psychological issue requiring attention. Such clinicians can also provide education to medical staff, designed to enable them to better understand and manage problems with patients. A second model is one in which the mental health practitioner is embedded within the specific service and is part of a multidisciplinary team, there to meet the needs of patients, families and staff. Programs based on those described in this book by Kraemer and Steinberg or O'Reilly-Landry are examples of how this approach can work effectively. In this model, a psychodynamically trained psychiatrist or psychologist is part of a multidisciplinary team on specialized, high-stress medical units, providing consultation to patients, families and professional staff. Fifth, it must be demonstrated more forcefully that the presence of psychologists and psychiatrists in the care of medical patients is cost-effective. Levitan and Kornfeld, for example, demonstrated that having a liaison psychiatrist on an orthopedic service resulted in a shorter length of stay and lower cost of care.[70]

CONCLUSION

The practice of medicine, like all human interpersonal experiences, can be symbolized and imbued with meaning. The research described in this chapter emphasizes that we know, feel and express more than we think we do, and that this psychological reality can both help and hinder the provision of good clinical care. It seems self-defeating to ignore the subjective and symbolic aspects of the clinical interaction and the advanced human ability to spontaneously and unconsciously evaluate situations. To be more self-aware and to recognize our own capacity for good clinical judgment, as well as our areas of vulnerability to distortion, is likely to foster improvement in the quality of care. It is therefore essential for medical practitioners and researchers to be mindful of the interpersonal and psychological dimensions of their work. The chapters that follow are an effort towards that end.

REFERENCES

1   Institute of Medicine. *Improving Medical Education: enhancing the behavioral and social science content of medical school curriculum*. Washington, DC: National Academies Press; 2004.
2   Wedding D, Stuber MI, editors. *Behavior and Medicine*. 4th ed. Gottengen, Germany: Hogrefe and Huber; 2006.
3   Maier T. Psychosocial and psychodynamic factors influencing health care utilization. *Health Care Anal*. 2006; **14**(2): 69–78.
4   Laederach-Hofmann K, Bunzel B. Noncompliance in organ transplant recipients: a literature review. *Gen Hosp Psychiatry*. 2000; **22**(6): 412–24.
5   Michelon TF, Plovesan F, Pozza R, *et al*. Noncompliance as a cause of renal graft loss. *Transplant Proc*. 2002; **34**(7): 2768–70.
6   Gaston R, Hudson S, Ward M, *et al*. Late renal allograft loss: noncompliance masquerading as chronic refection. *Transplant Proc*. 1999; **31**(Suppl 4A): S21–S23.
7   Shapiro PA, Williams DL, Foray AT, *et al*. Psychosocial evaluation and prediction

of compliance problems and morbidity after heart transplantation. *Transplantation.* 1995; **60**(12): 1462–6.

8   Cameron D. Patient compliance: recognition of factors involved and suggestions for promoting compliance with therapeutic regimens. *J Adv Nurs.* 1997; **24**(2): 244–50.

9   Van Hecke A, Grypdonck M, Defloor T. A review of why patients with leg ulcers do not adhere to treatment. *J Clin Nurs.* 2009; **18**: 337–49.

10 Sontag S. *AIDS and its Metaphors.* New York: Farrar, Strauss and Giroux; 1988.

11 Sontag S. *Illness as Metaphor.* New York: Farrar, Strauss and Giroux: 1977.

12 Clow B. Who's afraid of Susan Sontag? Or, the myths and metaphors of cancer reconsidered. *Soc Hist Med.* 2001; **14**(2): 293–312.

13 Moerman DE. *Meaning, Medicine and the Placebo Effect.* Cambridge, UK: Cambridge University Press; 2002.

14 Charon R. *Narrative Medicine: honoring the stories of illness.* New York: Oxford University Press; 2006.

15 Charon R. Narrative medicine: a model for empathy, reflection, protection and trust. *JAMA.* 2001; **286**(15): 1897–902.

16 Moerman DE, *op. cit.*

17 Blackwell B, Bloomfield SS, Buncher CR. Demonstration to medical students of placebo responses and non-drug factors. *Lancet.* 1972; **1**(763): 1279–82.

18 Grenfell RF, Briggs AH, Holland WC. A double blind study of the treatment of hypertension. *JAMA.* 1961; **176**: 124–8.

19 Hussain MZ, Ahad A. Tablet color in anxiety states. *BMJ.* 1970; **3**(720): 466.

20 Atwood JD, Weinstein E. Chronic illness and the family meaning system. In: Atwood JD, Gallo C, editors. *Family Therapy and Chronic Illness.* New Brunswick, NJ: Transaction Publishers; 2010.

21 Dura JR, Stukenberg KW, Kiecolt-Glaser JK. Anxiety and depressive disorders in adult children caring for demented parents. *Psychol Aging.* 1991; **6**: 467–73.

22 Harmell All, Chattillion EA, Roepke SK, *et al.* A review of the psychobiology of dementia caregiving: a focus on resilience factors. *Curr Psychiatry Rep.* 2011; **13**: 219–24.

23 Lovell B, Wetherell MA. The cost of caregiving: endocrine and immune implications in elderly and non-elderly caregivers. *Neurosci Biobehav Rev.* 2011; **35**(6): 1342–52.

24 Schultz R, Maritire LM. Family caregiving of persons with dementia: prevalence, health effects, and support strategies. *Am J Geriatr Psychiatry.* 2004; **12**(3): 240–9.

25 Kiecolt-Glaser JK, Jarucha PT, Malarky WB, *et al.* Slowing of wound healing by psychological stress. *Lancet.* 1995; **346**: 1194–6.

26 Smith GR, Williamson GM, Miller LS, *et al.* Depression and quality of informal care: a longitudinal investigation of caregiving stressors. *Psychol Aging.* 2011; 26(3): 584–91.

27 Houston WR. The doctor himself as therapeutic agent. *Ann Intern Med.* 1938; **11**(8): 1416–25.

28 Stewart MA. Effective physician–patient communication and health outcomes: a review. *CMAJ.* 1995; **152**(9): 1423–33.

29 Adler HM. The sociophysiology of caring in the doctor patient relationship. *J Gen Intern Med.* 2001; **17**: 883–90.

30 Ciechanowski PS, Katon WJ. The interpersonal experience of health care through the eyes of patients with diabetes. *Soc Sci Med.* 2006; **63**(12): 3067–79.

31 Kenworthy D, Kirkham M. *Midwives Coping with Loss and Grief*. London: Radcliffe Publishing; 2011.

32 Kahn MW. Etiquette-based medicine. *N Engl J Med*. 2008; **357**: 1988–9.

33 Strasser F, Palmer JL, Willey J, *et al*. Impact of physician sitting vs standing during inpatient oncology consultations: patients' preference and perception of compassion and duration: a randomized trial. *J Pain Symptom Manage*. 2005; **29**(5): 489–97.

34 Wechsler ME, Kelley JM, Boyd IOSE *et al*. Active albuterol or placebo, sham acupuncture, or no intervention in asthma. *N Engl J Med*. 2011; **365**: 119–26.

35 Moerman DE. Meaningful placebos – controlling the uncontrollable. *N Engl J Med*. 2011; **365**: 171–2.

36 Meltzer JI. Physician–patient interaction in the treatment of hypertension. In: Laragh JH, Brenner BM, editors. *Hypertension: pathophysiology, diagnosis, and management*. 2nd ed. New York: Raven Press; 1995.

37 Thomas JH. The surgical personality: fact or fiction? *Am J Surg*.1997; **174**(6): 573–7.

38 Banks D. Are surgeons capable of introspection? *Surg Clin North Am*. 2011; **91**(2): 293–304.

39 Freud S. The unconscious. In: Strachey J, editor/translator. *Standard Edition of the Complete Psychological Works of Sigmund Freud*. London: Hogarth Press; 1966. (Original work published in 1915.)

40 Sullivan HS. *The Interpersonal Theory of Psychiatry*. New York: Norton; 1953.

41 PDM Task Force. *Psychodynamic Diagnostic Manual*. Silver Spring, MD: Alliance of Psychoanalytic Organizations; 2006.

42 American Psychiatric Association. *Diagnostic and Statistical Manual of Mental Disorders*. Revised 4th ed. Washington, DC: American Psychiatric Association.

43 Kandel ER. *Psychiatry, Psychoanalysis, and the New Biology of Mind*. Washington, DC: American Psychiatric Publishing; 2005.

44 Schore AN. Relational trauma and the developing right brain: an interface of psychoanalytic self psychology and neuroscience. *Ann NY Acad Sci*. 2009; **1159**: 189–203.

45 Vuilleumier P. Hysterical conversion and brain function. *Prog Brain Res*. 2005; **150**: 309–29.

46 Solms M, Turnall O. *The Brain and the Inner World*. New York: Other Press; 2002.

47 Shedler JK. The efficacy of psychodynamic psychotherapy. *Am Psychol*. 2010; **65**(2): 98–109.

48 Leichsenring F, Rabung S. Long-term psychodynamic psychotherapy in complex mental disorders: update of a meta-analysis. *Br J Psychiatry*. 2011; **199**: 15–22.

49 Bateman A, Fonagy P. 8-year follow-up of patients treated for borderline personality disorder: mentalization based treatment vs treatment as usual. *Am J Psychiatry*. 2008; **165**(5): 631–8.

50 Knekt P, Lindfors O, Laaksonen MA, *et al*. Quasi-experimental study of the effectiveness of psychoanalysis, long-term and short-term psychotherapy on psychiatric symptoms, work ability and functional capacity during a 5-year follow-up. *J Affect Disord*. 2011; **132**(1-2): 37–47.

51 Luborsky L, Luborsky E. *Research and Psychotherapy: the vital link*. New York: Jason Aronson; 2006.

52 Maier T, *op. cit.*

53 Greenberg JR, Mitchell SA. *Object Relations in Psychoanalytic Theory*. Cambridge, MA: Harvard University Press; 1983.

54 Maunder RG, Hunter JJ. Attachment and psychosomatic medicine: developmental contributions to stress and disease. *Psychosom Med.* 2001; **63**(4): 556–67.

55 Ciechanowski PS. As fundamental as nouns and verbs? Towards an integration of attachment theory and medical training. *Med Educ.* 2010; **44**(2): 122–4.

56 Felitti VJ, Anda RF, Nordenberg D, *et al.* Relationship of childhood abuse and household dysfunction to many of the leading causes of deaths in adults: the adverse childhood experiences (ACE) study. *Am J Prev Med.* 1998; **14**(4): 245–58.

57 Vaillant GE, Vaillant CO. Natural history of male psychological health. XII: a 45-year study of predictors of successful aging at age 65. *Am J Psychiatry.* 1990; **14**(1): 31–7.

58 Vaillant GE. *Aging Well*. Boston: Little, Brown; 2002.

59 Kachele H, Schachter J, Thoma H, editors. *From Psychoanalytic Narrative to Empirical Single Case Research: implications for psychoanalytic practice*. New York: Routledge; 2009.

60 Rudnytsky PL, Charon R, editors. *Psychoanalysis and Narrative Medicine*. Albany, NY: State University of New York Press; 2008.

61 Meza JP, Passerman DS. *Integrating Narrative Medicine and Evidence-Based Medicine*. London: Radcliffe Publishing; 2011.

62 Moss AH, Ganjoo J, Sharma S, *et al.* Utility of the 'Surprise' question to identify dialysis patients with high mortality. *Clin J Am Soc Nephrol.* 2008; **3**(5): 1379–84.

63 Moss AH, Lunney JR, Culp S, *et al.* Prognostic significance of the 'Surprise' question in cancer patients. *J Palliat Med.* 2010; **13**(7): 837–40.

64 Cohen LM, Ruthazer R, Moss AH, *et al.* Predicting six-month mortality for patients who are on maintenance hemodialysis. *Clin J Am Soc Nephrol.* 2010; **5**(1): 72–9.

65 Teglas E, Vul E, Girotto V, *et al.* Pure reasoning in 12-month-old infants as probabilistic inference. *Science.* 2011; **332**(6033): 1054–9.

66 Banaji MR, Lemm KM, Carpenter SJ. The social unconscious. In: Tesser A, Schwartz N, editors. *Blackwell Handbook of Social Psychology: intraindividual processes*. Malden, MA: Blackwell Publishers; 2007.

67 Sue DW, Capodilupo CM, Torino GC, *et al.* Racial microaggression in everyday life: implications for clinical practice. *Am Psychol.* 2007: **62**(4): 271–86.

68 Kornfeld DS, Muskin PR, Tahil FA. Psychiatric evaluation of mental capacity in the general hospital: a significant teaching opportunity. *Psychosomatics.* 2009; **50**(5): 468–73.

69 Martin V. *Developing a Narrative Approach to Healthcare Research*. London: Radcliffe Publishing; 2011.

70 Levitan SJ, Kornfeld DS. A study of liaison psychiatry effectiveness: clinical and cost benefits of liaison psychiatry. *Am J Psychiatry.* 1981; **138**:790–3.

CHAPTER 2

Contemporary Psychodynamic Concepts and Modern Medicine

Ellen B. Luborsky

> It wasn't worth waiting. After pacing the doctor's office for nine minutes with no doctor in sight, he left. He wasn't about to miss work for this. Probably they wouldn't figure it out anyway, why he kept getting that strange sensation shooting through his gut. Maybe it was nothing.

What do psychodynamics have to do with that situation? What good does psychoanalytic thinking do for the nurse who went to find him or the doctor who could barely fit him into his schedule anyway? What good could it do the patient?

In an era when time for patient care has become as rare as a home-made pie, considering the emotions of the patient and the meanings of his behavior might seem like an arcane luxury. But that luxury could be a necessity when feelings get in the way of coping with illness. Consider the patient just described, who walked out of the doctor's office. His frustration landed him in the emergency room (ER), weeks later. He couldn't walk out that time.

What made waiting so impossible for him? He didn't know himself. But something about waiting had always infuriated him. It wasn't until he began to talk with a therapist while recuperating from surgery that he began to recall the ways he waited long ago – waiting for rides home from school that left without him; waiting for his mother to get home from work while his father just lay there, getting worse. The dread of what he might find out about his health blended with a vestige of those old feelings as he paced the doctor's office. Rather than memories, they emerged as a rush of emotion.

The medical situation brings all aspects of the self to the same moment. The physical self and the emotional self both react to the signal that something is wrong, but it takes a different lens to understand their workings. A symptom in medicine is a clue to a diagnosis, but a symptom seen through the psychodynamic lens is a very different kind of clue. It may be feelings in disguise, as in a headache that emerges during a 'headache' of a meeting. Or it may be a defense against feelings, as could have been the case with the patient who left before his appointment began. In bringing a psychodynamic perspective to the medical situation, both the medical and dynamic forms of understanding apply.

Finding out what is beneath the surface of behavior is facilitated by empathy. 'Getting a feel' for a patient's experience brings an emotional source of information, as well as a sense of partnership with the patient. That helps to create a *therapeutic alliance*, which psychotherapy research shows to be an important factor in the progress of treatment.[1]

The other aspect of the alliance is the joint effort of patient and therapist to understand the problems that the patient has been living with. That form of inquiry, inaugurated by Freud's writings over a century ago, seeks to decode the meanings of behavior that elude a rational lens. Rather than identify a problem and give it a label, a psychodynamic approach is a kind of detective work. As Freud described it: 'We seek not merely to describe and classify the phenomena, but to understand them as signs of the interplay of forces in the mind…'[2]

Just 'saying what comes to mind' serves as the classic source of information in psychoanalytic treatments. The patient's unedited thoughts allow for a *free association* between problems, feelings, memories, daydreams, real dreams, and desires. The seemingly random or illogical can begin to make sense when it is not dismissed, but becomes instead a clue to other aspects of the self. For example, a patient who had been ashamed of dropping out of college with just a year to go was able to finish once he faced the fears and *inner conflict* that had been in his way. Conflict between parts of the self may be expressed through psychological symptoms or emotional states. Anxiety, inability to move forward in life, and self-defeating behavior are some of the ways in which such conflicts may show up in a person's life.

Problems in relationships become a crucial form of data in psychodynamic approaches. People bring their hopes and their expectations to relationships, along with their habitual ways of responding. Frequent clashes with others or a frustration at not being heard may be clues to a pattern of responding that is on 'autopilot.' Freud's insight that people may remember by repeating informed his finding of the *transference* of old patterns onto new people. The transference becomes evident in treatment relationships, where hopes for help, love or acceptance may collide with past patterns.

In medical situations, there is no care without some kind of relationship to a doctor or a 'treating other,' and there is no medical situation without expectations. That means that interpersonal challenges will inevitably affect the medical situation. In this volume, the authors reveal the kinds of problems that occur in the midst of medical crises. They serve as *participant-observers*, who seek to understand through their own experience. Psychoanalytic thinking serves as the basis for the approaches these authors take but, contrary to common belief, psychoanalysis is not a unified canon. It includes different approaches, each of which has taken off from earlier forms. For example, *relational* and *interpersonal* approaches make active use of the analyst's and the patient's experience in a *two-person process*. The interpersonal perspective uses the current interactions as a prime source of understanding.[3] *Selective inattention,* which refers to a shift away from anxiety-provoking topics, is noted in action. The relational perspective works with the ways in which *intrapsychic* or inner mental processes combine with interpersonal ones.[4]

Many current approaches have integrated more recent discoveries into their thinking, notably those from attachment theory and neuroscience. Different points of view now live together in the 'big tent' of psychoanalytically based approaches[5] but they all share basic principles and ways of understanding.

The authors of this book each describe the psychological challenges for both patients and practitioners of different medical conditions and differing states of mind. In order to appreciate their insights and make use of their contributions, it is important to understand their concepts and their language. What follows are explanations of terms and ideas that are common to a psychodynamic understanding.

CENTRAL CONCEPTS

The unconscious

> The division of the psychical into what is conscious and what is unconscious is the fundamental premise of psychoanalysis.[6]

The *unconscious mind* includes states of mind and emotional processes that are out of awareness but still influence thinking and behavior. The power of the unconscious to serve as an unknown source of people's motivations and problems is a prime tenet of psychoanalytic thinking. Fears or desires that are out of awareness can seep into behavior, as in the young woman who kept leaving jobs and relationships. She was *remembering by repeating* the change and loss that she lived through in her own early life, as her family moved from place to place.

The *anniversary reaction* is a common example of the unconscious at work. Consider the woman whose mood sank as July began. It was only when she looked at the calendar that she realized what her unconscious had already recalled – she was approaching the anniversary of her first husband's death, many years ago.

In treatment, a goal is to gain awareness of a fuller range of inner experience, so that it can be used 'in the service of the ego' rather than as a source of problems or psychological symptoms. While Freud's ideas about the unconscious have been challenged, the basic concept has received support from neuroscience.

Westen describes the consensus among cognitive scientists that memory and thinking involve a conscious (explicit) and unconscious (implicit) system.[7] Implicit memory refers to memories that become apparent through behavior but bypass awareness. They serve as clues to the presence of a non-conscious process.

Transference

The *transference* of old patterns onto new people is a crucial concept in psychoanalysis. People's expectations in relationships are colored by earlier experience, so that a patient might find herself in the same kind of dead-end relationships without understanding how she got there. Early relationships have an influence on those expectations but the links are typically not intentional or conscious.

Clinical research on patterns in relationships using methods such as the core conflictual relationship theme method (CCRT) confirms that people tend toward such patterns.[8] They are often acted out or experienced through enactment, something that ends up as a source of information in treatment: '... the patient does not say that he remembers that he used to be defiant and critical toward his parents' authority; instead he acts that way toward the doctor.'[9]

In dynamic treatments, discovering the personal transference pattern is part of a process that can help to diminish its hold. Research with the CCRT finds that in a successful treatment, the patient keeps alive what he wishes for himself but is able to transform his expectations and responses toward more positive ones.[10]

Countertransference

Countertransference refers to the therapist's emotional response to the patient. It is necessary for the therapist to pay attention to such responses so that they do not interfere with the treatment. Instead, that awareness can be used to gain insight into the patient's relationship problems.

Countertransference reactions may occur when a patient brings out the therapist's own patterns in responding, by reminding him or 'ringing a bell' from his own past. Or, he may have a *resonant response* to the way the patient relates. That means that he reacts to the sway of the patient's attitude toward him, and ends up responding in ways that fit with those expectations. When the patient and therapist realize this, they have 'live information' about the ways the patient's relationship problems happen.

Transference and countertransference reactions are more common than many people realize. Like an actor in an improvisational drama, we all pick up clues and cues from other people. Consider a day in a medical practice. Why does one patient draw a smile and the other a nod? Why do you welcome one patient's questions but feel annoyed by those of another?

People carry their expectations in relationships along with them. Without realizing it, we all get pulled by the emotional draw of those expectations. That opens a door to a relational world where past patterns in relationships and past problems are enacted in the present. In treatment, those enactments become pivotal to understanding. By finding himself temporarily transformed, the analyst can decode the process that keeps happening to this patient. The patient and analyst can use that shared experience to work toward change.

Defense mechanisms

Defense mechanisms are automatic strategies that people use to respond to 'felt danger'. That means, for example, that instead of feeling the stress that would come from acknowledging a change in vision, someone might get very busy and forget to call the doctor for weeks. She would be using the defense of *avoidance*. Someone else might respond to the same situation by making several appointments with specialists, doing research online, and spending every spare moment looking into possible causes of the problem. He would be using an *obsessive-compulsive* defense in response to the same problem.

Defenses come into play automatically to diminish a sense of *psychic* danger.[11] But the more they obscure or distort reality, the more they create problems. For example, the defense of *denial* is typical in addictions, adding to the difficulty of recovery. The defense of *projection* means that extreme feelings or impulses are projected onto someone or something else. The other person may be seen as evil or dangerous, when they have simply said something the patient didn't like. Projection is the defense used in paranoia.

Dissociation refers to forms of disconnection between the self and the temporal world, or between parts of the self. Someone may get lost from the coordinates of time and place that we use to stay grounded. He may find himself in the next week without having been able to move the fog from his mind. He could have been in a *fugue state*, which shifts the mental gears away from awareness. Or someone may find herself at a meeting, having a conversation but feeling like it is not her that is speaking, just some pop-up version of herself. She may be in a state of *depersonalization*.

All forms of dissociation serve to protect the ego from being flooded with acute anxiety or a vestige of painful experience. Recent research links the use of dissociation with problems in the early attachment relationship.[12] The more severe forms of dissociation are common in those who have endured trauma or abuse, as a mental form of escape from that which could not be escaped in the real world. Understanding those processes of mind and tolerating the knowledge is a gradual but essential part of recovery.

OTHER PROCESSES AND SYSTEMS

Mentalization

How can you cope with a patient who thinks you have done her wrong? How can you feel alive while your body is in chronic pain? Without an ability to hold in mind different forms of understanding, some kinds of situations feel intolerable. *Mentalization* and *reflective functioning* pertain to the ability to be aware of and to 'get' the states of others, so that instead of feeling like an intrusion, they can become a source of empathy. These terms refer to the same kind of understanding when applied to one's own experience, so that there is an awareness of feelings and reactions as not synonymous with the self.[13]

Intellectualization could be seen as a second cousin of mentalization. It refers to considering things intellectually but leaving out their emotional meaning. It is a defense mechanism whose function is to avoid feeling painful emotion. However, when used as a primary defense, it can end up stripping the felt meaning from the person's life, by focusing on the facts and intellectual understanding alone.

Acting out refers to taking hot themes or impulses into action without considering their consequences. For example, a patient who is experiencing her therapist as unresponsive doesn't show up for their session and goes to a movie instead. She is acting out her anger at him, replacing the therapist with a more immediate experience. Recognizing her feelings and their links to her actions can tame the process of acting out. So can a process of *rupture and repair*[14] in which problems between therapist and patient are acknowledged and a deeper understanding begins. These processes grow the ability to mentalize.

Object relations

An *object* in psychoanalytic lingo does not reside on your table; it resides in your mind. It refers to a primary object of affection, often the person who was the early source of connection and care. *Object relations* theory begins with the premise that relationships, starting with the mother–infant bond, are themselves a basic motivating force.[15] That premise contrasts with the earlier psychoanalytic writings that emphasized drives or instincts as primary. This concept has 'grandmothered' current theories that focus on the central role of relationships in psychic life.

An *internal object* refers to the sense that a loved or important person has an inner presence in our lives. The process of *internalization* was explored in Margaret Mahler's writings on the *separation-individuation* process.[16] During the first three years of life, that process gradually allows the child to develop his own *sense of self*, holding onto an inner connection with the parent while she is not actually present. That process was renamed *attachment-individuation* by Lyons-Ruth, who suggests that the individuation process grows out of the attachment bond.[17]

Winnicott brought his experience as a pediatrician to object relations. He noted the ways in which a baby develops the ability to tolerate separation from the mother through the use of a *transitional object*, which is a treasured teddy bear or toy the baby imbues with fond feeling. Play itself serves as transitional experience, helping a child work through feelings without the consequences that come with reality.[18] It develops a *potential space*, between reality and fantasy, where imagination and new forms of experience can grow. That serves as a way to consider psychotherapy itself.

Patterns of attachment

When Bowlby first wrote about his theory of how we develop attachments to other people, many psychoanalysts dismissed his ideas. But 50 years later, the turn-around is substantial. Attachment theory and research have been recognized as a system for understanding that complements psychodynamic thinking.[19] This has prompted a number of the authors in this book to bring an attachment perspective to their work.

The parallels between the findings of attachment research and some psychodynamic ideas are striking. Attachment research shows the impact of early relationships on feeling secure or insecure, as well as more serious psychopathology. The 'long view' of attachment research looks at the durability of people's patterns over time. Each attachment pattern serves as a prototype of ways of handling emotions, stress, and distress. That means a very different response to a psychoanalyst or therapist in the form of transference, as well as to medical problems. An understanding of attachment patterns can help to elucidate the patient's ways of coping, as can the varied forms of psychodynamic theory described in this volume. The attachment and psychodynamic perspectives come together in seeking a deeper look at the ways in which people respond to stress, pain, and problems.

Many of the chapters that follow integrate the findings of attachment research with a psychodynamic understanding. All the chapters seek to keep alive the person within illness and medical care. That brings back what it's all about.

REFERENCES

1   Luborsky L, Luborsky E. *Research and Psychotherapy: the vital link*. Lanham, MD: Jason Aronson; 2006.
2   Freud S. Introductory lectures in psychoanalysis. In: Strachey J, editor. *Standard Edition of the Complete Psychological Works of Sigmund Freud*. Volume 15. London: Hogarth; 1961. p. 67.
3   Sullivan H.S. *The Interpersonal Theory of Psychiatry*. New York: Norton; 1954.
4   Mitchell S. *Relational Concepts in Psychoanalysis: an integration*. Cambridge, MA: Harvard University Press; 1988.

5   Orfanos S. 'On Such a Full Sea': advances in psychoanalytic psychology. *NY State Psychol.* 2006; **8** (4): 2–8.

6   Freud S. The ego and the id. In: Strachey J, editor. *Standard Edition of the Complete Psychological Works of Sigmund Freud.* Volume 19. London: Hogarth; 1961. p. 15.

7   Westen D. The scientific status of unconscious processes. Paper presented at the Annual Meeting of the Rapaport-Klein Study Group, June 11–13 1999.

8   Luborsky L, Crits-Christoph P. *Understanding Transference: the CCRT method.* 2nd ed. Washington, DC: American Psychological Association; 1998.

9   Freud S. On narcissism: an introduction. In: Strachey J, editor. *Standard Edition of the Complete Psychological Works of Sigmund Freud.* Volume 14. London: Hogarth; 1961. p. 150.

10 Luborsky L, Luborsky E. *op. cit.*

11 Freud A. *The Ego and the Mechanisms of Defense.* New York: International Universities Press; 1966.

12 Lyons-Ruth K. Dissociation and the parent-infant dialogue: a longitudinal perspective from attachment research. *J Am Psychoanal Assoc.* 2003; **51**(3): 883–911.

13 Fonagy P, Gergely G, Jurist E, Target M. *Affect Regulation, Mentalization, and the Development of The Self.* New York: Other Press; 2002.

14 Safran J, Muran J, Samstag L, Steven C. Repairing alliance ruptures. *Psychother: Theory Res Pract Train.* 2001; **38**(4): 406–41.

15 Fairbairn WRD. *An Object Relations Theory of the Personality.* New York: Basic Books; 1954.

16 Mahler M, Pine F, Berman A. *The Psychological Birth of the Human Infant: symbiosis and individuation.* New York: Basic Books; 1975.

17 Lyons-Ruth K. Rapprochment or approchment: Mahler's theory reconsidered from the vantage point of recent research on early attachment relationships. *Psychoanalyt Psychol.* 1991; **8**: 1–23.

18 Winnicott DW. Transitional objects and transitional phenomena: a study of the first not-me possession. *Int J Psychoanal.* 1953; **34**: 89–97.

19 Slade A. The development and organization of attachment: implications for psychoanalysis. *J Am Psychoanal Assoc.* 2001; **48**(4): 1147–74.

Subjectivity, Personal Meaning and the Medical Experience

Creating Security by Exploring the Personal Meaning of Chronic Illness in Adolescent Patients

Norka Malberg and Peter Fonagy

What are my hopes for my daughter? Well, really, that someday she can go to a party and drink and eat anything she wants, that she can go on holiday far, far away and send me postcards and that she can worry me sick because she is coming home late. Really, I just want to worry about normal things. I know it is strange that I want to worry about things most parents dread ... it is silly, isn't it?

Michelle, aged 43, is the mother of Brianna, a 14-year-old girl attending a pediatric hemodialysis outpatient unit in London. At the age of two, Brianna received a kidney transplant from her mother, only to return to the dialysis unit months later after it failed. A quiet and shy girl, Brianna is home schooled and has only one friend who visits her during her hemodialysis session on Saturdays. Michelle feels helpless about Brianna's non-compliance with her medical regime and constant fights between the two of them upset the other children in the family. Feeling overwhelmed, Michelle requested support from the psychosocial renal team in charge of Brianna's case. Michelle often felt that medical personnel and extended family blamed her for Brianna's behavior and ill health. During our conversations, she often said she felt very much alone and did not want to think any more.

The experience of chronic illness during childhood and adolescence goes against all that a parent hopes and wants for his/her child. It rewrites the narrative of both the child and the family. It challenges all coping mechanisms. Non-compliance with a medical regime reflects the interaction of diverse emotional and physical factors that medical professionals face. Michelle and Brianna's example highlights the importance of focusing on the quality of interpersonal exchanges in this context, and illustrates the ongoing impact that chronic illness has on relationships. An inability to think about states of mind and the difficult feelings that accompany them is common amongst the child, family and medical personnel. Emotional support available to the young person often remains at a very concrete and physical level. In a situation where action is vital to the survival of the young body, providing a safe and reciprocal relational experience that promotes emotional development is a real challenge. So, how can a psychoanalytic relational approach contribute in this context?

A good example comes from the field of attachment theory. In his 1988 book *A Secure Base*,[1] John Bowlby reminds psychotherapists to explore an individual's representational models (one's image of oneself in the context of each important relationship). In order to provide a 'secure base,' which feels safe and protected, the caregiver, medical clinician or therapist must be as reliable, attentive and sympathetically responsive to the individual as possible. The shift from a one-person psychology (the therapist who listens to the patient) to an active two-person relational story (where each participant contributes thoughts and feelings involved in the process of psychotherapy) has enabled psychoanalytic thinking to be applied in a wide variety of settings.[2] Bowlby's goal highlights the need for a dynamic and evolving relationship within a safe environment. Accomplishing this goal becomes especially challenging when delivering outreach clinical interventions.

How do we provide such experience in the context of an often unpredictable and busy inpatient medical unit? This chapter illustrates an application of attachment theory, namely mentalization-based therapy, in such an outreach setting. This approach represents a progression in psychoanalysis towards a relational understanding of psychological dynamics. This integrative model has proven particularly successful in non-traditional settings such as hospital units with their need for multiple collaborations.[3,4] The following pages explore the usefulness of such an approach in an adolescent hemodialysis unit. We highlight themes that emerged during our intervention by using clinical vignettes, and reflect on them from a 'mentalizing stance.'

So, what is mentalization? The concept of mentalization is based on the belief that we all have the innate capacity to relate.[5] A mentalization-based intervention seeks to activate such capacity by inviting people to actively think about their own mental states (beliefs, motives, feelings, desires and needs) and those of others, and about our mutual responses to one another. This approach attempts to create an awareness of the opaqueness of mental states (one can never be certain what others are thinking or feeling). It posits that it is more effective to wonder about someone's feelings and motivations than to express certainty about them or simply react to the behavior. Our personal histories significantly influence the way we mentalize. Our culture, race, religious beliefs and relational histories all influence the way we think of ourselves in relationships and how we react to unpredictable and stressful situations.

In the context of chronic illness, the child's support system (parents, teachers and medical personnel) often has difficulty responding in ways that consider the child's experience of the illness from his or her perspective. When a young body fails, it results in a constant sense of urgency and a rather concrete and non-mentalizing stance. Solutions to concrete problems are the focus: how to get the young person to take his medicine, for example. Staff and family meetings focus on what is conscious and rational – a new plan, a new medication, speculation that the young patient does not understand the seriousness of his illness or is just being a teenager!

Sharing the concept of mentalization with staff and families and including it in the daily language of the system helps to promote support for and an understanding of what one is trying to accomplish. The mentalization-based intervention is an invitation to young people to dare to start thinking about their minds and the impact that the 'unspoken feelings' have on their behavior. Through the use of playful activities and conversations, we seek to activate their motivation to reflect on the ways they cope with the stress of relationships. Recent applications of mentalization[6] integrate ideas from social-cognitive psychology with a psychodynamic framework. They link mentalizing to intersubjective experience – that is, the assumed subjective experience of another person in relation to oneself, the constant effort to identify and create a dialogue with the impact one is trying to have on another person. Subjectively this feels like 'being in touch' with someone or being 'attuned' to them. However, underpinning that emotional state that we take so much for granted are complex computations of, in effect, modeling or simulating the other person's experience both automatically (online) and reflectively (offline). The mentalization-based group seeks a reparative experience by encouraging the participant to develop a stronger sense of self through exploration of the personal meaning of the illness. Most importantly, it focuses on exploring the motivations for the young person's non-compliant behavior as well as his/her capacity to relate to the world of peers and family in a way that promotes growth and development.

According to Fiumara,[7] mentalization is a private psychological experience but we can attempt to share it with others. The adolescent's mentalizing efforts will be approved and encouraged only to the extent that these capacities are spontaneously active in the other members of the family and medical community. Much has been written about the passive role of the chronically ill adolescent and the high prevalence of depression and anxiety and the impact of chronic illness on the psychosocial functioning of the family.[8,9] We often talk about the meaning of the illness for the person affected; that kind of meaning may be more or less mentalized in the sense that subjective experiences linked to the disease are reflected on as related to the disease or experienced directly. For example, feeling pain and reflecting on that experience of pain as part of the illness is quite different from unmentalized pain experienced directly and without the benefit of the buffer of representation. The unmentalized experience of pain is more readily distorted to become part of meaning domains unrelated to the disease, for example, pain as a persecutory experience, pain as a signal of danger, pain as indicator of physical frailty. Failure of mentalization can promote a 'false self' in which one loses touch with oneself and behaves, and even feels, according to what pleases others.[10] This is how many young people survive within the medical system. This tendency contributes to an institutional culture in which parents, siblings and friends feel criticized and blamed for the young person's failure to follow medical advice. Thinking about medical compliance in this way helps us understand it as a coping measure designed to gain a sense of control and a partial confirmation of self boundaries and stability.

The mentalization-based intervention seeks to provide a space where all these issues can be explored. The mentalization-based therapy group model emphasizes the sharing of thoughts and feelings in the context of conflicts arising in everyday social situations. The focus of the group is in the here and now. What is going on between people in the group? How are members feeling in reaction to someone's comment? How does this person understand the other person's comment? Can one guess how this person might be feeling or what he might be thinking? Exchanges in the group allow for consideration of cultural understanding and relevant individual values (e.g. ethnic traditions, spiritual beliefs) and are respectful and attentive to the personal meaning of the experience. Our approach is meant to be a relational laboratory, a playground of ideas and an exchange of experiences guided by basic aims in the facilitators' minds. The group leader serves as a facilitator and model of mentalizing. There is a horizontal approach where the facilitator offers facts about their own experiences and reflects on their own non-mentalizing impasses during the group. The aim is to create a community where the focus on mentalizing and what inhibits its functioning becomes everyday language: a 'new developmental experience' conducive to new ways of thinking about feeling and of responding in relationships for the young person.

In a nutshell, the mentalization-based therapy group seeks to provide a relational restorative and repairing experience. Here, the young person can explore conflicting feelings, become aware of motivations behind non-mentalizing behavior and its consequences, and ultimately become aware of the negative triggers in his/her environment. We will now illustrate the design and implementation process of such an approach in a local pediatric hemodialysis unit, working with six adolescents (aged 12–17) suffering from end-stage renal disease. The development of this intervention required close attention to both systemic and individual aspects of the experience of adolescent chronic illness.

As the child reaches adolescence, he/she begins to think abstractly. General principles are used to understand emotions, rather than merely concrete aspects of the specific situation. As the adolescent experiences feelings in himself and others, the world is suddenly much more complicated, confusing and over-whelming. A defensive move towards non-mentalizing behavior takes place when the person feels unable to cope with the psychological impact of any one of a number of life experiences, but often life experiences directly linked to the chronic illness. A traumatic event such as chronic illness compromises the capacity for mentalization, particularly during periods of interpersonal stress. Providing a safe and predictable emotional environment (secure base) facili-tates the capacity to reflect on mental states and to tolerate the difficult feelings that accompany them. How the environment responds to the young person's newly acquired desire to explore new ways of thinking and feeling in relation-ships will ultimately determine the outcome.

Therefore, prior to beginning the mentalization-based group therapy, we set out to explore the various relationships that exist for people within the renal pediatric unit. The group leader needs to take these themes and concerns into consideration as she tries to elaborate for participants their thoughts and feel-ings about each other and others in their lives, attachment figures as well as professionals they have regular contact with in the unit.

It was very important that we have an understanding of the perceived needs of children, family and medical personnel. We presented our ideas for the project to the medical staff and gave multiple presentations regarding the con-cept of mentalization, making links between the issue of medical compliance, adolescence and attachment theory. By focusing on the relational aspect of the intervention, we were able to initiate an important dialogue among health professionals regarding what they perceived as the relational needs of young people suffering from end-stage renal disease.

Adolescents with chronic renal failure are 'outsiders' in many ways. They tend to be shorter than their peers and have, in their own words, 'battle scars' on display in their arms and torso from years of fistulas, feeding lines and inva-sive procedures. They are also different within their families, some enjoying 'special' status, others perceiving themselves as the family's 'damaged goods.' As a result, being part of a discussion group that brings out issues other than the experience of being ill produced a great deal of anxiety for this group of young people. Prior to the beginning of the group, there were concerns about what to do if an argument occurred or what would happen if someone disclosed things that made the others feel bad.

The idea of the group was presented to the six potential participants who were given time to discuss and ask questions. It was welcomed by all young people as they had been wondering what the main investigator had been doing all those months around the unit. A young man put it thus: 'We started to think you were a new piece of furniture.' This comment was understood by our team as an indication of the importance young people place on the physical setting of their unit, in which they spend an average of 12 hours per week. Visitors, changes in furniture or dialysis machines are all observed and ascribed a diverse set of attributions by both patients and staff.

The issue of physical setting became very real as well for us when our proposed treatment protocol was challenged by physical constraints, namely the loud sounds of the dialysis machines, the overall physical set-up of the unit and the ongoing traffic of service providers, family and friends. We needed to find ways in which we could promote a mentalizing group environment amid all these interferences. One of the main purposes of a mentalizing-based intervention is to promote a shift in the way participants and the supportive systems around them deal with daily challenges. We therefore decided to become creative, adapting to these constraints and satisfying issues of confidentiality and logistics in ways that could promote long-term shifts in relational and problem-solving strategies within the unit.

For example, we developed a system where we could communicate with young people in a separate room through the use of a walkie-talkie during our group sessions. This practice was later adopted by the nurses as a good alternative to having to attend to the screams of a young patient feeling excluded in the 'sick room.' We also discussed ways in which participants could opt out of the group by closing their privacy curtain or wearing earphones and watching a movie. It was very important that group participants felt free to refuse to attend without feeling punished or ashamed. In a setting where one's right to say no is often not perceived as an option, having others trying to understand and allowing one that right was incredibly relevant.

During this initial period, parents were given a chance to ask questions and express concerns. The level of openness and responsiveness varied from family to family, depending on the current state of their child's treatment, level of non-compliant behavior, relational history of family members with medical personnel, and cultural background. Many of the young people were brought by older siblings, creating an interesting dynamic during our meetings, as cultural and generational issues were often openly discussed. For instance, issues regarding bodyweight and image in young people were perceived radically differently by parents and older siblings. For example, an older sibling was concerned with her mother's constant angst over how skinny her ill brother looked, when in fact the child had serious difficulties keeping his weight down. Issues regarding what constitutes beauty and health were discussed casually in the context of medical consequences with the facilitator providing a 'mentalizing model' that allowed and reflected on the multiple beliefs and ideas.

These initial meetings enriched our understanding of the personal meaning that medical staff, patients and families gave to the illness and its treatment processes. Most relevant to our work was how different understandings and sets of beliefs often got in the way of the emergence within the system of the capacity to mentalize. We believed these discussions facilitated the creation of a secure base within the unit, one which provided the group with a safe vehicle for discussion, sharing and modeling new strategies when faced with interpersonal stressors.

On the first day of the group, we began by choosing a name for it, and the decision was easily reached by five eager participants and a reluctant one hiding under the sheets. Our name would be: *The Lords of the Machine*. The machines in the hemodialysis unit produce an annoying sound and are often spoken to by nurses and patients when they get stuck or run slowly. Our name established a hierarchy in which our voices would be stronger than those of the life-giving machines. The group leader reflected on this by saying that we seemed to seize power from the machines, and both nurses and patients seemed pleased with this comment.

Group sessions began with all members and the leader sharing something good and something bad that occurred during the past week. The challenge during our group became how to 'normalize' our discussions and explore age-appropriate issues outside the context of illness in order to promote a mentalizing stance when confronted with interpersonal stresses such as dating and fighting with friends. The young people of the renal unit explored their difficulties understanding some of their peers' behaviors during activities and group discussions. These discussions enabled the group leader to challenge members' assumptions about their peers' attitudes, beliefs and feelings, and to validate the young people's experience before offering alternative perspectives. Developing a new way of thinking about oneself in relationships and experiencing a stronger sense of agency (capacity to effect change in one's self and others) can be a strong protective factor when faced with adversity.

Our model emphasized the importance of working with all relational systems supporting the young person through the process of illness. After all, what good is it to foster a mentalizing stance in a young person if the home and hospital environments are not able to reinforce their efforts?

As the group's dynamics developed, issues relating to family dynamics and ways of coping with them, and how the 'hospital family' understood and reacted to such dynamics, became a very important topic. The experience of chronic renal disease has an impact on the young person's physical appearance, capacity to become autonomous, sense of control and self-reliance. At times, the culture of the hospital clashes with the ways in which the family copes with this situation, especially in multicultural environments. Frequently, the sense of urgency over issues of non-compliance inhibits the capacity of health care providers to mentalize the personal meaning the situation holds for the young person and his family.

Attachment research regarding the importance of what a culture values interpersonally can inform our understanding.[11] We know that attachment is a universal phenomenon but its evolution takes many forms, which is evident when it comes to the understanding of parent–child interaction in the context and culture of chronic illness.

Parental reactions to chronic illness may affect their children's capacity to achieve a sense of autonomy and self-sufficiency. Parents' fear and anxiety about losing their children can foster a pattern of overcontrol that may interfere with the young person's need to separate and become his own person. The following example illustrates the need to approach patients and families with humility and willingness to learn by adopting a 'not knowing' stance.

Clinical example: a good little girl

Aruna was a young-looking 15 year old who had been in and out of the hospital since the day she was born. Her case was of interest in the hospital as she was not supposed to survive beyond her fifth birthday. Aruna had by far the best medical compliance in the group. She was extremely close to her mother, calling her many times during the dialysis sessions. The nursing staff found this unbearable and recalled how difficult it was to convince her parents that teaching her to give herself needles would be good for her self-confidence. Aruna's mother explained to me and two other mothers visiting the unit that in her country, nurses and doctors give needles, not the patient. Lana's mother explained that in the hospital, the kids were supposed to be dependent patients when it was convenient and independent when it served the medical staff. I said it is difficult when you are trying to be a good parent and you feel the world outside thinks you are being overprotective or not letting your child grow. The other mothers nod and the only father in the group added that sometimes it felt like people think you caused your child to be sick, and it was worse when the child was included in those who think it was your fault. I added that it was difficult as a parent to know with whom to be angry, so imagine how the children must feel. Aruna's mother said she felt Aruna found safety in her relationship with her family who treated her as a normal child. She added she was scared Aruna would like hurting herself by using the needle and become one of those sick girls who cut themselves. She said because expectations have always been low for her outside, they had high expectations for her at home and she responded well to them. She thought Aruna felt special as she should, because she was a reminder to all of us that the human spirit can achieve anything. Lana's mother wondered if Aruna ever got angry and wanted to just stop it all. Aruna's mother said she did and that was when they sat and felt sad and angry together and thought of all the things they couldn't do because she was sick. Lana's mother challenged Aruna's mum by saying it was not that easy when they were not taking their medication. Aruna's mother replied by adding: 'It is her life, it is her body. When she chooses to stop we have no choice but to let her know what will happen...'

Aruna's mother seemed aware of her daughter's difficulties in expressing affect and regularly lent her own capacity to manage difficult feelings to her daughter. Problem solving for her daughter, however, perhaps did not give her the space to develop her own ways of dealing with anxiety and anger in a developmentally expected fashion. Aruna's development was atypical and therefore, she was not able to get beyond relying on her mother's capacities and paradoxically became quite dependent on this family role assigned to her by her mother of being resilient despite adversity. This identity has provided Aruna with the capacity to feel a sense of responsibility over her body that allows her to feel in control. Her mother's concern over needles was interpreted by the psychosocial renal team as an attempt to keep her daughter infantilized and dependent. However, one could also understand her fear regarding Aruna's potential for self-harming as a communication of her awareness of her daughter's emotional fragility and her difficulty reconciling clashing cultural beliefs regarding adolescent autonomy and family responsibilities for care.

For young patients, the process of making meaning from one's experiences takes place in the context of an emerging sense of self within the immediate environment, the family and all the meanings contained in them. Traumatic experiences such as chronic illness challenge existing beliefs and values of the system, creating confusion and upheaval. Providing a mentalizing environment in which to untangle the different meanings and work out who they belong to is pivotal in the process of strengthening young persons' capacity to cope.

Most adolescents view their illness as an external danger, even though it is located in their own bodies. They usually understand the malady as being imposed from an external source such as parents, God or fate. When listening to discussions between chronically ill adolescents, one discovers the many ways in which they avoid placing the sense of blame on themselves and their closest loved ones. Spirituality and religious beliefs can help them to cope but are these always just ways of coping or are they ways of making sense of an overwhelming experience? This question is pivotal to guiding the way we encourage mentalizing and the process of exploring the personal meaning of being ill. Uribe's story illustrates this point.

Clinical example: Uribe

Uribe was a 17 year old who became ill three years ago while on vacation with her family. The eldest of three children, she was the pride and joy of her parents and extended family in Kenya. The family had moved to the UK five years ago in order to improve the quality of life of the children and the professional prospects of both parents who were health professionals working in AIDS research. Uribe was very proud of her family's intellectual status and often used irony and sarcasm to cope with her feelings of helplessness. This tendency had made her increasingly unpopular with the nurses who found her condescending and ungrateful.

Our project began six months after Uribe had been transferred from another hospital. She had spent her first months in complete isolation, not speaking and refusing to show any independence in control of any of her medical care. She demanded that the nurses insert all her needles and complained constantly of their ineptness to do so on the first attempt. She insisted they were envious of her and enjoyed inflicting pain. Her initial feistiness was, however, quickly replaced by a state of depression accompanied by dangerous neglect of her medical regime. As we got to know each other in the unit, she recruited me as an intellectual equal with whom she could discuss matters of interest such as local politics, but she would dismiss me when she became bored by lying down on her side and looking away. Uribe never had visitors during her dialysis sessions and often complained about the loud chatter of siblings and friends who often inhabited the Saturday hemo session.

During the first group sessions, she was extremely verbal about her belief that this illness was a way for God to make her stronger. When one of the boys jokingly replied: 'What won't kill ya will make ya stronger, is that it?' she became enraged and offended. I wondered if anyone in the group could try to understand why Joe's joke had made Uribe so angry. Lana thought that for Uribe, making fun of God was a sin. I wondered if Uribe's family was very religious and she began to tell us how church had always been very important. In fact, now that she was sick she had the support of her church friends after she had lost all her friends at school. I said that it must be difficult to make sense sometimes of all of this when you are taught to be humble and accept God's will. Uribe agreed. Amir said his mum had slapped him when he said that heaven and Allah did not exist. I wondered if others shared this experience and how they thought Amir felt when this happened? Aruna asked: 'Norka, what do you think heaven is like?' I said that I was raised with the belief that heaven was a place where people had no pain and found people gone before them and this belief helped me when I lost people I loved. The conversation continued as everybody shared their ideas and beliefs about heaven. However, I felt it was important for us to think together about how Uribe and Amir felt and pointed out how we were moving away from thinking about painful feelings. Uribe agreed and said she felt like she was the only person in the group who was not angry with God. I invited others to share their reactions to Uribe's comment. Towards the end of the session, Lana turned to Uribe and said: 'My mum says God forgives everything, so I think it is OK if you get angry with him sometimes.' Uribe smiled and later on shared the fact that it felt pretty good to share how lonely and guilty she felt.

In time, I came to wonder if Uribe experienced her family's absence from the renal unit as a message that this was her cross to bear and that she was expected to do so quietly. Furthermore, as she saw her parents working to fight the spread of AIDS in Africa, I wondered what it meant for Uribe that they did not accompany her in her fight against her own weak and deteriorating body. Was her non-compliance with medical instructions a way of letting them know she needed to be taken care of? The nurses shared with me later that day that they hadn't realized that Uribe felt like that and that perhaps sometimes they were quite mean to her because they felt she was ungrateful.

Such reflections by the nursing staff as a result of listening to the young people share their thoughts and feelings became common during the whole intervention and in our opinion helped to activate the nurses' mentalizing capacity when confronted with patients' 'difficult behaviors.' In other words, they began to look beyond the young person's actions and words. In time, I came to understand Uribe's question as wondering, 'Do I still deserve to go to heaven when I feel so angry and resentful towards God?' For Uribe, her religious beliefs were a source of strength but also a burden. Overwhelmed by her conflict and confronted by a lack of family support, she turned her anger towards herself, becoming depressed, terrified and unable to take care of herself.

Uribe's story shows the value of listening to the personal meaning of the experience when attempting to make sense of behavioral manifestations such as non-compliance with a medical regime. It is a process that certainly demands much more emotionally and psychologically from all involved, but one that usually results in long-term improvement in behavior, health and quality of interpersonal exchanges.

CONCLUSION

The mentalization-based intervention seeks to promote a growing sense of agency and self-esteem in the chronically ill young person. Initially, the mentalizing group leader serves as a model of new ways of wondering about other people's thoughts and feelings; however, as the group evolves, members play different roles and slowly incorporate the new way of relating into their repertoire. As we hope we have illustrated, it is through this process, which aims to provide a playful and flexible framework, that meaning making occurs. By reflecting on the diverse meanings given to the same experience, one can access the hidden motivations behind challenging behaviors that often make us feel 'stuck.' Only in this way are we able to effect genuine change individually and systemically.

The mentalization-based intervention invites us to maintain a posture of 'not knowing' by remaining curious about the stories that our patients and families tell. This curiosity helps us ask questions and respond in ways that enable patients and families to expand the domain of the not yet said in their own chronic illness situation. When we invite young people to tell and retell, write and rewrite the narratives of their illness and life journeys, new meanings emerge that often help them and their families move past stuck points or enter periods of transition and change.

REFERENCES

1 Bowlby J. *A Secure Base: clinical applications of attachment theory*. London: Routledge: 1988.
2 Greenberg JR, Mitchell SA. *Object Relations in Psychoanalytic Theory*. Cambridge, MA: Harvard University Press; 1983.
3 Vermote R, Lowyck B, Vandeneede B, *et al*. Psychodynamically oriented therapeutic settings. In: Bateman A, Fonagy P, editors. *Handbook of Mentalization in Mental Health Practice*. Arlington, VA: American Psychiatric Association; 2011. pp.247–72.
4 Bales D, Bateman A. Partial hospitalisation settings. In: Bateman A, Fonagy P, editors. *Mentalization in Mental Health Practice*. Arlington, VA: American Psychiatric Association; 2011. pp.197–226.
5 Bowlby J. The role of attachment in personality development. In: Bowlby J, editor. *Parent Child Attachment and Human Health Development*. London: Routledge; 1988.
6 Allen J, Fonagy P, Bateman A. *Mentalizing in Clinical Practice*. Washington, DC: American Psychiatric Press; 2008.
7 Fiumara GC. Self formation, symbolic capacity and spontaneity. In: Ambrosio G, Argentieri S, Canestri J, editors. *Language, Symbolization and Psychosis*. London: Karnac Books; 2008. pp.42–56.
8 Brownbridge G, Fielding DM. Psychosocial adjustment and compliance to dialysis treatment regimes. *Pediatr Nephrol*. 1994; **8**: 744–9.
9 Bennet DS. Depression among children with chronic medical problems: a meta-analysis. *J Pediatr Psychol*.1994; **19**: 149–69.
10 Winnicott DW. Ego distortion in terms of true and false self. In: *The Maturational Processes and the Facilitating Environment*. New York: International Universities Press; 1960. pp.140–52.
11 White K. *Unmasking Race, Culture, and Attachment in the Psychoanalytic Space*. London: Karnac; 2006.

CHAPTER 4

Mobility Matters: The Intrapsychic and Interpersonal Dimensions of Walking

Ruth H. Livingston

A child takes her first step. It is a developmental milestone, proclaiming the peak of what Margaret Mahler termed 'separation and individuation,'[1] a period in which the child 'practices'; that is, she practices moving away from her mother and creates her own world, as distinct from her mother. With these steps, this child begins a 'love affair with the world.'[2] For the first time, she walks freely, upright, expanding her environment, enlarging her sense of her own power and independence, learning new perspectives, experiencing her body on a new plane, meeting boundaries with kinesthetic energy, relishing her sense of omnipotence. Her parents and others ooh and aah. 'She's walking!' Everyone is overjoyed, and our child takes delight in this exhilarating adventure into a new phase of her life.

This chapter is about walking and the psychological aspects of losing this potent symbol of empowerment and generativity. Mobility matters. Self-loco-motion is a biological adaptation for survival. Animals must propel to locate food and suitable habitats, to escape predators, and to find acceptable mates. As human animals, we use our legs to carry us through life, to be independent, to self-protect, to create an identity in work and social relationships, to main-tain boundaries, to be sexually desirable.

'Erectness is moral, existential, no less than physical' wrote neurologist Oli-ver Sacks after a temporary paralysis.[3] When fully mobile, we may not appreci-ate the privilege of walking freely, and how much one's sense of body integrity is embedded with this function. In fact, we tend to take walking for granted; we do not think about it. We do not think about it, that is, until something happens: a broken ankle, leg or hip, diagnosis of an illness that threatens one's mobility, an ongoing condition that gradually interferes with walking, an acci-dent that renders one unable to walk or just plain aging. Suddenly, what we've done so effortlessly for so long is no longer possible. In America, nearly 7% of those living outside institutions have physical conditions that impede their mobility.[4]

In truth, when walking fails, shifts in the relationship to oneself and often others emerge, sometimes powerfully.

Our culture champions mobility. In our society, walking is used to define autonomy, strength, stoicism, positivity, and success. Take, for example, some of our common aphorisms, all of them illustrative of these values: 'standing on your own two feet,' 'stepping up to the plate,' 'walking tall,' 'taking things in your stride,' 'climbing the ladder of success' and 'having a spring in one's step.'[5] Impairments in mobility, such as problems in balance, steadiness and stability, may be seen as signs of emotional weakness. Those who do not walk well may be labeled 'crippled' or 'gimp'; they may stagger, slip, misstep, blunder, 'trip up,' 'limp along' or 'fall flat' – none considered skills in negotiating life's challenges.

Clearly, then, we revere walking as a symbol not only of physical vitality but of mental and emotional vitality as well. That is, not being fully mobile has multiple meanings. The body with mobility impairments becomes a reflection of the self intrapsychically and interpersonally. Leg weakness or paralysis may be equated with weakness of soul, strength, and spirit. Persons who cannot walk fluently (or at all) are sometimes isolated and marginalized, viewed in terms of their disability, rather than as real people.

Losing one's ability to walk may be sudden, a shock, as in a fall or an accident, or gradual, with ever increasing disability, as in many chronic medical conditions such as arthritis, multiple sclerosis, Parkinson's disease and diabetes. While the experience may differ depending on the cause, the timing and the degree of functional limitation, loss and mourning are frequent themes, although not universal.[6,7] What *is* true is that the loss of easy walking often adds new complexities to our psychology. Even those who handle other challenges with aplomb may find that losing their ability to ambulate has an effect on their core identity – how they view themselves as independent individuals, in space, in time, and relationally. S. Kay Toombs, a philosopher, writes:

> (the) ... loss of mobility includes a change in the character of surrounding space, an alteration in one's taken-for-granted awareness of (and interaction with) objects, the disruption of corporeal identity, a disturbance in one's relations with others, and a change in the character of temporal experience (p.9).[8]

Indeed, the onset of a mobility impairment may exacerbate existing conflicts and reactivate previously worked-through issues of grief, anxiety, self-esteem and self-identity, shame, anger and interpersonal relatedness, all now seen through the lens of the condition. The loss of mobility is often a template on to which each person fixes his or her personal psychodynamics and pre-existing coping skills. In some cases, one's tendency to dissociate is highlighted, or perhaps other conflicts that have been dormant now press into the foreground, leading the person to project beyond the more tangible physical issue. The condition may be 'blamed' for unresolved problems in living, or external people or events may be blamed for the condition, even when it did not occur as a result of an accident or behavior of others. Internalizing the culture's stigmas of the mobility impaired, the individual may blame him or herself not only for the condition but for the clumsiness it creates, the dependency it fosters, and a host of other targets.

Let me put this in a personal context. Many years ago, when an adolescent, I was hit by a car while walking along a snowy road on my way to ice skating. The shock of this was compounded by the realization that I could not right myself, that one leg was simply not working: I had ruptured my muscle. Told by the doctor that the treatment was ice, elevation, rest and time, I mastered the use of crutches, enjoyed the special attention, and waited. When the day came to put weight on my leg, I discovered that I had no idea how to walk. It never occurred to me that there was any intentionality involved in putting one foot in front of the other. Concentrating on sending the 'walk' message from my brain to my dormant leg nerves yielded nothing. This I found extremely disturbing, perhaps more traumatic than the actual accident. How could the action of walking, so automatic, so much a part of me, be ineffectual? And what did this mean to my self-image as an active teenager?

In time I recovered, or my muscle memory recovered, and I went on to run and dance. I didn't consider the meaning of mobility again until much later when I was diagnosed with multiple sclerosis (MS) and faced some of the psychological effects that I discuss in this chapter. Soon I began working with patients who, like me, have a wide range of mobility impairments, from minor difficulty in walking smoothly to an inability to walk at all. My work on myself and with these patients centers on how mobility issues intersect with other aspects of everyday living and lives, as well as with one's internal and external sense of bodily self and identity.

Dynamics that arise in working with patients who have mobility impairments may not actually be so different from any psychoanalytic dyad, but some themes are especially poignant and prominent: mourning, identity shift, shame, dependence, anger, envy, pity, and family/interpersonal issues. Questions of how one is seen by self and others, concerns about how one will adjust over time, uncertainty about the future, and fears of burdening others predominate. I choose to tell my disabled patients that I have MS, not only because my disability is visible but also because it would seem withholding not to do so. This, of course, adds another layer to the interplay of transference and countertransference: both I and my patient hold assumptions on both sides of the shared experience as well as assumptions of experiences not shared.

As noted above, no matter how minor the mobility impairment, its effects may be major and should not be overlooked. Among the therapist's tasks, then, are the following:

➤ a recognition of the magnitude of loss associated with mobility impairment
➤ a detailed inquiry into the person's experience of loss of mobility and other life losses
➤ an exploration of each person's auxiliary support (including medical professionals, family/friends/caregivers) and how each of these systems is perceived as helping or hindering
➤ a keen attunement to the ways in which the loss of fluid walking emerges in one's interactions with others and in one's inner life through the relationship with the therapist, transference/countertransference, and through such tools as dreams and fantasies.

In the vignettes that follow, I discuss only a few of the many psychological challenges that may arise in those who have conditions that hamper their ability to walk. These cases illustrate the significance of past experience and core dynamics in how one negotiates the loss of mobility, shining a light on how one's prior history intersects with the loss, and how each person's emotional strengths and weaknesses, dependency needs/attachment style, and body awareness, among other issues, spring into the foreground when one can no longer fluidly walk.

COMPLICATED MOURNING

In 'Mourning and melancholia,'[9] Freud distinguished between healthy mourning and pathological mourning which he termed 'melancholia.' More recently, melancholia has been referred to as 'acute'[10] or 'pathological' grief,'[11] 'chronic mourning'[12,13] or 'complicated mourning.'[14] Bereavement theorists[10,14,15] describe this as prolonged, unresolved grief and the signs are many: anger, depression, irritability, fearfulness, social withdrawal, isolation, self-absorption, clinging dependence, appetite disturbances, fatigue and lethargy, sleep disturbances, increased illness, difficulty concentrating, short attention span, and confusion. As noted above, not all those who lose their mobility deeply mourn their lost functioning and among those who do, many cope with this grief without long-standing effects. Yet again, there are people like Carla, a classic example of someone in a state of complicated mourning.

A striking woman of 37, Carla suffers from a rare neurological disorder in which her lower limbs are so numb that she is unable to walk. The onset was sudden and there is no known cure, only palliative treatment.

When we met, Carla was on disability and used a walker. Through many tears and outbreaks of rage, Carla recounted her experience with doctors, her family's response to her illness, and her shame about using an assistive device to navigate. Before her legs failed her, Carla led an enviable life, traveling extensively, with many romantic relationships. She was, and is, theatrical: 'When I walked into a room,' said Carla, 'I was always noticed.' Now, she would rather not be noticed. Since her illness, Carla mostly stays at home, only emerging to attend doctor's appointments. Friends have disappeared. She leans, in all ways, on her most recent boyfriend, Jeff, a man whom she met after her diagnosis and whom, she confides, she does not find particularly attractive. She stays with Jeff because she feels no one else will have her.

Carla, grieving for her lost walking and inflated sense of self as well as her 'lost' life, is depressed and angry. She berates herself for clumsiness and her inability to self-motivate. She is constantly irritable, stays up all night and sleeps during the day. It is a challenge for Carla to harness the energy to handle even the most routine activity of daily living.

Complicated mourning theorists often refer to one's previous traumas in predicting whether or not one will successfully negotiate loss.[14-16] Carla comes from a broken family. She remembers her father as domineering and sometimes cruel; her parents fought constantly. When Carla was 14, her mother, frustrated with the father's abusiveness, abruptly left, abandoning Carla. The trauma of this still plagues her. She expects to be failed: to Carla, doctors fail her, family and friends fail her, Jeff fails her, I fail her, her body fails her. 'Why me?' is her mantra. Carla's failed legs are a metaphor for all the failures in her life, including what she sees as her failed former identity. Her loss of mobility is a narcissistic injury.

Indeed, there is a sense of helplessness in working with Carla. She cannot recapture her previous life; I cannot rescue her. My efforts to encourage Carla to rejoin the world are often met with hostility – how can I expect her to do this? Yet she uses our sessions to vent. I am her witness.[17] We are working together to integrate her melancholia into appropriate mourning, yet this is hard going. Carla, it seems, cannot relinquish her grief.

SHAME/DOUBT/CONTROL

In elaborating his theory of psychosocial development, Erik Erikson located mobility in stage two which he labeled 'autonomy vs shame and doubt,' the life-stage challenge of the toddler just learning to walk.[18] Writing about the tension between 'holding on and letting go' (p.251), Erikson considered the child's wish to 'stand on his own two feet' while simultaneously protecting himself from the shame and doubt that arises from this hard-won but potentially fleeting control. Such is the dilemma of Nancy.

Nancy came to therapy shortly after receiving a diagnosis of MS. She was just 27, with a stressful career and a new, yet committed relationship. Although her symptoms were relatively slight (she walked with a barely discernible limp), Nancy was all too aware of intermittent balance impediments, fatigue, and the occasional tingling in her legs that characterize relapsing remitting MS. Nonetheless, she put on a good face, kept pace with her job and told no one except her boyfriend. She was grateful for his acceptance of her mobility challenges.

Nancy had always been independent, in control. Her mother, a fragile woman, was hospitalized shortly after Nancy's birth for depression. Throughout Nancy's childhood, her mother suffered recurrences of this depression during which she would first completely withdraw, then be hospitalized. Nancy soldiered on. She recalls feeling as if she had to be 'the perfect daughter,' cheering up her despondent mother and consoling her heart-broken father who leaned on Nancy for companionship. She was very good at this. Nancy's natural resilience carried her through: she excelled in school, in relationships, and ultimately, her career.

Yet now, Nancy was in my office. Her MS diagnosis, she said, had 'thrown' her in ways that were far more disorganizing than her mother's frequent hospitalizations, her father's neediness, the demands at work or relationship disappointments. She suddenly felt resentful of requests from superiors and found herself envying those who seemed, at least to her, without trials in their lives. She noticed that she was becoming more dependent on her boyfriend and less trusting; she fantasized that he was about to leave her and confronted him when she felt he was not sufficiently attentive. When the boyfriend, confused by the changes in his independent partner, broke off the relationship, Nancy was devastated. She saw herself as 'damaged goods' and envisioned an uncertain and lonely future.

Nancy's diagnosis and her mobility difficulties set off a flood of doubt in her competence as an autonomous and 'in control' woman. It was, in Bromberg's words,[19] her 'tsunami,' unleashing her dissociation – all the ways in which she warded off shameful feelings related to those early years. The limp represented the imperfections of her upbringing. With the loss of full mobility, and thus control, Nancy associated to the shame her childhood experience evoked in her. She spoke of how she protected herself from the reality of her home life, for example never telling friends about her mother's depression or hospitalizations. She regretted how she denied her mother's experience but also, perhaps more important, how she submerged her own needs in the service of protecting a carefully constructed sense of herself and family.

Nancy was looking for a mother and I was all too happy to comply. Also, I identified with her. I remember those early days after diagnosis. I, too, came to MS with the delusion of perfection, not in terms of my body but in terms of what I expected to do in the outside world. My tendency with Nancy was to reassure and comfort rather than to look beneath her new, more vulnerable identity. Yet, ultimately, my job was to help her live with uncertainty and accept her physical and psychological 'flaws.' We mourned her gradual loss of mobility and the changes she was confronting. We also grieved that 'perfect child,' simultaneously celebrating her resilience. For Nancy, mobility has many meanings. Can she move on in life? Can she create and sustain an identity of someone who limps but still marches forward?

ANGER

John Bowlby[16] made a distinction between functional and dysfunctional anger in a child who has been separated from her mother: 'Sometimes it is the anger of hope; sometimes the anger of despair' (p.246). Functional anger, he wrote, is the hope of overcoming obstacles to a 'reunion' with the lost 'object' (here, the lost ability to walk effectively or at all). Other thinkers such as Bonime[20] have viewed anger as a tool to maintain the integrity of one's self-identity or as a way of combating anxiety.[21] Anger, then, may represent a cohesion of the self, and be motivating and protective.[22]

Indeed, in a person who has lost his or her mobility, anger may provide a host of constructive functions. Emerging first, perhaps as a response to the loss, anger may also be extended as a way to fight through sorrow or anxiety and as a response to external factors – such as frustration at physical limitations or society's perception of the condition. Yet anger is 'rarely tolerated, accepted, or understood' among those with disabilities[6] and, moreover, the person with impairment is often expected to be cheerful to accommodate society's discomfort towards those who cannot walk.

Michael fought this every day. An artist, Michael lost his ability to walk when he was 16. The cause was an accident when a drunk driver swerved off the road and rammed into Michael who was riding his bicycle. Michael's lower spine was severed and he no longer had use of his legs. He propelled himself in a beaten-up manual wheelchair, to which he had a strong attachment.

Michael was engaging, intelligent and psychologically minded. Early in his therapy, he let me know that he was not interested in discussing his inability to walk, that he'd only chosen me because my office was wheelchair accessible, and that he had other issues to discuss, among them, his relationship with his mother and his efforts to make a name for himself in the art world. He said he had done the hard work of coping with his parapalegia when in rehab following the accident. He did not want to be defined by his condition and made scant mention of it. I followed his lead.

On the surface at least, Michael was the poster child for healthy adaptation to his mobility loss. He and his wife appeared to negotiate their relationship easily and he was beginning to get more work as we explored career goals. There were signs, though, that something was missing. We wandered into the past: Michael's parents divorced when he was just four years old. Although he saw his father frequently, he did not much like him, nor did he care for the three stepfathers who followed. Moreover, Michael had a highly conflicted relationship with his mother, a severely narcissistic and dependent woman who, he revealed, overidentified with his experience and who had 'borrowed' money for cosmetic surgery from his 'accident trust' (the money received in settlement). She never repaid the trust. Perhaps this was why his mobility was off limits; perhaps he saw me as his mother, a woman who co-opted the life-changing experience of the accident, claiming it as her own.

Michael's artist studio was in the neighborhood of my office and I would, on occasion, see him on the street. We would speak about these off-site encounters but, at first, they seemed inconsequential; we learned to acknowledge each other and 'move' on. In time, however, I began to notice a persona about Michael in the outdoors that had not entered my consulting room. Observing Michael on the street, I saw a snarl on his face and an aggression that was absent in his behavior with me. A number of times I watched him nearly run down pedestrians and, more than once, I heard him initiate angry verbal exchanges. I worried about his safety and the safety of others in his path.

I considered Michael's transference to his wheelchair. It was an extension of himself. Using it outside, he could act out hostile impulses that were too dangerous to express 'inside.'

Agreeing with Michael that his feelings were justified more often than not, I opened the discussion to the ways in which the aggression I observed gave him a feeling of power and control. Michael agreed that his 'street' persona fueled a part of him that was otherwise submerged under a societal demand that he not appear 'the angry guy in the wheelchair.' Among strangers, Michael could express his anger, create distinct boundaries, and assert himself fully without risk to important relationships or his identity.

Now naming his anger, Michael found himself speaking openly about his feelings regarding mobility. He began sharing his frustrations and his surprise at his 'wheelchair' identity. For example, he once caught sight of himself in a full-length mirror and was shocked to see himself sitting in the chair; he noted that he had his own biases against being 'disabled' and thought this might be tied to the anger. Michael also became more attuned to his mobility limitations: he worried about the child that he and his wife were expecting and how he would manage holding her; he was able to share feelings about mobility with his wife and to hear her experience of his impairments without becoming defensive.

PITY/ACCEPTANCE/ATTITUDE

'Of all the human emotions,' Steven Mitchell wrote, 'we are perhaps most ambivalent about pity ... a tricky business because it sustains a tension between identification and differentiation, shared vulnerabilities and divergent fates'[23] (p.728).

In general, pity is not appreciated by people who have trouble walking, especially since it often 'presumes a status relationship in which the other person looks down upon the recipient'[7] (p.318). But to Mitchell, self-pity, or 'pathos' as he called it, has another function.

> Pathos vis-à-vis oneself – the capacity to acknowledge and accept one's suffering as real and poignant and sometimes unjustified – may be extremely important and constructive. A sense of pathos represents coming to terms with our relative helplessness in the face of many aspects of our lives.[23] (p.729)

George, who has a rapidly progressive form of MS, is someone who has 'self-pathos,' self-compassion, but who denies the label 'self-pitying.' He does not waste time feeling sorry for himself or for anyone else in his predicament. He urges members of his MS support group to 'pull up your socks and get on with it!' and is impatient with anyone who cannot heed his advice.

This is not to say that George is 'in denial.' He knows he was 'dealt a bad deck of cards' and often expresses sadness for the loss of his physical vitality. But here is George, 'waiting for the boom to fall,' acknowledging 'the black cloud hanging over my head' yet in the next breath saying 'but it's OK; what's meant to be is meant to be.' Situations that might create resentment in others who cannot easily walk are, for George, causes for merriment. He regales friends and family with his escapades of motor disability: falling into funny positions, knocking things over, attempting feats like climbing stairs, for example. He speaks of the advantages of his mobility impairment more often than the disadvantages: beating airport lines, having an excuse to take cabs rather than the subway, being home reading rather than having to work at a job he found tedious.

George does not like *not* being able to walk but he accepts his condition unconditionally, somehow remaining upbeat, centered and engaged with life, grateful that he ambulates at all (albeit clumsily) with two canes for support. He calls himself a pragmatist and George's optimism does not seem effortful. In his dreams, from which he awakes happily, he is always joyously running.

How does one account for George's attitude? George, a scientist, is the only son of devoted parents, with whom he is close. Prior to his birth, his mother suffered a series of miscarriages, so he was especially treasured by both parents and felt so. He led a happy childhood, with a large family and friends. The only painful memory George accesses is the death of a college friend in a car accident. The circumstances shape much of George's perspective. He intended to drive with his friend back to school but his mother, concerned about icy roads, suggested he take the train instead. George believes that fate and his mother's intuition saved him from the accident that led to his friend's death. Since then, he believes in destiny – he was destined to live then and to have MS now. To him it seems a small price to pay.

Given his sunny outlook, one might wonder what George seeks in his MS support groups and in his therapy. There are few conflicts in George's life that call for analysis: he is happily married, has many friends, and enjoys entertaining and traveling. In years of working with George, his anger only emerges when he senses that people are feeling sorry for themselves (self-pitying) or when others treat him as 'disabled', that is, with pity. We often discuss these moments as narcissistic injuries, as if people see themselves or him only through the lens of walking ability. He calls others who have MS his 'brethren': the support group and I symbolically bolster his wobbly legs.

Yet support can have its downsides. In simply propping up George (which I sometimes feel I'm doing), I wonder if I'm doing the same for myself. George reminds me of my own MS progression; our shared 'destiny' cannot be denied. Are we colluding to protect ourselves from reality? George would say no: 'As a scientist,' he says, 'I look at the hard facts. We both have MS and that's it!'

DEPENDENCY/BURDEN/COMPROMISE

Loss of mobility, especially when it's major, is a family affair, as the cliché goes. Those who have mobility impairments must depend on others to help with even the most routine activities of daily living – for example, anything that requires balance such as lifting without toppling, shopping or standing for long periods when cooking, etc.

Maria, who contracted polio when she was 10, knows how dramatically her inability to walk affects her relationships. She keenly recalls her ordeal as a child with polio – the pain, the hospital, the iron lung, the braces, the shock of not being able to walk, and the responses from her family and everyone else around her. Maria's parents, of strong Irish stock, treated her like the rest of her siblings. She was expected to do all the same chores, even if they would have to make special accommodations because she could not stand or walk without support. This was, by her account, good for Maria; she took her inability to walk 'in stride,' became strong and independent, eventually went off to college, then moved to New York where she became a teacher and writer.

Maria, however, most wanted a relationship and a family. Although men liked her, she was repeatedly jilted which she attributed to the polio. When one short-lived but intimate relationship resulted in pregnancy, Maria was thrilled; she felt, she said, 'finally whole.' Others were not thrilled: Maria's family, friends and even her ob/gyn expressed horror at the prospect of her as a single mother with a severe mobility impairment. They urged her to have an abortion; Maria refused. Nine months later she gave birth to a healthy boy, Adam.

Caring for an infant and toddler is challenging for parents who are fully mobile. Maria, who could not walk, took twice as long and required three times the effort to complete her child-rearing tasks. Her health began to deteriorate and she contracted diabetes. Out of necessity, she began leaning more on her friends, but often felt they interfered with her mothering. She no longer felt competent, independent or empowered. Instead, Maria found herself compromising, allowing others to make decisions regarding Adam in exchange for their physical support.

Still, there were many positives and Maria has never regretted her decision. In the early days, Adam 'enjoyed' his mother's disability, perching on the back of her scooter, squealing with delight, as the two of them zipped through city streets. He loved helping her and thought she was especially 'cool' because she could do things with her scooter that other mothers, without such a contraption, could not. He also enjoyed the attentions of Maria's friends who spoiled and doted on him.

As Adam grew into his teens, however, the relationship with Maria unraveled. He refused to help her and was vocal about his shame, not wanting to be seen with her. He favored her 'abled' friends. For Maria, losing the symbiotic relationship with Adam was devastating. 'Adam just doesn't want to look after me any more,' she wailed.

Throughout Adam's childhood, Maria sacrificed her health to show the world that she could manage. This, combined with the loss of Adam's attention, weighs heavily. Maria's physical condition is more fragile than ever. I encourage her to focus on herself now and to trust that Adam will grow out of this phase. But Maria's retraumatization has taken on a life of its own; she recalls her experience of that little girl, all alone with the loss of her legs, and how she had to find ways to cope with her motor impairment and to depend on those around her. I must help her mourn.

EPILOGUE

I now walk with a cane. It is a part of 'me,' much more than an accessory, something that makes me feel less vulnerable (I no longer fall) and more vulnerable (it's a sign of my disability). With it, I am both stronger (I can walk longer and faster) and weaker (why do I need a cane?). At times, my journey from the child who took her first step to today is overwhelming. I cope with many of the same challenges as my patients: mourning, shame, anger, denial, dependence. I, like my patients, must continually adapt to changes in my body, my psyche, and to the image others hold of me.

For those of us who cannot walk fluidly, these are expected. Our experiences differ but we all share one awareness: we do not take walking for granted. We know what we knew as toddlers: mobility matters.

REFERENCES

1   Mahler M, Pine F, Bergman A. *The Psychological Birth of the Human Infant*. New York: Basic Books; 1975.

2   Greenacre P. The childhood of the artist: libidinal phase development and giftedness. *Psychoanal Study Child*. 1957; **12**: 47–72.

3   Sacks O. *A Leg to Stand On*. New York: Touchstone; 1984.

4   Erikson W, Lee C, von Schrader S. *Disability Status Report: the United States*. Ithaca, NY: Cornell University Rehabilitation Research and Training Center on Disability Demographics and Statistics; 2010.

5   Iezzoni L. *When Walking Fails: mobility problems of adults with chronic conditions*. Berkeley, CA: University of California Press; 2003.

6   Olkin R. *What Psychotherapists Should Know About Disability*. New York: Guilford Press; 1999.

7   Wright BA. *Physical Disability: a psychosocial approach*. Cambridge, MA: Harper and Row; 1983.

8   Toombs SK. The lived experience of disability. *Human Studies*. 1995; **18**: 9–23.

9   Freud S. Mourning and melancholia. In: Strachey J, editor. *The Standard Edition of the Complete Psychological Works of Sigmund Freud, Volume XIV: on the history of the psycho-analytic movement, papers on metapsychology and other works*. New York: W.W. Norton; 1917. pp. 237–58.

10 Lindemann E. Symptomatology and management of acute grief. *Am J Psychiatry*. 1944; **101**: 141–8.

11 Gort G. Pathological grief: causes, recognition, and treatment. *Can Fam Physician*. 1984; **30**: 914–24.

12 Bowlby J. Processes of mourning. *Int J Psychoanal*. 1961; **42**: 317–40.

13 Bowlby J. *Attachment and Loss: vol 3. Loss: sadness and depression*. London: Hogarth Press; 1980.

14 Rando TA. *Treatment of Complicated Mourning*. Champaign, IL: Research Press; 1993.

15 Anderson C. Aspects of pathological grief and mourning. *Int J Psychoanal*. 1949; **30**: 48–55.

16 Bowlby J. *Attachment and Loss: vol 2. Separation: anxiety and anger*. New York: Basic Books; 1973.

17 Stern DB. *Partners in Thought: working with unformulated experience, dissociation, and enactment*. New York: Routledge; 2009.

18 Erikson EH. *Childhood and Society*. New York: W.W. Norton; 1950.

19 Bromberg PM. Shrinking the tsunami: affect regulation, dissociation and the shadow of the flood. *Contemp Psychoanal*. 2008; **44**: 329–50.

20 Bonime W. Anger as a basis for a sense of self. *J Am Acad Psychoanal Dyn Psychiatry*. 1976; **4**: 7–12.

21 Sullivan HS. *Clinical Studies in Psychiatry*. New York: W.W. Norton; 1956.

22 Buechler S. *Making a Difference in Patients' Lives: emotional experience in the therapeutic setting*. New York: Routledge; 2008.

23 Mitchell S. You've got to suffer if you want to sing the blues: psychoanalytic reflections on guilt and self-pity. *Contemp Psychoanal*. 2000; **10**: 713–33.

CHAPTER 5

When the Body Fails Us: Living with a Chronic Illness

Patricia B. Vitacco

I'd like to tell you about Mary, a young woman who was diagnosed with a chronic illness four years into our work together. These are Mary's recollections as she told them to me.

> I can still remember that day. I was so anxious as I sat in the rheumatologist's office waiting to hear the results of tests that I hoped would explain my three years of fatigue, pain, flu-like symptoms and weird rashes. This was the seventh doctor that I had consulted and I was hoping that I would finally receive an explanation other than 'It's stress, it's nerves or it's all in your head.' The doctor came in with my chart, sat down, looked me straight in the eye and said, 'Well, all the test results point to a diagnosis of systemic lupus.' I was numb and speechless. I needed to catch my breath. I felt like a bomb was exploding in my brain. While I was relieved to finally have a name for my symptoms and to have my experiences validated, I was simultaneously devastated by the diagnosis of lupus.
>
> In the silence that followed the doctor said, 'You are still you' but I knew that the person who had walked into this room no longer existed. Disease, like a thief in the night, had stolen me from me. Who was I now?

And so Mary began her journey, a journey to mourn the loss of her old self and discover her new self, a journey to take back and reclaim those parts of her life that she was still capable of living and a journey to discover new aspects of herself that the disease enabled her to find. This is the journey that anyone diagnosed and living with a chronic illness knows only too well.

Mary was a beautiful, single, 26-year-old attorney working a 24/7 week at the time she was diagnosed with lupus. After years of hard work and study, her efforts had been rewarded with an enviable partner-track position at a major corporate law firm. Lupus, however, was quickly leaving her both physically and mentally exhausted, as well as in constant pain. Maintaining the life she had worked so hard to achieve was becoming progressively more and more difficult. As Mary explained, the culture of her profession was one of fierce competition and left no room for those with vulnerabilities. Mary chose to keep her condition a secret but as she became less able to work the demanding hours, she resigned. Re-evaluating her professional goals, she took another position as an attorney with hours she could physically manage and health benefits that would cover her costly medical care.

Initially treated with high-dose prednisone, Mary quickly gained weight and developed the typical 'moon face' seen in patients on steroids. At times, she became agitated and had difficulty sleeping. She exhibited severe mood swings. Looking at her previously lean and agile gymnast daughter, her mother would cry, 'What has happened to my daughter? Where has my beautiful daughter gone?' It soon became clear that it was not only Mary who was devastated by the changes and losses brought on by lupus. Mary's mother, who had lived vicariously through her daughter, was also deeply traumatized by the illness. Lupus had stolen Mary's professional goal, her physical attractiveness and vitality, and her mother's admiration and support. Since Mary and her mother had shared an enmeshed relationship, these losses were even more dramatically experienced. In sessions Mary would cry, 'If my own mother can't love and accept me for who I am now, will there ever be a man who will?' She desperately wanted to marry and have children but given her diagnosis and medications, could or should she ever have children? I pondered, could Mary come to accept and love her new self?

Mary is one of over 50 million Americans living with an autoimmune disease. Women comprise 75% of this population.[1] Lupus, multiple sclerosis, rheumatoid arthritis, and Crohn's disease are just a few of the more than 100 identified autoimmune diseases. These diseases occur when a person's immune system becomes derailed and instead attacks healthy tissue. They are chronic, meaning there is no cure. At best, there are drug-induced remissions that can modify symptoms and slow the progression of the disease's destruction but their effectiveness is unpredictable; there may be side-effects of cancer and severe immune suppression, and sometimes the drugs just stop working. Since autoimmune diseases can strike any part of the body, there are wide variations in presenting symptomatology and this makes diagnosis and treatment very difficult. It is common for patients to be seen by multiple specialists and to undergo myriad diagnostic procedures over many years before an accurate diagnosis can be made. During these prediagnosis years, patients frequently report that they are made to feel like hypochondriacs, and this feeling compromises their ability to read their own bodies and trust their self-knowledge. During the lengthy diagnosis process, their disease can evolve unchecked in its attack on the body. These diseases can cause debilitating pain, deformity and death. Fortunately, current medical research is enabling patients to be diagnosed and treated earlier, and new medications and treatment protocols are changing the prognosis for many patients, enabling them to live their lives more fully.

The trauma of living with an autoimmune disease occurs within a social context. In my work with adults living with autoimmune diseases and chronic illnesses, a theme that consistently emerges is that of the feeling of aloneness in their illness. While family and friends may be available and supportive during the diagnosis and acute initial phase of the disease, this support frequently recedes during the life-long chronic phase or until a serious flare or hospitalization occurs. It is important to remember that those who know and love the patient have also suffered a loss. They anxiously await the return of their loved one's former self when an apparent medical crisis subsides, wanting the disease that will never go away to just disappear and for life to be as it was before the illness. It is during this very same period of time that the patient is struggling to surrender their former self, the person they used to be, in order to discover a new viable sense of self. Frank conceptualizes this as finding a grateful life in conditions that their previously healthy self would have considered unacceptable.[2] The conflicting needs of the patient on the one hand, to discover and embrace their new and changed self, and the family on the other, to resist or deny this change, frequently create tensions which then leave the patient feeling even more alone and disconnected from the very love and support of family and friends that they now need most. Not surprisingly, it has been reported that up to 75% of marriages in which one member develops a chronic illness end in separation or divorce.[3]

Some patients speak mournfully of family and friends who fail to make an effort to learn about their disease: 'Why don't they just google it?' Frequently, they can only experience this as a lack of caring or indifference. Many patients have a resigned wish that those closest to them would 'somehow just get it' and understand how challenging living each day of their life has become. Because of this, it frequently doesn't feel helpful or even safe for them to talk about their experiences of living with their diseases, and at worse they can feel painfully rejected, dismissed and even more alone with their illnesses.

We live in a culture with a strong bias against the old, the ill and the disabled. People living with chronic illnesses are marginalized because they are different and/or they make others feel anxious. These attitudes are internalized by the patient and can become sources of self-hatred and shame. Ninety-five percent of autoimmune diseases are invisible. Fearing labeling, job loss, social exclusion and discrimination, the patient, like Mary, may choose to 'pass'; however, this choice carries a heavy emotional price. Alpert[4] has written about the depression that frequently can accompany this choice, while others have discussed how isolating it can be. Many who choose to disclose their illnesses report feeling pitied or alternatively experience responses that are meant to be sympathetic as 'put-downs.' 'You look good' may feel like an invalidation of the pain and seriousness of their illness or the suffering that they cope with daily. Workplace accommodations are commonly met with eventual co-worker resentment and the accommodated worker may feel guilty for not 'pulling their weight.'

Being diagnosed and living with an autoimmune disease derails and unravels one's sense of self. Interpersonal relationships change as well as one's relationship to one's own body. Many have described this experience as feeling like a stranger in an unpredictable, undependable and unfamiliar place. Bromberg discusses the shock of strangeness when one's body doesn't do what it's supposed to.[5] Even among the most emotionally stable individuals, living with a chronic illness can be a serious disruptor and shatter a sense of self developed over a lifetime. Consider a complex puzzle as a metaphor for the self: the puzzle falls, it comes apart and scatters into many pieces. Some of the puzzle pieces remain connected, others easily fit back together, others no longer fit, some pieces are lost, and some new pieces get worked in, but the new puzzle is different and the old puzzle is changed forever. The experience of being diagnosed and living with an autoimmune disease is like that puzzle. 'What has happened to me, who am I now?' This is the trauma of living one's life with an autoimmune disease or indeed with any chronic illness.

Trauma, as frequently discussed in early psychoanalytic literature, refers primarily to repressed, cumulative or childhood trauma. While these early traumas definitely impact and configure the experience of later life traumas, this is not how I am using the term today. Rather, my conceptualization of trauma in this instance is more in line with Boulanger's[6] construct of adult-onset trauma. In her model, trauma is conceived as the psychological and physical reaction to an overwhelming external event in reality, something occurring in the here and now which undermines the very foundation on which a previously stable sense of self and self in relation to others existed. She believes that these adult traumas can and do shape subsequent adult development and may exert as much force as childhood events. Other contemporary theorists speak of the defensive use of dissociation in trauma and how this can make abstract thinking difficult and leave the survivor in a state of confusion. Greenberg specifically addresses the trauma of illness and how it impacts motor, sensory and affective systems and leaves us feeling a loss of connection with our former selves.[7]

In a paper discussing acute and chronic illness, Courtois conceptualizes illnesses that require intensive medical interventions and/or in which there is a single calamitous traumatic event as a complex trauma, a form of post-traumatic stress syndrome.[8] In many adults, regardless of their character type and prior pathology, a specific set of symptoms can be anticipated as a response to a life-threatening trauma. The probability that these symptoms will occur increases in proportion to the intensity and duration of the trauma, and they can last indefinitely. That said, it is important to be mindful that many patients who live with autoimmune diseases have been able to remarkably integrate the experience of their illnesses into their new sense of self and are able, for periods of time, to live each day with the reality of their disease taking a backstage position. At some points, though, many of these patients may experience post-traumatic stress disorder (PTSD) symptoms. Patients speak of the terror they feel when their diseases flare. 'Will I helplessly have to depend on others for even my most basic needs? Will I be hospitalized? Will there be any medication that can help me this time? Will my insurance continue to pay for my treatments? How will I support my family? How much pain will I suffer?' What the patient truly fears at these times is not so much their physical extinction but, more significantly, the loss of their humanness.

A number of factors shape the way in which people experience and internalize the trauma of bodily assault caused by an autoimmune disease or any chronic illness: the severity of the disease process, the stage of life when diagnosed, the pre-existing personality structure, and the social and emotional relationships and supports.

Let's return to Mary. Even though her initial lupus symptoms of fatigue, severe joint pain and rashes were helped by steroids and other medications, she was not able to continue working in her high-pressure position. Once she became physically more stable and made a job change, she was able to continue working as an attorney. This minimized the shift she had to make in her professional identity and self-representation.

Contrast this with another attorney, William, who experienced a rapid onset of myasthenia gravis. This severely compromised his breathing and left him with double vision. Multiple medications were tried but none was successful in controlling the progression of his disease. One year after an initial diagnosis, this 43-year-old man was unable to work and was placed on permanent disability. His illness profoundly altered his life, shattering his self experience and sense of self.

In each of these instances, the severity of the disease's pathology shaped how the trauma of illness unfolded and was experienced in the patient's psyche.

Mary was in the prime of her adulthood when she was diagnosed with lupus. Similarly, at 22, Harry was diagnosed with Crohn's disease and was treated with a colostomy. Reflecting back now as a 73 year old, he laments, 'What gal wanted to date a guy who carried his shit around in a bag?' He experienced his surgery as a sexual castration and this trauma has continued to dramatically shape his experience of his sexuality and to compromise his capacity to maintain healthy adult intimate relationships. Another patient, Bert, a happily married, retired engineer, was diagnosed in his later 60s with myositis, a rare autoimmune disease. He had achieved both professional and personal goals during his lifetime and was planning ways in which he and his wife could enjoy the time they had remaining. He had reached the phase in his life cycle when one normally begins to consider and accept one's mortality, and his illness brought this into sharper focus. He was able to adaptively use the crisis of his diagnosis and disease as an opportunity to evaluate and redirect his life priorities. Each patient's unique response to his or her illness was shaped in part by where they were in their life's developmental journey. For Harry, the timing was devastating. For Bert, it provided an opportunity and in Mary's case, the outcome is yet to be discovered.

The experience of a trauma is molded by one's personality structure and cumulative life experiences. Mary, a bright, beautiful and charismatic only daughter, was 'the apple of her parents' eye.' Her relationship with her mother had been narcissistically organized. To survive in this relationship, Mary had to become skilled at reading people and behaving in ways that insured their recognition, praise and admiration. This dynamic, however, severely compromised Mary's capacity to develop a stable sense of self. Thus when lupus limited Mary's ability to continue to receive many of these narcissistic gratifications, she was left struggling with feelings of emptiness, confusion and depression.

Autoimmune diseases frequently run in families, as it did in Mary's. Her paternal grandmother had developed rheumatoid arthritis when Mary was seven. Growing up, Mary had witnessed her grandmother become gradually more deformed and debilitated, finally ending up in a wheelchair and then dying in a nursing home. When Mary developed lupus, this ghost from her past reappeared; it haunted her and profoundly affected the formation of fantasies she developed about her own illness and life. Determined not to become disabled and like her grandmother, Mary used her good intellect and perseverance to educate herself about her illness and became a proactive collaborator with all prescribed medical protocols. Not only did these actions provide Mary with an opportunity to achieve a sense of mastery and control over her illness, but they helped to insure an optimum medical outcome.

Living with chronic illness can be very lonely and active social and emotional supports can be critically important in the process, experience and negotiation of the trauma. Mary experienced major shifts in her support system after her diagnosis. Debilitating fatigue and pain compromised her efforts at socializing with her friends and colleagues and over time these relationships waned. More challenging for Mary was the end of her relationship with her fiancé. Mary's mother, devastated by the lupus diagnosis, became severely depressed and physically and emotionally withdrew. This shift in the family constellation created an emotional space that enabled her father to become more involved in her life than had been previously possible. As a successful attorney, he was able to guide Mary through her professional decisions but, more importantly, he was emotionally available when she needed him. Living with the challenges of lupus provided an opportunity for Mary and her father to create a new relationship and in the process it changed both of them. Most significantly for Mary, it provided her with a new relationship template that was more mutually mature and respectful of the other. Mary had seen many doctors on her journey to a diagnosis, but the rheumatologist who ultimately diagnosed her illness had a temperament that worked well with Mary's personality. This relationship enabled Mary to feel supported and safely grounded in her medical care.

Mary and I had been working together for four years at the time she was diagnosed with lupus. Initially, I had assumed a more classic theoretical position in my work with her. Believing that many of Mary's presenting bodily complaints were psychosomatic reactions to her highly stressful, anxiety-ridden life and underlying personality dynamics, I had diligently listened for conflicts that I might interpret. This approach, however, failed to provide her with any measurable relief from her physical symptoms. Once multiple medical tests confirmed a lupus diagnosis, I knew that I had to rethink my therapeutic stance. How could I help Mary bear this assault to her body? How could I be more effective in our work together? I was deeply saddened by the realization that my work with her was not providing the help that she needed at this time. Stepping back and reflecting on our work together, I recognized that I frequently used interpretations as a way to distance and protect myself from the intensity of the painfully overwhelming affects that emerged in our sessions. Bergner[9] refers to this dynamic as the 'anxiety-reducing psychological function of our theories' (p.270). Once I became aware of this dynamic, I began to interpret less, while I simultaneously struggled to contain and bear within myself affects which emerged in our sessions. I hoped that by doing this, Mary would be eventually enabled to tolerate and handle them within herself.

Mary was depressed, overwhelmed and terrified by her diagnosis. Initially, to defend against the confusion created by the trauma of her illness, she used her good intellect and became obsessionally driven to research her illness. This spilled into our sessions and I felt barraged by the onslaught of minute details. Mary was in an emotional struggle to stay afloat and survive this assault on her body and her mind. At times, like Mary, I felt like I was drowning and it became difficult for me to remain focused and emotionally connected with her, while at the same time trying to understand and process her chaos within myself. She needed me to be ego supportive, to help her to anticipate and to organize, and to contain and to hold the terrors within myself that she could not bear at these times. This was very difficult to witness and there were times when I just didn't want to hear it. I struggled to stay connected, knowing that to do less would recreate in our relationship what she was experiencing in so many others in her present life.

Mary was someone who had always been in control, and now she was controlled by unwelcomed invaders of her body. At times she acted out and would become sexually promiscuous and use excessive amounts of alcohol and marijuana. I understood these behaviors to have many possible psychological meanings: a counterphobic reaction to being controlled by lupus and medications; a maladaptive attempt to self-soothe; a confirmation that she was still sexually desirable; and an attack on the body that had betrayed her. I also was aware that these behaviors could be a side-effect of her medications. At these moments, not only would an interpretation be useless, but it could be experienced as yet another assault or an intrusion or leave her with the aloneness that comes with feeling not understood. I had to hold my dynamic speculations in mind while simultaneously remaining affectively connected with Mary, bearing witness to her trauma and waiting for the time when her capacity for reflective thinking re-emerged, and an interpretation might be helpful.

Gradually Mary's symptoms were brought under control and contained by medications. There were times, however, when her lupus would flare and she would become frightened and depressed again. At these times the confluence of her symptoms was challenging for me to understand, untangle and comprehend. For instance, were her depressive mood, fatigue and pain a reflection of her underlying personality organization, a bodily communication of her trauma that could not be symbolized and put into words at this time, a symptom of her medical illness and/or a side-effect of her medications? I struggled to understand these presenting symptoms so I might be guided in how best to intervene.

Mary felt a deep shame because of her bodily changes and her experience of being damaged. She would have terrifying fantasies about 'evil things' happening inside her body, 'ugly black monsters' or cancers that she couldn't see but feared would kill her. Her dreams were flooded with themes of overwhelming bodily destruction. Especially at these times, Mary hated herself and her life as it had changed. I experienced a parallel loss of hope and, like Mary, felt helpless and traumatized by her illness. Bach speaks of the need to balance what he calls the 'mutually living through' with the patient at times like this, and recommends that the analyst seek support in supervision, a peer group and/or with their analyst when their countertransference proves overwhelming.[10]

As the time between lupus flares increased and Mary's health became more predictably stable, many of her former capacities began to re-emerge and in our work together, we began to find hope, hope for a life that included a serious illness but that did not have to be defined by it. Like the reconstructed puzzle, Mary had changed. She had been able to move to a more accepting and integrated experience of her body and developed the capacity to have new relationships that were mature and rewarding. This change was reflected in our relationship too. In these new relationships she was seen and cared for as the person she is today, a professional woman who also has lupus. It's ironic that, while lupus stole her former life, it also provided Mary with new opportunities, the opportunity to begin to know and accept herself for all that she is and is not. But most importantly, the opportunity to develop new relationships in which, for perhaps the first time, she feels seen, accepted and loved for who she is, something her mother had been unable to provide.

Paraphrasing Anna from *The King and I*, '... by our patients we'll be taught.' My work with Mary has taught me a considerable amount about living one's life with a chronic illness, about the losses, the fears, the loneliness, the anger, the frustrations, the pain and, yes, the opportunities too. Learning to understand, manage and work with my countertransference with a medically traumatized patient was not only illuminating but essential in guiding our work together. Most importantly, Mary taught me about the value of hope, what Slochower[11] calls 'the capacity to envision a different way of being' and of our human capacities for resilience.

Acknowledgment

I wish to both acknowledge and thank rheumatologist Grace C Wright MD PhD for her support and encouragement. Her assistance in recruiting interviewees for this paper was invaluable.

REFERENCES

1   American Autoimmune Related Diseases Association. www.aarda.org

2   Frank AW. Just listening: narrative and deep illness. *Families, Systems Health.* 1998; **16**(3): 197–212.

3   Copin L. Who hates to hear they look great? Over half of the chronically ill. *Scleroderma Newsbrief* 2007; 1–2.

4   Alpert J. Chronic illness as trauma: falseness keeps one alive and makes one feel dead. Paper presented at the 28th Annual Spring Meeting of the Division of Psychoanalysis of the American Psychological Association, April 2008.

5   Bromberg P. One need not be a house to be haunted: on enactment, dissociation and the dread of 'not me'– a case study. *Psychoanal Dialog.* 1994; 4: 689–709.

6   Boulanger G. *Wounded by Reality: understanding and treating adult onset trauma.* New Jersey: Psychology Press; 2009.

7   Greenberg TM. *Psychodynamic Perspectives on Aging and Illness.* New York: Springer; 2009.

8   Courtois CA. Complex trauma, complex reactions: assessment and treatment. *Psychol Trauma Theory Res Pract Policy.* 2008; **Suppl 1**: 86–100.

9   Bergner S. Seductive symbolism: psychoanalysis in the context of oncology. *Psychoanal Psychol.* 2011; **28**(2): 267–92.

10   Bach S. *Getting from Here to There.* New Jersey: Analytic Press; 2006.

11   Slochower J. *Psychoanalytic Collisions.* New Jersey: Analytic Press; 2006.

CHAPTER 6

Managing Patients with Orofacial Pain: Psychodynamic Explorations

Ruth Freeman

Dentistry is associated with pain – painful teeth, painful jaws and disagreeable treatments to rectify these physical pains. If toothache is at one end of an oral disease spectrum then at the other end are a variety of conditions which may have an emotional causation.[1] These 'painful conditions' have been given a variety of names including somatic symptoms, functional problems, psychogenic symptoms, psychosomatic symptoms or medically unexplained symptoms. They are in essence 'psychical pain syndromes' and in dentistry, they are encapsulated within the family of conditions known as orofacial pain.[2]

Orofacial pain includes a number of conditions, such as atypical facial pain, burning mouth syndrome, temporomandibular dysfunction, phantom toothache, etc.[3] It has been estimated that 10% of an adult population will experience orofacial pain, with prevalence levels rising to 50% in older age groups.[4] Therefore, all patients with orofacial pain are not the same.[1] The label 'syndrome' is quite appropriate for this family of conditions since their causation lies on an etiological continuum[5] from physical to psychical within the construct of a 'mind–body continuum.'[6] Henningsen, Zipfel and Herzog have perceived the mind–body continuum as a 'psychosomatic interface' between body and mind[7] and it is through this interface that emotional problems – unacceptable fantasies, unbearable thoughts and unresolved conflicts – are deposited in the body and experienced as physical pains.[8,9]

The clinician (the term 'clinician' is used in place of dentist/doctor/nurse/health care practitioner) who is faced with a patient presenting with orofacial pain is set a series of formidable tasks, the least of which is to ensure the correctness of the patient's diagnosis.[1] The appropriateness of the diagnosis is just one of many difficulties that the clinician experiences. Concerns that the patient may have a physical ailment may blind the clinician to the underlying emotional elements of the patient's presenting symptom. Moreover, a referral for medical investigation will lend a sense of reality, reinforcing the patient's belief that their pain is, after all, physical. Consequently, clinicians who encounter patients with orofacial pain are confronted with a patient who experiences facial (bodily) pain where emotional pain and anxiety should be.[8] Stuck in this confused discourse, there is little space to negotiate a treatment alliance (that is, the patient accepting the treatment the clinician is offering). If a working relationship is to be achieved, the clinician must be in a position to encourage the patient to speak, to hear the history of her orofacial pain and to understand the hidden meaning of the physical pain as a bodily expression of emotional pain.

Being psychodynamically informed will allow clinicians to assess the degree to which patients will accept an emotional explanation for the cause of their orofacial pain.[1,8] The advantage of this approach is that clinicians will be more able to recognize the course of the patient's psychosomatic illness which, being distinct from a physical illness, allows them to be confident in their diagnosis of a functional disorder. It is necessary to examine orofacial pain from the experiences of the patient and from the emotional and treatment decisions of the clinician if a psychodynamically informed management protocol is to be realized.

THE PATIENT EXPERIENCE: DETERMINANTS OF OROFACIAL PAIN

To develop an awareness of the interplay between unconscious motivations and emotions (that is, a psychodynamic understanding), the clinician needs to appreciate why the patient presents with physical or bodily symptoms when an emotional response or feeling would be appropriate.[8] The ability of the clinician to realize why a patient presents with a physical symptom in the place of an emotional one is the first step in devising appropriate patient management. It is important, therefore, at the outset to appreciate that a pathway exists from the original physical trauma (somatic compliance) through the build-up of unpleasurable thoughts and feelings and physiological regression to the bodily symptom in psychosomatic illness.[10,11] For this course of events to occur, predisposing emotional and cognitive factors must be in position. It is these predisposing factors, together with the traumatic power of the physical event, that act as an immediate cause of the illness. In this formulation, it is the traumatic event which reawakens this archaic or bodily means (the predisposing factors) of coping with emotional pain.

To understand the archaic nature of bodily symptoms, it is necessary to address the mind–body question. The mind–body question is at the center of the debate about whether an archaic connection exists between mind and body. Conceptualized as a closed circuit, the mind was considered not just to be located in the brain but dispersed throughout the body.[12] It followed, therefore, that in early life the mind and body functioned as one, reflecting the process of birth when the infant became physically separate but remained emotionally bound to the mother. Thinking in this way allowed the suggestion to be made that the infant's mind and body at birth were similarly merged and intimately connected with the mind and body of the mother.[12] Therefore, within this closed circuit, connections existed between mind and body and so bodily feelings could be released as affects and emotional upsets released as bodily discomforts.[13]

In this formulation a communication route existed – a door connecting body with mind and mind with body. With psychological development, a separation occurred and gradually emotional upsets were discharged through psychological pathways and by using thoughts, words and action.[13] In other words, with development the individual was able to think or mentalize and gain the ability to understand themselves and other people in terms of thoughts and feelings.[14,15] Recent psychophysiological research with adult pain patients supports these clinical observations as it demonstrated atypical brain activity in areas engaged in cognitive/emotional expressions of pain.[16,17]

For the child to be able to think and experience emotion, two additional elements needed to be in place. The first was the child's cognitive functioning. The child's ability to speak, to verbalize and communicate their feelings was essential if discharge of affect was to be achieved through thoughts and words.[13] The second element was the relationship between parent and child. Lacan proposed a central role for the parent with whom the infant identified.[18] In Lacan's view, it is the identified parent who makes available language to the infant that will be used to express thoughts and feelings to make sense of her inner world.[18] Children, however, caught up in an aggressive and/or anxious parent–child dyad, could have parents unable to find appropriate words to give to the child to allow the child to express her emotions. With disturbed early life experiences, these children would find themselves in an unsafe place with uncommunicative parents who would be unable to contain their children's fears and anxieties.[19,20] Being unable to communicate,[21] the vulnerable child would become stuck in a helpless state of heightened anxiety, and without a safe parental object, regress or fall back from thinking or mentalizing to experiencing bodily symptoms or somatizing.[10,22] Placed in anxious situations, the child would once more feel the full force of her emotions as bodily symptoms. The scene would now be set, consistent with the framework above, for bodily pain to be experienced in the place of words to express emotional upset.[23] As a result, there would be a tendency for psychosomatic illness in adulthood and the propensity for the formation of somatic compliance.[13,22]

Freud described how bodily functions or physical illness associated with any of the bodily organs could result in a significant psychological meaning and as such, act as the basis of a somatic compliance.[24] For example, a physical trauma – an actual event – associated with a significant emotional event would provide the nexus for somatic compliance and allow unconscious feelings a means of physical discharge or release. The choice of symptom was of central importance in understanding the event(s) which give rise to the presenting symptom. The consequence of the physical trauma for the vulnerable adult was that their unconscious conflicts, thoughts and wishes would remain unevenly distributed between body and mind.[8] With the unconscious conflicts[8] confined and located in the body, they would be unable to gain a quality of consciousness to be expressed as words and actions and remain dammed up and released as physical symptoms.[9]

The case of Kathy is illustrative. Kathy, a 40-year-old separated woman, presented with orofacial pain. She was 'miserable' on account of the pain but acknowledged that it seemed incomprehensible to her since it was located to her nose. It had started 'out of the blue' some 6 months previously. Kathy was living 'happily' with her present partner, son and daughter. While she insisted that the pain was 'completely physical,' she entertained the notion that her painful nose might be connected, in some way, to her former husband. Their relationship had been 'stormy and violent' and Kathy recalled, with ease, being hospitalized after her husband broke her nose. Kathy had heard nothing from her husband for years and then out of the blue six months ago he had contacted her. He wished for reconciliation. Kathy was terrified. It was clear that the onset of her symptoms (the painful nose) hid the psychical pain she experienced – the memory of her husband's violent attack, her anxieties and her unbearable wish for revenge. For Kathy, the physical trauma was the broken nose (somatic compliance); her unacceptable vengeful wish – 'to give him a bloody nose' – unable to be verbalized, remained dammed up, to be discharged through the pain in her nose.

Orofacial pain may be understood in terms of aberrations in psychological and cognitive development, which have contributed to maintaining an archaic connection between mind and body and for bodily symptoms or somatization to stand in the place of thoughts and feelings or mentalization. This is compounded by a child's emotional environment in which they may be unable to verbalize their emotional upset. A sense of reality is provided by the physical trauma which acts as a stimulus for the emotional pain to be displaced and condensed onto the injured part, permitting the creation of a somatic compliance. The result of these events is an adult patient unable to think and feel their emotions which remain dammed up and discharged as orofacial pain.[9]

THE CLINICIAN'S PERSPECTIVE: EMOTIONAL RESPONSES AND TREATMENT DECISIONS

At the center of the relational difficulties clinicians encounter with orofacial pain patients are those associated with words, language and communication.

Patients who communicate their feelings of pain and unhappiness as bodily symptoms may seem incomprehensible[21] but the clinician must try to decipher and understand the patient's pain in order to identify the various elements which gave rise to the presenting symptom. In this maelstrom of managing the patient's miscommunications, clinicians must also control their own annoyance and irritations at the patient's perplexing attacks.

Jane had a long history of orofacial pain. She traveled from her dentist to pain clinic to hospital trying to find a cure for her painful jaw. Sixteen healthy teeth had been extracted, investigative surgery conducted, antidepressants and anxiolytics prescribed but her pain and suffering remained. Jane had developed an 'obsessional antipathy' towards her dentist. In her opinion, it was the dentist who was the cause and source of her pain. In her fury against him, she insisted that he had refused to provide the 'correct treatment' that would have rendered her pain free.

In this vignette, Jane foisted her suffering upon the person of the dentist and inveigled him into her psychical reality. Unable to tolerate Jane's complaints against him, the dentist had reacted by extracting teeth and, when all else failed, referring her for investigative surgery. How can such apparent mismanagement of orofacial pain be understood? There is little doubt that Jane's interaction with her dentist was characterized by complaints, frustration and discontents, leaving her dentist depleted and angry. It is possible that the dentist's subsequent clinical decisions were an indicator of his unconscious vengeful wishes cloaked in the best of intentions to provide evidence-based treatment for Jane's pain.

Salmon and colleagues would suggest an alternative behavioral formulation for Jane's interaction with her dentist.[25,26] They propose that primary care physicians mishear their patients' emotional cues and communications. As a consequence, they block any affective communication, only note the patient's physical complaints and refer the patient for further medical investigation. These authors observed that the longer the consultation time, the more likely it was that the patient would be referred to secondary care. It seemed that the physicians' behavior betrayed their unconscious wishes to be rid of their complaining patients.

Using a psychodynamic formulation, however, the physician's blocking may be perceived as the clinician acting as the unattainable parent who blocks the infant's attachment and mishears their communications.[18,21] Being unable to find words and language to speak, and with a clinician who blocks their attempts at communication, the patient is returned to an earlier time with an unresponsive parent where their feelings of isolation and anxiety were experienced as bodily pain. This is a transference situation where the clinician is placed, by the patient, in the role of the non-responsive and unattainable parent. The provision of inappropriate physical treatments serves to capture the clinician and patient in this emotional web where the clinician is at the mercy of the patient's hostile responses. Whether the clinician–patient relationship is formulated in terms of transference or projections from the past, what is apparent is that within their interaction, an unconscious play is being performed which is reflected in the patient's anxieties and hostile responses, on the one hand, and the clinician's blocking reactions, on the other.

It is the clinician's ability to cope with this irritation, frustration and even anxiety stirred up in him by the patient which is a second step in the appropriate management for orofacial pain patients.[23] The clinician's ability to identify and subsequently contain the patient's complaints and discontents (projections) and transference reactions is of central importance in the management of the patient. It is necessary that the clinician hears the patient's communications to understand the emotional meaning of the physical symptom. After all, the physical pain experienced by the patient is a coded message with the many turns and twists reflecting the archaic communication between body and mind.

In the following vignette, Tillie's experiences of being bullied as a girl, 'keeping her feelings to herself' and her mother's illness provided the necessary ingredients for her to experience facial pain where affect should have been.

Tillie, a 21-year-old single woman, lived with her mother. She presented with left-sided facial pain mirroring the distribution of the facial nerve. She had been in constant pain for several months. After extensive physical examination and neurological tests, no physical explanation for the pain was found and so she agreed, reluctantly, with her doctor who suggested she was 'stressed'. Tillie, the youngest of three, had left school at 16 to escape being picked on and physically bullied. She had always kept her feelings to herself. The onset of Tillie's pain coincided with her mother having a tumor removed from her left parotid gland. Tillie had been relieved when her mother's tumor proved benign but was distressed by the facial paralysis as a result of the unavoidable damage to the facial nerve during the operation. Tillie accepted the idea that the pain on the left-hand side of her face was connected with her mother's operation. Since the operation, her mother had been angry and had picked on Tillie. This reminded Tillie of being picked on at school and her daydreams of 'smashing the bullies in the face'. She was shocked when she realized that she had the same thoughts and wishes for her mother.

At this time Tillie reported a dream. She is at the clinic. Her left jaw bone is at right angles to her face. She implores people to notice how distorted her face has become. In the dream she says, 'Look at my face, it is all changed.' Everyone tells her it's just toothache, it's stress. Tillie's associations were as follows: she had been thinking about coming to the clinic; she feared that, like her mother, she had a tumor growing inside her head but no one would listen to her. She recalled her mother's ruminations: 'Has my face changed?'

Tillie accepted the psychological element in the onset of her facial pain as illustrated by her dream and a propensity to mentalize. She recognized that her anger and fears for her mother acted as the immediate cause for the onset of her pain and that the distribution of the pain, together with fears of malignancy and facial disfigurement (representing her fears of loss of mother and punishment for vengeful wishes), mirrored her mother's pain and paralysis after the removal of the tumor. Unlike many other patients, Tillie was able to entertain a psychological causation for her orofacial pain because of the availability of her unconscious thoughts to consciousness. As Solms[8] has proposed, it is the patient's awareness (as in the case of Tillie) of their thoughts and feelings which acts as an indicator as to whether the patient is able to accept a psychological intervention for their orofacial pain.

MANAGING THE OROFACIAL PAIN PATIENT

Clinicians who encounter patients with orofacial pain are presented with difficulties concerning their management. First, patients may be resistant to the idea that their facial pain has an emotional element; secondly, their insistence that a physical origin exists interferes with the treatment alliance and generally destroys it; and finally, the patient's relationship ties may not be strong due to disturbed early life experiences. Acknowledging the difficulties in developing a treatment alliance with orofacial pain patients, clinicians should adopt an expectant attitude and wait for the patient to reveal their difficulties. Adopting an expectant attitude is encapsulated in Halliday's questions[27]:

➤ why does the patient fall ill when (s)he does?
➤ why does (s)he come now for treatment?
➤ what sort of person is this?

thus allowing the clinician to uncover the emotional determinants of the presenting bodily complaint.

The clinician who adopts this approach and uses the above questions in a conversational style can assist the patient to put into words the distressing events which gave rise to their pain, assist the patient to recognize the difficulty of their current life situation[21] and assess the degree to which the patient will entertain a psychological origin to her orofacial pain.

Facilitating the treatment alliance and encouraging the patient to speak utilizing Halliday's approach[27] was adopted by a specialist dentist (D) when Norah (N) was referred to his clinic with pain on the right side of her face along her jaw line.

> D: So to recap – you've had this pain for several months on the lower right side which is getting increasingly more painful. What do you think has caused the pain?

N: Well, it's obvious, isn't it? It was the tooth extraction two months ago. The dentist left infection down there and that's why it's so painful!

D: Well, everything does seem well healed. There is no pain when I palpate the area where the tooth was extracted and the X-ray shows no infection. So, I think we must think that maybe the pain might be to do with something else? Do you know sometimes this sort of pain can come about because of clenching and grinding your teeth? People often grind their teeth when they feel stressed about something.

N: I don't feel stressed about anything, everything's good. I'm getting married, even if it is the second time – I just hope it will be more successful than the first! (*Silence and after some time*) My former husband (*laughing*) could be described as having 'more faces than a clock tower.' At the start he was like my fiancé, attentive and loving, but our separation was messy. Do you know, I went back to get some clothes and my front door was opened by this young woman with a child of about 3 years old on her hip. The child was the spitting image of my former husband – not much wonder he hadn't been very interested in me for a long time (*laughing*). (*Silence*) He hit me … you know that night he hit me … he hit on my jaw … he hit me on my jaw on the right side – now I remember it was bruised for some time – at least a month.

D: That's interesting, isn't it – he hit you on the right side of your jaw. Perhaps the pain has something to do with that … something to do with being married?

N: Now you mention it, I've been thinking about getting married again and to be honest, I am worried that it will go wrong again. You know now when I come to think of it – I've had the pain – it's been on and off but recently it has gotten so much worse. I've had it since we've been talking about a date for the wedding.

The dentist recognized the emotional element in Norah's orofacial pain not only by the absence of physical signs but by the course of the illness – the increasing intensity of the pain since the extraction of the tooth some months previously. During the consultation, the dentist noted that once Norah started to speak of her unhappy first marriage and her fears and worries that her fiancé would be like her first husband, attentive at the start but would eventually leave her alone and isolated, the pain in her face started to ease. It was clear that Norah 'fell ill' because of her impending marriage and her fears that her second marriage would fail, leaving her alone and isolated as before. Norah was the sort of person who believed that she needed to 'put a good face on it' and she did so by making light of her violent husband and unhappy first marriage. She hid the true distress she had experienced. The traumatic power of the tooth extraction reawakened her bodily means of coping with emotional pain and together with Norah's convictions of 'putting a brave face on it,' provided all the necessary ingredients for her to experience orofacial pain.

Adopting an expectant approach based on a psychodynamic understanding of orofacial pain and the relational difficulties that may exist between clinician and patient has the potential to consolidate the treatment alliance and to facilitate the patient to speak and communicate in words their emotional concerns and feelings. This approach to the patient presenting with orofacial pain provides the clinician with a pathway to explore the immediate cause of the illness and the predisposing factors that allow the reawakening of an archaic or bodily means of coping with emotional pain. Working in this way provides the basis of an appropriate management protocol for patients who present with orofacial pain of an emotional origin.

REFERENCES

1   Freeman R, Lamey PL. Clinical and theoretical observations on atypical facial pain. *Psychoanal Psychother.* 2000; **14**(1): 23–36.
2   Lamey PJ, Lewis M. *Oral Medicine in Practice.* London: British Dental Journal; 1991.
3   Woda A, Tubert-Jeannin S, Bouhassira D, *et al.* Towards a taxonomy of idopathic orofacial pain. *Pain* 2005; **116**(3): 396–406.
4   Madland G, Feinmann C. Chronic facial pain: a multidisciplinary problem. *J Neurol Neurosurg Psychiatry.* 2001; **71**(6): 716–19.
5   Freeman R. A psychotherapeutic approach to the understanding and treatment of a psychosomatic disorder: the case of burning mouth syndrome. In: Ekins R, Freeman R, editors. *Centres and Peripheries of Psychoanalysis: an introduction to psychoanalytic studies.* London: H. Karnac (Books) Ltd; 1994. pp.129–40.
6   Gaddini E. Notes on the mind–body question. *Int J Psychoanal.* 1987; **68**(3): 315–29.
7   Henningsen P, Zipfel S, Herzog W. Management of functional somatic syndromes. *Lancet.* 2007; **369**(9565): 946–55.
8   Solms M. What is affect? In: Ekins R, editor. *Unconscious Mental Life and Reality.* London: H. Karnac (Books) Ltd; 2002. pp.45–82.
9   Fenichel O. *The Psychoanalytic Theory of the Neurosis.* London: Routledge and Kegan Paul; 1946.
10 Deutsch F, Thomas D, Pinderhughes C. *Body, Mind and the Sensory Gateways.* New York: S. Karger; 1962.
11 Freud S. *Introductory Lectures on Psychoanalysis.* London: Hogarth Press; 1916–1917.
12 Gaddini E. Early defensive fantasies and the psychoanalytic process. *Int J Psychoanal.* 1982; **63**(3): 379–88.
13 Freud A. The symptomatology of childhood: a preliminary attempt at classification. *Psychoanal Stud Child.* 1970; **25**: 19–41.
14 UCL Division of Psychology and Language Sciences: Psychoanalysis Unit. Mentalization-based treatment for borderline personality disorder. www.ucl.ac.uk/psychoanalysis/research/mbt.htm
15 Fonagy P, Bateman A, Bateman A. The widening scope of mentalizing: a discussion. *Psychol Psychother.* 2011; **84**(1): 98–110.

16 Hennington P, Creed F. The genetic, physiological and psychological mechanisms underlying disabling medically unexplained symptoms and somatisation. *J Psychosom Res.* 2010; **68**(5): 395–7.

17 Farmer AD, Aziz Q, Tack J, *et al*. The future of neuroscientific research in functional gastrointestinal disorders: integration towards multidimensional (visceral) pain endophenotypes? *J Psychosom Res.* 2010; **68**(5): 475–81.

18 Lacan J. The mirror stage as formative of the function of I. In: Fink B, translator/editor. *Ecrits: the first complete edition in English.* New York: Horton; 2006. pp.75–81.

19 Dumas J, LaFreniere P, Seketich W. 'Balance of power': a transactional analysis of control in mother–child dyads involving socially competent, aggressive and anxious children. *J Abnorm Psychol.* 1995; **104**(1): 104–17.

20 Hummel R, Gross A. Socially anxious children: an observational study of parent–child interaction. *Child Fam Behav Ther.* 2001; **23**(1): 19–41.

21 Vanheule S, Verhaeghe P, Desmet M. In search of a framework for the treatment of alexithymia. *Psychol Psychother.* 2011; **84**(1): 84–97.

22 Freud A. Psychopathology seen against the background of normal development. *Br J Psychiatry.* 1976; **129**(Nov): 401–6.

23 Pines D. *Woman's Unconscious Use of Her Body.* New Haven: Yale University Press; 1994.

24 Freud S. *Fragment of an Analysis of a Case of Hysteria.* London: Hogarth Press; 1905. pp.7–122.

25 Salmon P, Humphris GM, Ring A, *et al*. Primary care consultations about medically unexplained symptoms: patient presentations and doctor responses that influence the probability of somatic intervention. *Psychosom Med.* 2007; **69**(6): 571–7.

26 Ring A, Dowrick CF, Humphris GM, *et al*. The somatising effect of clinical consultation: what patients and doctors say and do not say when patients present medically unexplained physical symptoms. *Soc Sci Med.* 2005; **61**(7): 1505–15.

27 Halliday JL. *Psychosocial Medicine: a study of the sick society.* London: William Heinemann; 1948.

CHAPTER 7

The Empty Chair: A Psychodynamic Formulation of a Dialysis Unit Death

Maureen O'Reilly-Landry

Conscious awareness of death demands from us an intimate encounter with our profound sense of vulnerability and impermanence in the world. Death challenges us to contend with our beliefs about the meaning of our lives and our place in the universe. As with all endings, death confronts us with anxieties related to separation and attachment, with feelings of abandonment and loss. Our sense of power and control is called into question at the same time that feelings of hope, disappointment, anger and guilt may rise to the surface. Living with an illness that is both chronic and potentially life threatening punctuates a life with intense episodes of anxiety. And such anxiety can provide strident background music in a life that may already feel seriously compromised.

Here I will discuss the psychological effects of living with the looming presence of death on a chronic dialysis unit. I will examine the impact of death from three vantage points. First is the impact of one patient's death on the surviving dialysis patients, who routinely bear witness to the deaths of their fellow patients. Second will be a glimpse into the emotional experience of medical caregivers, who develop attachments to the patients to whom they have been ministering, sometimes for years. Finally there is the dialysis unit as a dynamic organized system which also becomes disrupted by death, and may develop symptoms expressive of this disturbance.

The treatment team on this dialysis unit includes nephrologists, nurses, a social worker, a dietician, medical technicians and me, a clinical psychologist and psychoanalyst. On the unit, patients and their families, along with the entire dialysis staff, struggle together toward a common goal – to keep the patients alive and as healthy as possible for as long as possible. The mutual engagement of patients, families and medical professionals in this challenging task encourages the formation of close emotional connections to one another forged around issues of sickness, vulnerability and death. Due to the intense nature of the work, explicit feelings and anxieties, as well as those that are less formulated or even unconscious, are very often in play. The psychological defense mechanisms utilized by patients and staff in their efforts to control potentially painful emotional states have an impact on how death is experienced individually and as a group. Anxieties surrounding the issue of death and the defensive efforts to contain them are frequently played out in the relational arena of the dialysis unit.

When a clinical psychologist in a medical setting is able to think psychoanalytically, she wields a powerful tool that can be used to improve the quality of patient care. The deep understanding of intrapsychic and interpersonal phenomena developed through training in psychoanalysis can be used to facilitate improved ways of relating between patients and medical staff. As the team psychologist on a chronic outpatient dialysis unit, I take on the role of participant-observer and will draw on my own experiences there to demonstrate my point.

As the team psychologist, I evaluate patients, provide individual and group psychotherapy and participate in treatment team meetings. In doing so, I attempt to attend to some of the unspoken and unformulated experiences in the unit that can lead to high stress, interpersonal conflict, depression, aggression and potentially compromised medical care, as well as to burnout or loss of will. Being able to think psychoanalytically has been invaluable. Paying attention to covert and unconscious aspects of human phenomena makes it possible to elucidate some of the more mystifying aspects of human behavior and relationships.

A psychoanalyst is concerned with subjective experience and symbolic or unconscious meaning. A chronic illness surrounds one with constant reminders of just how vulnerable and dependent we are as human beings. For the person who is very sick, each aspect of the illness can have meaning. There are the pills and other medications that signify the illness itself; a special diet may provide a daily reminder of the special care that must be put into staying alive; trips to the doctor can highlight the newly created dependency; the need to submit to invasive medical procedures can demonstrate the sense of helplessness and lack of control over so much of what is happening; and close involvement with the machinery of modern medical technology may come to symbolize the cold, stark reality that one's fantasies and dreams will not be realized, and that what might have been, never will be.

Sickness also affects social relationships. To live in close contact with someone who is chronically ill demands that one confront a large world of deep and possibly newly considered emotions and anxieties. Becoming a caregiver for a family member means having to cope with an onslaught of unexpected and possibly shameful feelings of anger and resentment toward a loved one who is helpless and not able to do any better or who may be taking his or her own anger and anxieties out on us. In essence, a serious illness threatens our sense of who we are or who we would like to be, while it undermines our sense of safety and security in the world.

Medical caregivers are affected by illness as well. A serious chronic illness is one from which there is no expectation of recovery. Medical practitioners often choose their professions hoping to cure and heal the sick and to alleviate human suffering, and they have spent many years in preparation for this. But with dialysis patients, they encounter their limitations, along with experiences of helplessness and powerlessness. They find they can help but they cannot cure.

My training as a psychoanalyst has taught me the importance of knowing myself. While the pursuit of self-understanding is a continual life-long process, in my work I do try to be aware of my own thoughts and feelings and to draw on my understanding of my psychological tendencies and defensive proclivities. My training has taught me that an analysis of my own emotional responses in a given situation can often lead to a deeper understanding of the emotional environment in which I am embedded.

When I first joined the multidisciplinary dialysis team, I spent a great deal of time listening to patients who would open up to me about how difficult life was for them. They sometimes told me things they did not share with anyone else. Although some members of the medical staff are quite attuned to the feelings of the patients, there are always others who seem intolerant of behavior they construe as excessively needy, demanding or manipulative. In my role of psychologist, I ended up feeling quite special and entertained a secret sense of superiority stemming from the belief that I alone understood the patients' suffering. It seemed to me that I was the one who cared, while the others did not.

Over time, this mild grandiosity began to fall away as I came to notice that I was going home at the end of the day feeling rather depressed and helpless. Eventually, it became apparent to me that since I was the team member who was there specifically to listen and to receive what was disturbing in the patients, I had become the holder of the depressive anxieties and the sense of hopelessness that were being defensively disavowed by many of the others on the team. Could my sense of specialness itself have been a defensive strategy designed to negate my own feelings of depression and powerlessness? Perhaps. But I was definitively cured of my exaggerated sense of importance when I realized that the physicians, nurses and technicians were not uncaring. Rather, they were the ones who were actually keeping these patients alive – and they needed those good defenses to maintain the psychological equilibrium required to stay focused on doing this very important job. Through attention to my own unbidden emotional responses, I was able to understand my colleagues' behavior in a deeper and ultimately more useful way.

Renal insufficiency involves a severe loss of kidney functioning, and end-stage renal disease (ESRD) is the point at which renal replacement therapy, or dialysis, is required. Being on dialysis is an arduous undertaking that generally proves disruptive to a person's life. Patients often seek in one way or another to get off dialysis.

For the many patients who long to be free of the need to come to the dialysis center three times every single week for the rest of their lives, there are essentially three options available to them. The first option is to transfer to a home-based dialysis treatment. While these dialysis modalities work for some, there are many patients for whom it is not a viable option. A second way to leave dialysis is to be a lucky recipient of a kidney transplant. The most successful transplants are those involving a living donor, most often a family member, who volunteers one of his or her own kidneys. A patient may also sign up with a local transplant center to be placed on a list to receive a kidney from a recently deceased organ donor. While not as high as with a kidney from a live donor, the success rate for a cadaveric kidney is still very good. But the wait for a kidney can be as long as seven years, while the average life expectancy for a person on dialysis is considerably shorter than that. So inevitably, the third, and statistically the most likely, way for a patient to stop dialysis treatments is to die.

But even the option to die involves choices. For those of us who are not so sick, if we want to kill ourselves, we have to put a considerable amount of effort into accomplishing the task. But dialysis patients do not have to work nearly so hard. They can die by just doing nothing at all. In these instances of passive suicide, the degree to which death is the result of conscious intent is often not so clear. And suicides that are unconsciously motivated may be even less obvious.

A typical hospital-based outpatient chronic dialysis unit consists of a very large room containing 10–20 oversized reclining chairs. Each chair is tethered to a large machine that cleanses and then returns the patient's blood. In a chronic unit, each patient is assigned to one of six shifts. He or she is designated to occupy a particular treatment chair at a specific time of day on three specific days every week. So each time a patient comes for treatment, it is with the same group of fellow patients and the same staff members attending to them. All medical procedures are accomplished while patients are awake. Many patients are bright and alert and pass the three or four hours they are there reading, knitting or watching TV, while others feel too sick, lethargic or physically distressed to do more than lie still. Still others just choose to nap. Conversations between patients can occur while they are in their chairs but this usually requires a degree of shouting, since the chairs are fairly far apart. But patients often get to know each other in the waiting room and greet one another as they go through the unit to their designated chair. Most patients are ambulatory but some require the assistance of a wheelchair, a family member or a health aid. Patients converse with the nurses and technicians about their immediate medical situation, as well as about topics of a more general or more personal nature.

Since the group of patients and staff who comprise a shift is fairly consistent over time, different shifts can develop particular personalities determined by the individuals on them and the chemistry that develops between them. Patients who are older and sicker may predominate on one shift to create an atmosphere that is relatively quiet and placid, or perhaps more depressed. In contrast, there will be a more energetic feel to a shift on which the patients are younger and livelier, or perhaps just angrier. Expressions of anger are common in dialysis, and verbal attacks on staff members occur; physical assaults are even known to happen. Sometimes people express their unhappiness passively or in a more hopeless or self-punitive way, by refusing to follow their restrictive diets or failing repeatedly to show up for treatments. With recurrent no-shows, the staff often work hard to devise ways to get them in.

It all began with conversations with Janice on the early morning Tuesday, Thursday, Saturday dialysis shift. Most mornings Janice found her friend Susan already seated in her dialysis chair, tubes connecting her veins to the dialyzing machine. But today, Susan's chair was empty. Janice had experienced empty chairs before and seeing one always made her uneasy. A dialysis chair might be empty for a host of reasons: transportation was late, the patient transferred to a different shift or was hospitalized, or was on vacation, or received a kidney transplant. But sometimes the chair is empty because its usual occupant has died and no new patient has yet been assigned to replace her.

Janice and Susan not only shared a dialysis shift. They also had rooms near each other on the same floor in the nursing home where they stayed because their multiple medical problems left them unable to care for themselves at home. Both in their fifties, they had become close friends and spoke to one another about all aspects of their lives. Janice was disappointed when Susan was not there because she had been feeling particularly distressed about a problem she was having and wanted to discuss it with Susan, who was easy to talk to and who often gave her useful advice.

Since Susan was frequently in and out of the hospital for one problem or another, Janice didn't make much of it when at first she didn't see her. But she became worried when she found herself unable to get a straight answer from anyone regarding Susan's whereabouts. As Janice continued to search for Susan, her anxiety escalated. Never one to keep her thoughts or complaints to herself, Janice persisted in her quest to find out about Susan. Back at the nursing home, the more she voiced her interest in finding out about Susan, the more dismissed and rebuffed she felt. Eventually, she became irritable, hostile and angrily disruptive. At dinner time, she refused to eat or even to come out of her room. When the next shift came on duty, they were not informed of the reasons Janice was upset. They attempted to engage her and convince her to eat, but Janice yelled at them and pushed them away. With the many worries and disappointments in her life, angry behavior was not unusual for Janice and this was the way she expressed her anguish and sense of helplessness. The staff had learned to keep away from her when she behaved like this.

A nursing home attendant new to the floor did not know Janice's reputation for being difficult and went in to find out what was wrong with her. Willing to weather the initial storm of Janice's wrath, this naïve attendant discovered what lay behind Janice's rude behavior. Janice felt the staff hated her and were refusing to help her. The attendant then explained to Janice, quite awkwardly and uncomfortably, that Susan had died in the hospital two days earlier. Her worst fears confirmed, Janice burst into tears and began to scream once again. She felt devastated to learn of the loss of her dear friend and felt betrayed by the medical and nursing home staff for having known and not told her.

In all of the clinical work I do, whether I am working with individuals, couples or families, and even in settings that are the furthest thing from a psychoanalytic consulting room, I find my training as a psychoanalyst to be invaluable. This is because psychoanalysis is not merely a particular modality of psychotherapeutic treatment, but it provides a conceptual framework for thinking about people and how they relate to themselves and to the people in their lives. A psychodynamic formulation is a tool that can provide insights into some of the more mystifying aspects of human behavior and relationships. Paying attention to covert and unconscious aspects of human phenomena makes it possible to elucidate behavior that would be otherwise enigmatic. When ignored, such silent feelings may make themselves known by resurfacing in disguised ways that can disrupt successful adjustment.

When Sigmund Freud introduced the field of psychoanalysis more than a century ago, he hypothesized that people are motivated by a quest for pleasure, which is achieved through the gratification of certain basic biological drives. Specific people become significant to a child, he surmised, because they satisfy his or her basic biological needs. A mother becomes important to a baby, for example, because she feeds him when he is hungry; this satisfies the child's need by removing the hunger and results in a state of tension reduction. The infant experiences this state as one of pleasure and is now happy, content and satisfied. The baby's love and attachment to the mother develop as a result of her ability to create this condition of pleasure and to repeatedly satisfy his primary, i.e. biological, needs.[1]

Freud revised and reworked his own theories over the course of his lifetime, adapting his ideas to accommodate new information. Psychoanalysts subsequent to Freud have continued to build on his ideas and further refined and expanded them. One group of post-Freudian psychoanalysts, known as 'relational psychoanalysts,' posit that from birth, people are motivated to maintain interpersonal connections with others.[2] They believe that this drive to be in a relationship is a primary and adaptive one that is not merely a secondary result of pleasure or drive reduction. Keeping with Freud's ideas, relational theory holds that patterns of relating established with one's earliest caregivers become generalized and form the basis of later adult relationships. Relational psychoanalysts emphasize the importance of the capacity of mothering figures to soothe the child's agitation and anxiety and to modulate the intensity of his or her emotions. These are capacities the child will internalize and eventually be able to perform without the mother's help.

Through her general availability and consistent, loving presence, the mothering figure provides a 'holding environment' in which the baby experiences a sense of safety and security.[3] In order to fulfill this function, the mother or other important caregiver need not be perfect but merely 'good enough'. Being a 'good enough mother' means being able to accept the child's intense love, whether it is soft and sweet or intense and passionate, and to withstand and endure the child's emotional storms, aggressive attacks, overt rejections and sadistic impulses, and to do so without either withdrawing completely, which causes him to feel abandoned and suggests to the child that he can destroy others with his anger, nor by retaliating with a response that is overly punitive, rejecting or excessively aggressive. The mother, then, must provide a safe space and serve as a container for the very young child's anxieties and most primitive and unbridled emotions. So just being a 'good enough' mother is neither an easy task nor a small accomplishment.

Though fairly calm most of the time, a chronic dialysis unit is a place where people feel strong emotions as they regularly confront issues of life and death and all that this evokes. The medical staff are highly trained and medically and technologically proficient. They have to monitor and respond appropriately at any moment to changes in a patient's status. The stress level can be high and so is the staff burnout rate. For their own self-protection, dialysis personnel need good defenses to keep the overwhelming feelings at bay. A dialysis unit is a community in need of a protective emotional 'holding environment,' one which can contain and neutralize anxieties and withstand the many expressions of emotions such as grief, rage and despair. These psychological states can be difficult to bear but are so much a part of the work.

Following Janice's brief recounting of what had happened to her in the time following Susan's death, I pondered what might have been going on to have resulted in such distress for everyone. I offer these as working hypotheses. It is always necessary when interpreting real-world events to highlight aspects that seem relevant to the problem at hand and then make some educated guesses regarding the subjective conscious and unconscious experiences of those involved. But since people are psychologically complex, and their interactions even more so, there are naturally many ways to conceptualize a single event.

It was quite clear that both patients and staff can react strongly when a patient dies, and they respond not only with grief but with anxiety. They attempt to reduce this anxiety by utilizing a variety of defense mechanisms.

In this instance, a number of people tried to avoid the issue altogether. This stance, despite its conscious goal of protecting the patient from being upset, only served to create more anxiety.

An imbalance of power that always exists between staff and patients became exacerbated the moment some people, notably the professionals, were given the information that Susan was dead, while the less powerful patients were not. Knowledge is power and Janice had less of both. She was left to feel ignorant and alone, all the time missing Susan. This differential between patient and staff reinforced the powerless, helpless and dependent feelings which were habitual states for Janice, as they are to some degree for all patients. But now, in response to the defensively avoidant way the staff had handled the communication of Susan's death, Janice's experience escalated from helplessness to impotent rage. She then withdrew, giving passive expression to her fury by refusing to eat. This negative behavior enabled her to regain some of the power she felt she had lost, as she was now able to prevent the staff from doing their job, which was to feed and take care of her.

The experience of the staff was difficult as well, but in a different way. In the period leading up to Susan's death, the medical personnel had derived satisfaction from their professional roles. During that period, the specialized knowledge afforded by their medical training brought with it the power to do good by helping to keep people, Janice and Susan included, alive. But now, the special knowledge that distinguished the professional from the patient was that Susan was dead. With this knowledge came profound anxiety and discomfort because it enabled them, they feared, to hurt Janice by telling her that her good friend had died. This shifting experience of their sense of power came along with the sadness and guilt that they had failed Susan in their inability to save her – this good and kind woman who was too young to die. The interpersonal dynamic based on differences in power and status may explain why it was a less informed and relatively less powerful aide who was able to get close enough to Janice to find out what was wrong and to give her the information she needed to know. The defensive attempts of other staff to distance themselves from their anxieties deeply affected the way Janice experienced that same death.

I believed that a structure was needed that could mitigate some of the negative interpersonal effects of the anxieties that death arouses. I recommended that the staff establish a clear and routine way for the news of a patient's death to be communicated to other patients. With such a structure in place for imparting knowledge about the loss of a group member, the anxiety will then be located in a single prepared individual. With everyone now feeling free to communicate openly, patients and staff will be able to come together in a supportive sense of community that could help to reduce the sense of aloneness that death can create.

I have just described for you my efforts to understand the meaning of a death on a chronic dialysis unit by examining the subjective and unconscious psychological ramifications of this one incident for patient, staff and the dialysis unit as a whole. It is a step toward developing a structure that will enable the dialysis unit to function as a 'holding environment' that is able to contain and soften the many disturbing emotions and anxieties that may erupt in the course of this very important but difficult work. Such a stable structure can enhance the sense of emotional safety and security felt by both patients and staff.

Acknowledgments

This chapter is reprinted from O'Reilly-Landry M. The empty chair: a psychodynamic formulation of a dialysis unit death. In: Souza M, Staudt C, editors. *The Many Ways We Talk About Death in Contemporary Society*. New York: Edwin Mellen Press, 2009, with permission from Edwin Mellen Press.

REFERENCES

1   Freud S. An outline of psychoanalysis. *Int J Psychoanal.* 1940; **21**: 27–84.
2   Greenberg JR, Mitchell SA. *Object Relations in Psychoanalytic Theory.* Cambridge, MA: Harvard University Press; 1983.
3   Winnicott DW. *Maturational Processes and the Facilitating Environment.* Madison, CT: International Universities Press: 1965.

CHAPTER 8

The Placebo Response: An Attachment Strategy to Counteract Emotional Stress?

Richard Kradin

There is a medieval Near Eastern folk tale in which a mother consults a local healer hoping to get her infant son to stop crying inconsolably.[1] The healer listens to her complaint, asks her to wait and retires behind a curtain to a back room. After some time, he emerges with an amulet. 'Take this,' he says, 'and place it at your son's bedside. It will cure him.' The woman pays the healer and does as he suggests. Shortly afterwards, her son stops crying. Fearing that he might start again, she leaves the amulet at his bedside for years. One day, after the boy has grown to be a healthy young man, and out of curiosity, she opens the amulet in order to see what was written on its parchment scroll, only to discover that the scroll is blank. Disgruntled by this discovery, she returns to the healer to complain that she had been misled. He, in turn, inquires as to whether the amulet had worked and she admits that it had. He looks at her quizzically and asks, 'Then why are you complaining?'

This tale is an example of what might currently be described as a *placebo effect*. Placebo effects are observed in all areas of therapeutics. The percentage of subjects that exhibit placebo effects in treatment studies can be quite high. Placebo effects are not limited to psychiatric disorders, and they occur regularly in patients treated for pain relief, and in roughly a third of patients with heart disease, peptic ulcers, arthritis, etc.[2] It is impossible to ascertain the frequency of placebo effects in uncontrolled clinical practice, but there is reason to think that it may be considerably higher.

A *placebo* is a drug or other therapeutic intervention known to have no innate efficacy. A *placebo response* develops in response to the administration of a placebo. It is an integrated mind–body activity evoked by the therapeutic dynamic. It is both automatic and subliminal; one neither observes it directly nor wills its development. Placebo effects, i.e. the salutary effects attributable to a placebo response, involve the subjective report of renewed wellbeing. However, objective changes can also be observed. *Negative placebo* or *nocebo effects* refer to an exacerbation of symptoms or to the development of new ones in response to a placebo.

A critical point with respect to placebo effects is that even when an *active* drug or intervention is administered, the concomitant offer to treat can, by itself, evoke placebo effects, so that the total therapeutic effect for an individual is an uncertain combination of effects attributable to the active intervention and those due to placebo effects.[2]

Although a large literature addresses its phenomenology, specific mechanisms that contribute to the placebo effect have received relatively little critical scientific attention. In this chapter, the current scientific status of the placebo response is examined, a novel theory with respect to its mechanism is expounded and finally, therapeutic stances that are likely to promote placebo effects usefully in the medical situation are discussed.

PLACEBO EFFECTS AND SCIENTIFIC SKEPTICISM

Whereas skepticism about placebo effects is often expressed publicly, few clinicians seriously doubt their existence. John Bailar, a rigorous epidemiologist, concluded that most clinicians are deeply convinced by personal experience that placebo responses are common and potent.[3] Yet like the woman in our folk tale, there is a nagging sense on the part of some medical scientists that in accepting the validity of placebo effects, they might be regressing to a prescientific magico-religious mode of thinking.

Another ancient tale highlights the fallacy of this concern.[4] In the Pali Canon, the Buddha recounts the parable of a warrior gravely wounded in battle by an arrow. When his aides rush to remove it, he stops them, insisting first on knowing more about the lethal weapon. 'What is its length? How was it constructed, etc.?' Before the answers can be ascertained, he dies of his wound.

Like the overly rational warrior, there is much that we do not yet know concerning how placebo responses develop. But that is not cause to ignore their importance. Reasons for our present limited knowledge concerning how placebo effects develop are worthy of consideration. One factor is personal bias on the part of some scientists, who resist the notion that therapeutic interventions could possibly work through mechanisms that currently have no clear scientific explanation. They may also have limited expertise in integrating the areas of medicine, neuroscience and psychology that likely underlie how these responses develop. A science of complex systems may be the best model for the activities of the nervous system, but few medical scientists are versed in this area and may tend to reject phenomena that do not exhibit linear behaviors.[5] However, the most serious obstacle encountered in placebo studies is likely confusion on the part of many medical scientists as to the critical difference between what is *imaginal* as opposed to *imaginary*. The former is rooted in the mental processes of imagination and represents an important achievement of the human nervous system; the latter is fictitious and lacks an ontological basis.

Presently, there are too many experimental data supporting the physiological basis of placebo effects for any intelligent observer to conclude that they are fictitious. The origins of the healing arts can be traced to the dawn of recorded history, but medicine as currently practiced is a relatively young science.[6] To dismiss placebo effects because their mechanism is not yet understood seems unwarranted. Many activities of the body are currently beyond our knowledge, but science demands that the unknown be confronted, appropriate questions be asked, and available technologies be adopted, in the service of unlocking the secrets of the body.

The underpinnings of evidence-based medicine are by no means fundamentally sound. Almost daily, new therapeutic claims and denials suggest that our current views of therapeutic efficacy are still in need of revision. Many popular therapies once widely accepted as beneficial have proved to be 'nothing but' placebos, after being subjected to critical examination.[2] A separate tome could be devoted to examples of how placebo effects have undermined therapeutic claims so I will limit my examples to two from the field of surgery, an area rarely considered to be subject to placebo effects. One recent report demonstrated that a widely popular and *rational* approach to the surgical removal of degenerated cartilage fragments in the knee joint was no more effective at providing long-term pain relief than sham surgery, in which the skin of the knee was incised without the subsequent extraction of the fragments thought to be causing symptoms.[7] An older but equally startling study found that an apparently successful surgical procedure designed to revascularize the ischemic heart was no more effective than making an incision in the chest wall with no additional surgery.[8]

Humans seek meaning, and find it difficult to accept that rational approaches may be no more effective than placebo. But history has repeatedly taught us that 'rational' ideas can be incorrect. For millennia, it was thought, based on reason and experience, that the sun orbited the earth; Einstein's theory of special relativity displaced Newton's perfectly rational approach to mechanics; and quantum mechanics and deterministic chaos have taught physical scientists that scientific explanation can extend beyond the realm of daily experience.

PLACEBO RESPONSE AND THE MIND–BODY PROBLEM

Traditionally, denigration of placebo effects by medical scientists has arisen from a failure to recognize that mind is rooted in a complex neurophysiology capable of influencing somatic physiology, although mental *experience* cannot be reduced to its constituents.

A number of poorly defined psychological factors have been implicated in the development of placebo responses. These include expectancy and hope, faith,[10] and belief.[11] In his article 'The powerful placebo,' Beecher suggested that placebo responses depended on the attitude that patients adopt towards caregivers.[12] Perceived competence, concern, empathy and trust by patients with respect to caregivers all increase the likelihood of positive therapeutic outcomes.[13,14]

Interestingly, many of these factors are identical to those aimed at in the practice of psychotherapy. Time spent with patients, empathic concern, and a milieu of established trust between patient and caregiver may all promote placebo effects. The current popularity of alternative/complementary practices, despite an abundance of evidence that these practices are not superior to placebo interventions, is likely a consequence of the increased time and attention allotted to patients by practitioners of these methods.[13]

Meaning, as the medical anthropologist Daniel Moerman argues, plays a critical role in the development of placebo responses.[15] Moerman has suggested that the term *placebo response* be changed to *meaning response,* in order to reflect this fact. There is evidence to support this opinion. For example, the size, shape, and method of drug administration all contribute to the size and direction of placebo, depending on their contextual meaning. However, Kaptchuk *et al*'s recent finding that subjects developed placebo effects even after being told that they would receive a placebo suggests that meaning and expectancy are not the only factors in their development.[16]

PLACEBO RESPONSES AND THE BRAIN

Studies in neuroscience suggest that placebo responses may be linked to pleasure pathways in the central nervous system[17] and that these are comparable to those activated during early development as part of the infant's learning to self-soothe.[18] In the psychiatric literature, it is well recognized that placebo effect rates are low in patients with obsessive compulsive disorder (OCD), as compared to patients with other anxiety-based Axis I disorders.[19] Most studies suggest that placebo response rates in attention-deficit hyperactivity disorder and schizophrenia[20] may be substantially lower than those seen in anxiety and depressive disorders.

Humans have the ability to create and respond to both social and psychological stressors. Repeated stress has the capacity to produce a shift in the normal responses of the body, as well as mental states of dysphoria. Repetitive stress increases the risk of developing chronic anxiety and depression, metabolic disturbances, pain syndromes, and a host of disorders showing no definite morbid anatomy, i.e. somatoform or functional disorders.[21] Placebo effects are most frequently observed in individuals suffering from functional disorders, an indication that placebo responses might play their primary role in counteracting the effects of chronic stress.[22,23] Of course, patients with organic disease can also manifest symptom exacerbations due to chronic stress, and these may respond to placebo effects.

It may be desirable to construct a theory of the placebo response that might account for the diversity of placebo effects, nocebo effects, and the limited predictability and reproducibility of placebo effects. The theory proposed here is rooted in the early developmental attachment in which infants learn to regulate their response to stress.

ATTACHMENT: THE BASIS OF THE PLACEBO RESPONSE?

Early experience plays a critical role in the configuration of somatic physiology and background mental states.[24,25] The behavioral correlates of the placebo response are perhaps best explicated by attachment theory. John Bowlby and Mary Ainsworth demonstrated that attachment behavior was a primary instinctually driven aspect of early development.[26,27] Bowlby theorized that newborns and mothers are driven towards secure attachment, which contributes to the child's increasing sense of autonomy, the ability to regulate affect, and achieving a comfortable balance between autonomy and mutuality. He suggested that the primary goals of attachment include seeking, monitoring, and attempting to maintain proximity to a protective attachment figure, identifying a secure base as the basis of an *exploratory behavioral system*, and fleeing to an attachment figure in moments of perceived danger and alarm. As will be argued, the latter strategy normally persists into adulthood and constitutes the basis of the placebo response.

Abnormalities in attachment styles increase susceptibility to adult psychopathology, vulnerability to somatization, and defects in the ability to self-soothe.[28-30] The styles of attachment have been classified primarily as *secure*, *avoidant*, *ambivalent* or *chaotic*.[30] Secure attachment is characterized by resilience on the part of the maternal caretaker, mirroring styles that are appropriate for the situation and that include the caretaker's ability to interpret and transform it, comparable to Wilfred Bion's concept of maternal alpha-functioning.[31]

Infants raised in a secure milieu tend to separate comfortably from a primary attachment figure, show increased acceptance of strangers and non-inhibited exploratory behavior of the environment, 'good enough' affect regulation, and the ability to self-soothe.[30] As adults, they tend to show good self-esteem and social adaptation, as well as positive affect. On the other hand, infants with avoidant attachment styles tend to show increased exploratory behaviors, with little interest or concern upon being reunited with the primary attachment figure. As adults, they show increased susceptibility to environmental and internal stressors.

Ambivalently attached infants show decreased exploratory behaviors and tend to be distressed when separated from their mother, but anxiously seek to be reunited with her. They also show increased vulnerability to stressors. More recently, a fourth attachment style, referred to as 'chaotic,' has been described. These infants show transient enigmatic, unexplainable, and bizarre behaviors when in proximity to their caretakers. The level of attunement between mother and infant is poor, and the child shows an increased susceptibility to stress and to the development of borderline spectrum mental disorders.

Fonagy has suggested that attunement and appropriate mirroring styles by caretakers are critical in the subsequent development of a coherent sense of self and in recognizing intersubjectivity.[30] The psychoanalyst Donald Winnicott described a sense of 'going on being.'[31] This can be conceived of as a sequence of implicitly remembered somatic states that are linked to a background feeling tone, which for most of us is experienced implicitly as wellbeing.[32]

The achievement of adequate symbolic mental self-representation may be the primary factor in regulating stress and dysphoric affect. When mirroring is defective either in quantity or style, Fonagy suggests that children and adults are prone to increased fantasy, concrete thinking, *alexithymia*, i.e. the inability to 'read' internal states, and to ineffective affect regulation. It is the present thesis that quality of attachment provides the basis for subsequent placebo responses.

But how might this apply to the placebo response? I am suggesting that the placebo response, like the stress response, is adaptive and that its essential role is the restoration of the sense of wellbeing, in response to the distress resulting from the impact of impinging stress. As Cannon noted, stress can trigger aggression, avoidance or inactivity (fight, flight or freeze)[33] but it also promotes affiliative behaviors in humans, as attachment theory suggests. Indeed, the placebo response is initiated by attachment behavior, insofar as one must identify a caretaker in the form of a physician, therapist, etc. in an effort to recapitulate a secure attachment and the reduction of stress.[34,35] Thus, patients who develop *nocebo responses*[36] are likely to have suffered disordered attachment leading to chronic anxiety, background feelings of negative affect, including emptiness, irritability, boredom, as well as an increased risk for alexithymia and somatization. From a physiological perspective, this may be conceived of as the effect of poorly modulated stress beginning in infancy. In these patients, efforts directed at alleviating distress would be predicted to be resisted or to result in exacerbations of dysphoria. As a consequence, efforts at evoking secure attachment are implicitly resisted. This may account for the 'help-rejecting' complaints of these patients that are encountered in medical practice, and for the 'negative therapeutic reactions' observed in psychotherapy.[37,38]

HARNESSING PLACEBO RESPONSES

Much has been written on the topic of 'harnessing' placebo responses.[39] If the theoretical underpinnings of the response are as described above, that is a substantial challenge due to their idiosyncratic features. However, it stands to reason that if the placebo response is evoked by early implicit memories of caretaking, then interventions that model 'good enough' caretaking might well be predicted to trigger the requisite associations.

The psychology and behavioral styles of 'good enough' attachment, as Winnicott referred to it, have been referred to in diverse ways within the psychoanalytical literature. These include the holding environment, maternal alpha-functioning, containment, attunement, mirroring and idealization, complex development, projective and introjective identifications.[30,31,40] With different inflections, these all refer to the diverse elements that contribute to the ability of the infant eventually to modulate anxiety, self-soothe with respect to distress, and ultimately to individuate optimally.

The experiences of early development likely contribute in overlapping ways to the achievement of adult mind–body states, but a number of early behavioral interventions are aimed specifically at reducing the undifferentiated distress of the infant. Interestingly, many of the specific elements aimed at achieving this goal are emphasized in psychotherapeutic theory and practice, and it is virtually certain that one important common factor of diverse modes of psychotherapy is their ability to evoke the placebo response.

What are the mental and behavioral approaches that tend to promote a beneficial therapeutic approach? Certainly, one major aim is to provide security and to establish trust, as this will alleviate distress. As Ainsworth suggests, the elements of secure attachment are flexible, not rigid; they are co-operative, not authoritarian; they are helpful, not rejecting; they promote trust rather than anxiety.[27] But how is this achieved in medical or other therapeutic endeavors outside psychotherapy? Obviously, a number of factors are involved but the process ideally begins with the initial contact with the patient. Efforts to respond promptly and predictably without undue lateness to appointments constitute a critical first step. In psychoanalysis, these elements are integrated within the framework of the treatment but whereas some of these might not be suited to other modes of treatment, the idea of meeting predictably, on time, in a defined location, etc. does tend to safeguard the secure base of any form of treatment.

The art of 'being there' for another, in ways that do not exhibit anxious preoccupation with other personal or professional concerns during the encounter with a patient, can do much to make them feel properly attended to and secure. If placebo effects result from the alleviation of stress, then a simple ground rule is that any behavior that promotes stress might be predicted to detract from the potency of therapeutic effects. The ability to be present as an empathic listener can successfully be achieved even in a brief visit, but it requires a full calm presence during the encounter.

The art of empathic listening to patient concerns should be consciously cultivated. When caregivers are attuned to what their patients are saying, they assume the role that Bion describes as 'maternal alpha-functioning,' i.e. working in a relaxed manner that can assist in processing the anxious concerns of patients.[40] This may include attentive listening, and achieving relaxed mental states that Freud termed *hovering attention*[38] and Bion referred to as *reverie*.[41] This promotes relaxation by providing a contained environment but also assists in the generation of meaningful thought. Well-timed interventions, which may include the compassionate communication of a diagnosis, can actually help patients make sense of dysphoric sensations, thereby promoting the placebo response.

As Paul Ekman and others have shown, negative affects, including impatience, contempt and irritability, are transmitted implicitly by facial expressions, tone of voice, failure to make eye contact, etc.[42] Supportive positive affects likely to evoke states of wellbeing in others are also transmitted by implicit facial and other somatic expressions. Many caregivers lack a clear awareness of how they communicate their presence and reactions via implicit somatic cues.

The British philosopher John Locke stated that there is nothing in the mind that was not first in the 'senses.'[43] There is much truth to this statement, and it can be helpful to review how a mindful approach to each of the senses can contribute to alleviating states of stress. The olfactory system is well integrated with limbic function. Although olfactory cues are perhaps not as important in humans as in some species, they do warrant consideration. Chronically stressed patients may be sensitive to odors, at times experiencing them as irritants. This is the primary symptom in patients with the 'multiple chemical sensitivity syndrome' but can also be seen in patients with chronic sinonasal disorders. Caretakers should be aware that aromas that appeal to them may be off-putting to others and the treatment room should ideally be 'neutral' in this regard. It has been demonstrated that infants can distinguish their mother from other caretakers via olfactory cues[24] and there is likely a great deal that still needs to be elucidated concerning pheromonal communication and the therapeutic role of the olfactory system. But as Marcel Proust has elucidated, the aromas of early development can be strongly evocative of affect for some individuals.[44]

As Stern and others have noted, the visual system rapidly achieves sensory primacy in humans during the first year of life.[45] Visual mirroring may be as critical during the therapeutic encounter as it is in maternal–infant attunement. It is important to promote the skill of making attuned eye contact with patients. Visual aversion, a behavioral communication of poor self-esteem, is associated with right frontal cortical dominance.[25] As such, the importance of making good eye contact is likely a factor in determining whether placebo responses are evoked.

Tactile contact is important in the promoting pathways of self-soothing.[46] Individuals who are unable to generate effective placebo responses, or instead develop nocebo responses, may have had disordered attachment characterized by little tactile soothing. Physicians and those who work primarily with the body have the opportunity to use touch in an effective manner, assuming, of course, that it is not overly intrusive and that it is being applied in a non-threatening way for a given patient. Here, a detailed history that includes the possibility of physical or sexual abuse can help caregivers determine how touch is applied.

Although taste rarely comes up as a factor in most modes of therapeutic practice, certainly medications can have pungent effects on the gustatory system. Pleasant-tasting remedies may be soothing. But whereas disgust is unlikely to contribute to placebo effects directly, the knowledge that medicines, although bad tasting, may also be good for you is a lesson learned early in life and as a consequence may contribute to placebo effects.

The ability to modulate behavior in the therapeutic encounter is a skill often referred to as the 'art of therapy.' But it is not an art *per se*. Rather, it is the behavioral science of optimal attachment, as it contributes to the psychoneuro-biology of placebo effects. These skills are by no means the sole province of psychotherapeutic 'technique.' One can identify them in lay individuals who excel in the capacity to soothe others, regardless of their professional training. Unfortunately, this is too often not a primary consideration in determining who is selected to train in the medical profession, a profession where these traits should represent important selection criteria.

CONCLUSION

This chapter proposes that individual styles of attachment are a strong predictor of response to placebos. Attachment styles are not 'pure.' They show considerable overlap and are prone to change with the level of stress. Having said this, it is hypothesized that patients with secure attachment, as well as those who show dominant ambivalent attachment, the latter due to their tendency actively to seek attachment, would be most prone to developing placebo responses. On the other hand, patients with dominant elements of resistant or chaotic attachment styles would be predicted to report lower placebo response rates. This may correlate with what has been observed in patients with rigid resistant and chaotic borderline personality styles.

Increased attention should be paid to the importance of stress and affect regulation in patients who develop placebo responses. Ideally, these assessments could be made via adult attachment style inventories.

The question of how to investigate non-linear responses at the integrative level is more complicated; however, it should be abundantly evident that the complexity of mind–body responses requires a non-linear approach. Probes of autonomic nervous system activity, e.g. assessments of heart rate variability, might be candidates for applying the methodologies of non-linear dynamics in carefully constructed placebo research.

Cannon was clear in his observation that too often healers are indifferent to the psychological factors that contribute to the overall distress of their patients.[47] As he noted, they are too frequently inclined to the notion that 'any state which has no distinct "pathology" appears to be unreal, or of minor significance.' Consequently, the anxieties and concerns of patients may be dismissed as unimportant. But Cannon argued emphatically that emotional concerns were indeed the proper focus of those in the helping professions, and he encouraged physicians to engage in research in this area.

> This field has not been well cultivated. Much work still needs to be done in it. It offers to all kinds of medical practitioners many opportunities for useful studies. There is no more fascinating realm of medicine in which to conduct investigation. I heartily commend it to you.

REFERENCES

1   Sabar S. Childbirth and magic. In: Biale, D, editor. *Cultures of the Jews.* New York: Schoken; 2002. pp. 671–724.
2   Shapiro AK, Shapiro E. *The Powerful Placebo: from ancient priest to modern physician.* Baltimore, MD: Johns Hopkins University Press; 1997.
3   Bailar JC 3rd. The powerful placebo and the Wizard of Oz. *N Engl J Med.* 2001; **344**: 1630–2.
4   Bodhi B. *In the Buddha's Own Words.* Boston: Wisdom; 2005.
5   Kradin R. The placebo response complex. *J Anal Psychol.* 2004; **49**: 617–34.
6   Osler W. *The Evolution of Modern Medicine.* New Haven: Yale Univerity Press; 1921.
7   Moseley JB, O'Malley K, Petersen NJ, *et al.* A controlled trial of arthroscopic surgery for osteoarthritis of the knee. *N Engl J Med.* 2002; **347**: 81–8.
8   Cobb L, Thomas GI, Dillard H, *et al.* An evaluation of internal mammary artery ligation by a double blind technique. *N Engl J Med.* 1959; **260**: 1115–18.
9   Humphrey N. *Great Expectations:the evolutionary psychology of faith healing and the placebo response.* Oxford: Oxford University Press; 2002.
10 Plotkin WB. A psychological approach to placebo: the role of faith in therapy treatment. In: White L, Turksy B, Schwartz GE, editors. *Placebo: theory, research, and mechanisms.* New York: Guilford Press; 1985.
11 Bertisch SM, Legedza AR, Phillips R, *et al.* The impact of psychological factors on placebo responses in a randomized controlled trial comparing sham device to dummy pill. *J Eval Clin Pract.* 2009; **15**: 14–19.
12 Beecher HK. The powerful placebo. *JAMA.* 1955; **159**: 1602–6.
13 Kradin R. *The Placebo Response: power of unconscious healing.* London: Routledge; 2008.
14 Kaptchuk TJ. The placebo effect in alternative medicine: can the performance of a healing ritual have clinical significance? *Ann Intern Med.* 2002; **136**(11): 817–25.

15 Moerman D. *Meaning, Medicine, and the Placebo Effect.* Cambridge: Cambridge University Press; 2002.

16 Kaptchuk TJ, Friedlander E, Kelley J, *et al.* Placebos without deception: a randomized controlled trial in irritable bowel syndrome. *PLoS One* 2010; **5**: 15591.

17 Benedetti F. Mechanisms of placebo and placebo-related effects across diseases and treatments. *Annu Rev Pharmacol Toxicol.* 2008; **48**: 33–60.

18 Schore A. *Affect Regulation and the Origin of the Self.* Mahwah, NJ: Lawrence Erlbaum; 1999.

19 McDougle CJ, Goodman WK, Price LH. The pharmacotherapy of obsessive-compulsive disorder. *Pharmacopsychiatry.* 1993; **26**: 24–9.

20 Pugh CR, Steinert J, Priest RG. Propranolol in schizophrenia: a double blind, placebo controlled trial of propranolol as an adjunct to neuroleptic medication. *Br J Psychiatry.* 1983; **143**: 151–5.

21 McEwen BS, Wingfield JC. The concept of allostasis in biology and biomedicine. *Horm Behav.* 2003; **43**: 2–15.

22 Benson H, Klemchuk HP, Graham JR. The usefulness of the relaxation response in the therapy of headache. *Headache.* 1974; **14**(1): 49–52.

23 Hrobjartsson A, Goetzsche PC. Is the placebo powerless? An analysis of clinical trials comparing placebo with no treatment. *N Engl J Med.* 2001; **344**: 1594–602.

24 Schore A. *Affect Dysregulation and Disorders of the Self.* New York: W.W. Norton; 2003.

25 Schore A. *Affect Regulation and the Repair of the Self.* New York: W.W. Norton; 2003.

26 Bowlby J. *Attachment and Loss.* New York: Basic Books; 1969.

27 Ainsworth M. Attachment across the life span. *Bull NY Acad Med.* 1985; **61**: 792–811.

28 Ainsworth M. *Patterns of Attachment: a psychological study of the strange situation.* Hillsdale, NJ: Lawrence Erlbaum; 1978.

29 Main M. Attachment: overview with implications for clinical work. In: Goldberg SC, Muir R, Kerr J, editors. *Attachment Theory: social, developmental, and clinical perspectives.* Hillsdale, NJ: Analytic Press; 1995.

30 Fonagy P. *Attachment Theory and Psychoanalysis.* New York: Other Press; 2001.

31 Winnicott D. *The Maturational Process and the Facilitating Environment.* New York: International Universities Press; 1960.

32 Sandler J, Sandler AM. *Internal Objects Revisited.* London: Karnac Books; 1998.

33 Cannon WB. *Wisdom of the Body.* New York: Norton; 1932.

34 Fisher P, Gunnar M, Dozier M, *et al.* Effects of therapeutic interventions for foster children on behavioral problems, caregiver attachment, and stress regulatory systems. *Ann NY Acad Sci.* 2006; **1094**: 215–25.

35 Maunder R, Hunter J. Attachment and psychosomatic medicine: developmental contributions to stress and disease. *Psychosom Med.* 2001; **63**: 556–67.

36 Shapiro AK, Frick R, Morris L. Placebo induced side effects. *J Operat Psychiatry.* 1974; **6**: 43–6.

37 Barsky AJ, Saintfort R, Rogers MP, Borus JF. Nonspecific medication side effects and the nocebo phenomenon. *JAMA.* 2002; **287**: 622–7.

38 Freud S. New outline of psychoanalysis. In: Strachey J, editor. *Standard Edition of the Works of Sigmund Freud.* London: Hogarth; 1936.

39 Brody H. Placebo response, sustained partnership, and emotional resilience in practice. *J Am Board Fam Pract.* 1997; **10**: 72–4.

40 Bion WR. *Elements of Psycho-Analysis.* London: Heinemann; 1963.

41 Bion WR. *Learning from Experience*. Northvale: Jason Aronson; 1962.

42 Ekman P. *Emotions Revealed*. New York: Times Books; 2003.

43 Clapp JG. *John Locke*. New York: Macmillan; 1967.

44 Proust M. *In Search of Lost Time*. New York: Modern Library; 1993.

45 Stern D. *The Interpersonal World of the Infant*. New York: Basic Books; 1985.

46 Fishman E, Turkheimer E, DeGood D. Touch relieves stress and pain. *J Behav Sci*. 1994; **1**: 69–79.

47 Cannon WB. The mechanisms of emotional disturbance of bodily functions. *N Engl J Med*. 1928; **198**: 877–84.

Medical Provider and Patient: Mutual Influence

CHAPTER 9

Adult Attachment and Health: The Interpersonal Dance in Medical Settings

Robert Maunder and Jon Hunter

Interpersonal patterns that are most evident in our closest relationships influence many aspects of health care. The ways in which our styles of relating to others affect health range from direct effects on interpersonal interactions between patients and those who support them, to patient–health care provider relationships and more subtle effects on experiencing and reporting symptoms and adhering to recommended treatments.

Attachment theory provides a useful framework for understanding how relationships affect health. Originally described by John Bowlby as a theory of the close relationship between infants and their parents,[1-3] attachment theory has been extended to explain individual differences in how adults approach intimate or confiding relationships.[4] Since the developmental underpinnings of attachment theory are extensively described elsewhere (for example, Cassidy[5]) and are beyond the scope of this chapter, we will review these concepts briefly when they are relevant to understanding interpersonal aspects of health.

ADULT ATTACHMENT STYLE

Attachment theory is especially concerned with interactions that relate to personal threat, loss, separation, rejection, vulnerability, reunion, and intimacy. States of mind that determine our response to these events can be summarized as an *attachment style*, which represents our patterns of trust or caution, dependency or self-reliance, and expression or suppression of feelings of distress. Therefore, patterns of adult attachment style describe attitudes, expectations, and behaviors that are associated with strong feelings in our closest relationships. Importantly, illness and its treatment are potent triggers of events of this kind, so attachment behavior is often evident in medical settings.

Attachment bonds between infants and their care-providing parents have been reinforced by evolution because of the survival value of an infant being able to signal distress to its parent at times of threat, thus drawing the protective adult into closer proximity. Depending on the infant's experience of his or her parent's responsiveness, biases as to the optimal way of expressing distress develop. For example, one infant learns that loud complaint is required to produce a response from a distracted parent, whereas another infant learns that high-volume complaint will be punished, rather than responded to, and that greater proximity is available when appearing unperturbed. This individual tendency towards expression or suppression of distress, which becomes embedded in the adult's interpersonal style, is particularly important in medical settings because it influences under-reporting or amplified reporting of symptoms, which can in turn explain individual differences in utilization of health care resources.

We will use clinical scenarios to illustrate four prototypic styles of attachment style in a hospital setting. In these examples the interactions we are describing are between first-year medical students and their newly assigned patients (a choice which allows us to describe interactions involving less interpersonal finesse than many readers will possess – it is helpful to start at the beginning). After introducing the four styles through case examples, we will return to elaborate on how attachment theory informs health care workers' understanding of their patients' interpersonal styles.

SECURE

In the cardiac care unit, Serena Panindar is on the phone when the students enter her room. She excuses herself and hangs up to greet them. Serena has been in the hospital for two days since being brought by an ambulance after experiencing sudden chest pain at work, which turned out to be due to a myocardial infarction. It is obvious that she is tired but she lets the students introduce themselves and direct the interview. One of the students, Esther, is a little more self-assured than the others, and she takes the lead.

Serena describes the events leading up to her dramatic trip to hospital. She had not been expecting to have heart trouble. She doesn't smoke and although she is a little heavier than she would like to be at 50, she is active and eats a sensible diet. When she suddenly started to feel unwell and nauseated, she excused herself from a business meeting and went back to her office. As the uncomfortable sensations started to include a feeling of pressure on her chest, she called a friend from an adjoining office to ask her to bring her to the hospital. By the time the friend arrived moments later, they agreed that it made more sense to call for an ambulance. The doctor in the emergency department told her that she had done exactly the right thing. There was some damage to the muscle of her heart but it could have been much worse had she not responded so quickly.

Esther asks Serena about risk factors for heart disease. Serena tells her that her father had high blood pressure and eventually died of heart failure but not until he was well into his 70s. Her mother had diabetes and died of a heart attack when she was 50, almost the same age that Serena is now, so that's a worry. A tear trails across her cheek as she talks about her mother. She smiles at Esther, acknowledging that they both know she is having tender feelings but that they have another job at hand. She wipes the tear away and they carry on. Esther asks if Serena has been tested for diabetes. Yes, with her mother's history she has been concerned, so her family doctor checks her blood sugar when she has a check-up, and it's been OK so far. They talk some more about the days before her hospitalization, as well as how she grew up, who's in her family, what she likes to do with her time, and what kinds of things she finds frustrating. Esther and the other two students are able to co-operatively conclude the interview at the end of the hour, with a sense that they understand Serena's cardiac status and even a little bit about her as a person.

A person who experienced consistent, responsive, attuned care in their early years and was also encouraged to play independently, to learn and explore, has been provided with the interpersonal experiences that reinforce a *secure* style of relating. A secure adult, like Serena, has a flexible approach to evaluating the need to report symptoms, distressing emotions and disability. She assesses her circumstances and adapts. She is flexible, feeling confidently able to handle many challenges independently without being inhibited about asking for help when it is needed.

PREOCCUPIED

Susan Szabo was admitted to hospital two days ago because of dizziness and a funny feeling in her chest. Although the medical team is already planning her discharge because tests showed nothing of concern, Susan didn't find those results reassuring. She thinks that something might have been missed. She still has no real explanation of her symptoms and no plan to deal with her distress and so talk about being discharged home has brought anxiety instead of relief.

When the students arrive, Susan motions them to gather closer around the head of her hospital bed. To their relief, she starts telling her story without waiting for them to figure out what the right questions might be. Their relief turns to concern a few minutes later when they realize that her story is long and complicated and that they don't have the skills yet to direct this interchange effectively. They lean forward and listen, writing notes feverishly as she proceeds. No one takes charge of the interview; it is a disorganized conversation.

Susan sees her family doctor frequently and has seen a few specialists as well, although she has never been clearly diagnosed with an illness as far as the students can gather. She mentions problems with dizziness, vomiting, and a disturbing sensation in her chest – and makes one of the students blush when she pulls her top way down to point to the spot where it hurts – but it doesn't sound like anything they've read about. Susan can't help them to organize her story. She speaks of her health and her interactions with the medical system in a confusing blur of anecdotes, worries, and conjectures. It is not long into her story when the students realize they have lost any sense of how long she's been having trouble, which anecdotes are recent, which are long past, and what things changed to make her decide to go to the emergency department.

Nonetheless, Susan is an engaging person. It is clear that she is suffering and the students feel sympathetic. They are keen to be helpful and they share her concern that she is being sent home before understanding what is wrong. The students don't know how to respond when Susan talks of how several doctors have let her down, promising to get to the bottom of things and then 'shuffling her off' to someone else without finding answers.

The end of the hour approaches and the students have no way to draw the interview to a close. Susan asks them what they think the problem is. None of them feels that it would be acceptable to admit that they have no idea. One of them mumbles that they will be conferring with her attending doctor. Susan goes on talking about her concerns as if the student hadn't spoken. In the end, the students do not bring the conversation to a close, they simply say they have to leave and go. It is an awkward, graceless finish and Susan sinks back into her pillow feeling worse than she did before they arrived.

An individual whose early experience was inconsistent, with a parent who was sometimes attentive, at other times unavailable, and still other times excessively protective when it was not required, is likely to develop a different stance towards the expression of problems than our secure patient did. On one hand, the inconsistent availability of others reinforces the value of sending distress signals frequently and intensely in order to keep others attentive and available. On the other hand, a sense of having little self-efficacy (because one's efforts do not consistently bring about the desired outcome) and little confidence (because of a paucity of experiences of mastering situations independently) interferes with this person's capacity to manage challenges alone. This cluster of attitudes and feelings, called *attachment anxiety*, results in a tendency to treat all challenges as if they are severe, to identify problems and symptoms frequently, to communicate them intensely, and to rely on others to provide comfort and solutions. Attachment anxiety is prominent in the *preoccupied* style.

DISMISSING

The third trio of medical students is assigned to the intensive care unit (ICU), where they meet William Cassidy. He was on a ventilator to assist his breathing until yesterday, which has left him hoarse, but he is able to talk. William has cancer. He tells the students about his medical care with a story that is careful, chronological and seemingly complete, leaving little left for the students to question.

When William was first diagnosed he was treated with chemotherapy. In his case, the chemotherapy killed so many cells that his kidneys were overwhelmed with cellular detritus and shut down. Kidney failure greatly amplified the sickness that he was already feeling. Far from complaining about the burden of these symptoms, however, William just put up with it. He didn't question that he was urinating less and feeling worse and worse until he eventually got a fever that wouldn't go away. Even then he was reluctant to come to the emergency department and 'bother the doctors' but his wife laid down the law, reminding him that they'd been told to look out for fever, so it was his obligation to go to the hospital. William apologized to the emergency department staff for needing help and minimized his suffering. The doctor in the emergency department was surprised to find out that not only was William in kidney failure, but he also had early indications of pneumonia brewing. Once he was admitted into the hospital, his condition deteriorated rapidly and he was soon in the ICU receiving dialysis to detoxify his blood and requiring a ventilator to breathe for him. To the students, this was hardcore medicine. They saw William almost like a character on a TV show, especially as he seemed so calm and cool.

William gave straight answers to their medical questions but when they asked about how he had felt about his extraordinary time in hospital or about his cancer, his answers were polite but brief. There was, it seemed, very little to say. Consecutive questions were required to get additional personal information. The conversation was pleasant; in fact, the students felt like they had a clear account of his illness by the time they'd finished. If they'd been asked to describe William as a person, however, and give some sense of what makes him tick, they'd have been at a loss.

A person like William, whose early experience was with a parent who was consistently punitive of expressions of distress or of the need for comfort, intimacy and soothing, is likely to have learned to suppress the expression of vulnerability or the desire for intimacy. Beyond this inhibition, he may have come to mistrust those who try to elicit negative feelings or who wish for more intimate contact, a cluster of attitudes and behaviors which is called *attachment avoidance*. Attachment avoidance is prominent in the *dismissing* style.

FEARFUL

Jodi Heatley was admitted to the hospital because of an infection beneath the skin of her abdomen. She had liposuction to remove fat from her belly at a private clinic the previous week and she had experienced unexpected complications. She is in her late 20s and hit the ward like a whirlwind, complaining about waiting for tests, her room, the food, and the nurses who fail to bring her medication at exactly the time she needs it. She hates being in the hospital and she can barely have a conversation without it turning into an argument. She is angry, disappointed, judgmental and secretive all at once. It would be a challenge for an experienced professional to find a way to converse with her so that she felt understood. The staff have already begun 'counting down' the time until her discharge. For the medical students, the challenge is much too great for their limited skills.

The students introduce themselves and Jodi acknowledges that she knew they were coming. They ask why she is in the hospital and she tells them she has an infection. One student notices her hands cupped lightly on her abdomen and asks if she is uncomfortable. 'Uncomfortable? I'm in pain! Have you ever had an abscess? Do you have any idea what you are doing?' The students have no way of knowing that just before they arrived, Jodi had an argument with her doctor about pain medication. He was concerned that she was using more pain medication than is usually required. She told him that she couldn't eat and walk and do the other things she was supposed to do if she was in agony. It doesn't get any better. Another student takes over the interview to take her colleague off the hot-seat.

'We are trying to understand why your stomach got infected.' Jodi can't calm down. 'Then you should read the chart. I've told this story a hundred times. Nobody listens. Nobody does their homework.'

Again, there is a back story but the students don't know it and Jodi isn't interested in trying to help them understand. Jodi has had liposuction twice. She hates the look of her belly and feels ugly. She had to talk the plastic surgeon into doing the procedure this time because he said that her abdomen looks fine and that her satisfaction after the first procedure was only temporary. Still, she saved up her money to have it done and allowed herself to hope that it would really change things for her – that she would like herself more afterwards and feel more comfortable being around people. Instead, she has an infection now that is sure to leave a scar. She is disappointed, angry and more frightened than she lets on. But Jodi isn't about to volunteer this angst to these strangers.

The students realize after 30 minutes or so that they seem to be making things worse for Jodi and they are definitely not getting the information they need to write up a medical history. Deflated, overwhelmed, and more than a little intimidated, they excuse themselves early and go to the cafeteria to regroup.

The *fearful* style represents a combination of attachment anxiety and attachment avoidance in which these dimensions of insecurity are both intense and about evenly balanced. There is a tension between attachment anxiety which provides a pull towards emotional (and often physical) proximity to others, and attachment avoidance which provides a push towards greater interpersonal distance. This tension can be expressed in different ways. Jodi keeps people at a distance with expressions of hostility, which confound her simultaneous demands for care and understanding. This pattern is called angry withdrawal. Other fearful people maintain interpersonal distance in the face of attachment anxiety by appearing very shy, a social strategy that passively communicates fear, worry and suffering.

Often, the combination of insecurities that are prototypic of the fearful pattern can be understood as the end result of an intention to maintain a dismissing stance which fails when the defensive avoidance is insufficient to mask underlying attachment anxiety. This failure of avoidance can occur in circumstances in which stressors are simply too challenging to allow for a better modulated response.

Having reviewed these vignettes, think of your own clinical work. Health care providers can usually readily identify patients from their own experiences who exemplify these patterns:

➤ the preoccupied patient, who is experienced as excessively dependent, who wishes to be too close, who uses medical resources (like appointments and tests) more than others, and who experiences frequent symptoms and reports them more dramatically than others

➤ the dismissing patient who is experienced as too distant and emotionally closed, rarely complains (even when problems would seem to others to merit some attention), and prefers not to take direction from others

➤ the fearful patient, who appears to be distressed or to need help but who also seems to thwart good-faith attempts to provide care.

We are setting aside any discussion of another kind of disorganized (or unresolved) attachment. This pattern is very important to mental health outcomes because it represents the most vulnerable of the insecure patterns[6-8] but is not well studied with respect to physical health and medical interactions, at least for now.

HOW ATTACHMENT STYLE AFFECTS MEDICAL CARE

A good place to start understanding the links between attachment and health in more depth is the ways in which people differ in their appreciation of sensations within their bodies, particularly the point at which they detect that a physical sensation is unusual and problematic, and when they seek medical help for it.

Symptoms

The first sign of disease is typically a physical sensation like a headache or a cough. Over the course of a week, most people will have experienced a new symptom[9] so symptoms and the minor injuries and illnesses that cause them are part of normal life. People differ greatly in how sensitive they are to detecting symptoms and seeking medical attention, largely because of differences in their interpretation of the meaning of symptoms. Symptom detection and reporting relate to attachment style because a person who feels more vulnerable, in general, will more often find physical sensations to be salient and threatening, and so will be more aware of the symptoms and more likely to treat them as medical problems. That is why the preoccupied attachment style is consistently associated with higher frequency and intensity of symptoms of all kinds, and greater use of health care resources.

Whether or not a person with a dismissing style detects symptoms more or less often is hard to say because they are quite unlikely to acknowledge it if they do. What is clear is that they are likely to avoid becoming patients when they can, and are relative underusers of the health care system. Interestingly, the combination of attachment anxiety and attachment avoidance that occurs in the fearful style results in a high prevalence of symptoms (just like the preoccupied style) but in spite of that, their strong tendency to not trust others leads them not to seek medical help (like the dismissing style). So the fearful style tends to result in suffering, but suffering in silence.

These biases are particularly important when dealing with chronic diseases, as doctors have to rely heavily on patients' reports of their symptoms to gauge patterns of relapse and remission and responses to changes in treatment. Since patients differ so widely in how severely they describe their symptoms, simply assessing 'how bad it sounds' on a given day doesn't provide enough information for health care workers to accurately judge someone's health. The solution for this is for the doctor to know her patient. Her interpretation of the patient's current state has to take into account how his symptoms *usually* relate to other measures of disease activity. Being able to put a person's report of their symptoms in context like this requires continuity of care.

MEDICAL DIRECTIONS AND ADVICE

Attachment style also affects how willing an individual patient is to follow the recommendations of a health care provider. Of course, by far the majority of people of any attachment style don't follow medical recommendations *completely* – pills are forgotten, lifestyle changes are difficult, other priorities intrude. Beyond those complexities, a person who has invested a great deal of their sense of personal security in a dismissing stance may tend to actively reject someone else's advice, especially when that advice means treating themselves like a sick person or relinquishing control to others. Again, the evidence backs up the prediction: attachment avoidance, in the dismissing and fearful patterns, reduces adherence to medical recommendations, which can have a major impact on health.

Attachment style even affects whether or not a person shows up to see the doctor for routine care. People with the preoccupied style have the highest frequency of scheduled appointments, whereas avoidant attachment leads to fewer scheduled appointments. People with the fearful style seem to experience the tension between approach and withdrawal here too; they have the highest frequency of making last-minute crisis appointments *and* the highest frequency of not showing up.[10]

THE INTERPERSONAL DANCE: HOW ATTACHMENT BEHAVIOR ELICITS RESPONSES FROM OTHERS

Since attachment theory is about relationships, it is insufficient to talk about one person's attachment style without talking about those with whom they interact. Attachment behaviors are usually very effective in eliciting emotional responses from others. Perhaps we are hard-wired as a species to respond to others' emotions since it is crucial to the evolutionary purpose of attachment behavior that an infant's signals reliably trigger a swift and appropriate parental response. Similarly, for adults in a relationship where one is facing a challenge to his or her wellbeing and another is providing care (which is a description of most provider–patient relationships), it is unusual for a care provider *not* to feel something when an ill person is expressing suffering, clinging to support or pushing away efforts to help.

It is helpful to appreciate the kinds of responses that attachment behaviors tend to elicit, which are sometimes referred to as the responses they 'pull for.' The 'pulls' that we are discussing are based on the Circumplex Model of Interpersonal Problems[11] which is not a theory of attachment but is complementary.[12] According to this model, interpersonal events that elicit emotional responses from others are described as points along a circle that has two axes, like a compass. Relationships of power are represented on the vertical north–south axis, where north represents dominance and south represents submission or passivity. Relationships of affiliation are represented on the horizontal or east–west axis, where west represents interpersonal distance and east represents interpersonal closeness. Behaviors on the north–south axis tend to pull for their complement – dominance pulls for passivity and vice versa. Behavior on the east–west axis tends to pull for a matching response – affiliation pulls for affiliation, distance for distance.

A patient with a preoccupied style who is suffering and in distress, like Susan when she is talking to the medical students, actively expresses her symptoms and fears. Although Susan does not experience herself as powerful (quite the opposite), her social behaviors are dominant. She controls the dialogue, is hard to interrupt and does not acknowledge constraints on the doctor's time or attention according to typical social conventions. Susan asks for connection, help, time, and understanding both explicitly and implicitly; she wants close contact. Her interpersonal stance is thus both dominant and affiliative. What response does Susan pull for? Dominance pulls for passivity, affiliation pulls for itself. Unless the students reflect on their options and make a different choice, their natural tendency will be to respond with a passive, affiliative response – listening, not interrupting, extending the length of the session, missing opportunities to take control and show leadership in addressing Susan's concerns. This response is automatic and natural, but it is not effective in meeting her medical needs.

A doctor who is more reflective may realize that it would be more useful to respond in another fashion. For example, he may try to provide an active (i.e. more dominant) and affiliative response by trying to take control of an interaction in a helpful manner. This may pose a challenge to the patient. When he tries to assume more control of the interaction, the doctor creates tension by opposing typical patterns of social interaction. He matches dominance to dominance, which means he will be introducing a conflict or power struggle to the interaction. He will need to be skillful to prevent Susan from either feeling thwarted and overpowered or amplifying her dominant behaviors in response to the implicit challenge.

If the doctor's effort fails, as an interpersonal strategy, or if he feels overpowered, he may react in a less constructive way. He might retreat from his dominance into a passive and distancing response, staying quietly disconnected. This move is likely to make things worse; the more he retreats, the more Susan will need to pursue, which creates a vicious circle. Finally, and most problematically, the doctor may elect to take control of the interaction in a manner which is both controlling and distancing. He may, for example, adopt the attitude that 'I'm the doctor, I'll tell you what to do and then we are done' – lecturing, interrupting without listening, and conveying a bulldozing lack of empathy towards Susan's suffering. One thing leads to another.

As an example of how the dismissing style affects the interpersonal dance in health care relationships, and ultimately patient outcomes, we can look at Paul Ciechanowski's studies of people with diabetes.[13-15] In diabetes, there is a close relationship between the course of disease and behaviors such as adjusting diet, monitoring blood glucose levels, taking medication and adjusting insulin dosages. Strong collaborations are required between patients and doctors, nurses and diabetes educators. Ciechanowski found that dismissing patients had substantially worse diabetic control than secure patients. This big difference was due to dismissing patients choosing not to go along with treatment recommendations regarding diet, exercise, smoking cessation and the use of medication.[16]

But it is a mistake to attribute all difficulties to the characteristics of the patient; it is how the health care providers and patients *interact* that matters. The data that emphasize the interactive nature of this process are that the biggest problems occurred among dismissing patients who were paired with physicians whom the patients did not find to be effective communicators.[15] A dismissing person, such as William, who has to live with a disease that demands collaborative care, is challenged to give up his self-reliance. He needs to recognize and accept that he has a serious disease and can't afford the luxury of maintaining an illusion of being invulnerable. If his doctor responds to his efforts to take control by engaging in a power struggle, demanding compliance instead of enquiring into the challenges he is experiencing, the patient is likely to respond with passive distancing, manifested perhaps by not showing up for a subsequent appointment or silently resolving to manage his diet and insulin in his own way without telling the doctor what he is doing. Since a passive, distancing response is an interpersonal position that feels very comfortable for someone like William, it takes a physician with strong interpersonal skills and insight beyond the details of glycemic control to help him find a better outcome.

Difficult interactions

Interpersonal problems between health care providers and patients are most evident in so-called 'difficult' interactions. Since blame and distancing are common responses to interpersonal friction, it is often the patient or the provider who is identified as 'difficult' rather than the interaction, but it takes two to tango. Difficult, unsatisfying interactions occur for many reasons, but patterns of attachment are one important contributor.

Annie Panzer and her colleagues studied these difficult interactions in the emergency department.[17] Emergency room assessments are often highly charged physician–patient interactions because the stakes can be high. Patients are in distress and often have to wait longer than they would like. Health care providers are busy, and the requirement to distinguish minor illnesses and injuries from major problems very quickly amplifies the tension. On top of that, the provider and patient are likely to be meeting each other for the first time. Strangers often find it hard to give each other the benefit of the doubt. In Panzer's study, emergency physicians were much more likely to find the interaction 'difficult' if the patient had an insecure attachment style, especially the fearful style. Difficult interactions occurred 39% of the time with fearful patients, and in more than 15% of interactions with preoccupied and dismissing patients, but with almost none of the secure patients.

In order for these emergency room interactions to go well, both the doctor and the patient have to 'take the other into account.' In an interaction with a secure patient, like Serena, this happens essentially seamlessly; she can appreciate the harried casualty officer's situation and not allow her own frustrations and worries to interfere with giving him the information that he needs to know. She moves quickly to a concise, understandable narrative that clearly describes her situation, pauses to allow the doctor to ask for clarifications, and focuses the interaction on her most pressing concerns. Neither party experiences this interaction as difficult. In fact, the doctor would report it as an efficient task-oriented interaction, with little interpersonal freight to it.

With a fearful patient like Jodi, however, the emotions not only run high but may push in opposite directions. One moment she emphasizes her autonomy and distrust of the doctor, while in the next breath her fear and dependency come to the fore. In this arena of high interpersonal tension, Jodi's physician may even find it difficult to clearly appreciate her chief complaint, much less formulate a shared understanding of her problem and management plan. The fearful patient can't step back from her fears of both her illness and of the inter-action with the doctor, to consider what the doctor needs in order to under-stand her. The resulting interaction is often unsatisfactory for both parties.

Since many interactions with patients who have insecure patterns of attach-ment (i.e. any pattern other than secure) are not difficult, it is apparent that other variables also contribute to the interactions. Amongst these is the style of the doctor, which leads us to consider how attachment styles that are matched or mismatched affect interpersonal interactions.

MATCHING AND MISMATCHING ATTACHMENT STYLES

Despite a paucity of empirical evidence, when we think about what might emerge from a partnership of two people who each have an insecure style, we can make a few generalizations. Good interactions between two people who both have a dismissing style are likely to emphasize respect for each other's autonomy and self-control as a central value; they may function as buddies or respectful competitors. Bad interactions are more likely to tend towards cool distance and disengagement. If they work well together, it is likely because the non-attachment aspects of their relationship keep them interested in maintain-ing their bond.

Two people who both have a preoccupied style face a very different chal-lenge. For them, the trouble is likely to lie in being intrusive – offering support and advice when it isn't welcome – or with the contagion of anxiety when neither person is able to put apprehension and worry in their place. Their part-nerships can be enmeshed, meaning each person is embroiled in the other's concerns. It is hard for either person to find a sense of security when each has anxieties that egg the other one on.

A partnership of one dismissing and one preoccupied person may be the most difficult of all to sustain. In essence, a relationship is set up in which one person is always in the role of seeking greater closeness and then being hurt or disappointed when it is not obtainable, while the other is in the role of trying to fend off unwanted demands for intimacy and support. One always chases and the other always flees or rejects. A partnership between two insecure adults in which at least one has a fearful style has even more complicated and unpredictable dynamics.

Matching and mismatching between providers' and patients' attachment styles

How does this apply to relationships between patients and health care providers? Of course, these relationships are not reciprocal. A patient may, as a result of fear, suffering or infirmity, take advantage of the safe haven that a health care provider can offer, but the provider is hopefully not counting on her patients to bolster her own sense of security. Nonetheless, provider–patient relationships are extraordinarily intimate compared to just about any other non-attachment collaboration and so the provider's attachment style may influence her approach to her relationships with patients.

The psychiatrist Jeremy Holmes was once asked about how the interaction between a therapist's attachment style and a patient's attachment style influences psychotherapy. He said, paraphrasing: dismissing plus dismissing – therapy never starts, preoccupied plus preoccupied – therapy never ends. Holmes was speaking about psychotherapy rather than medical care in general, and he was being a little facetious; still, there is something important in his aphorism. If both the health care provider and the patient are too invested in maintaining relationships, seeking and obtaining approval, avoiding criticism and rejection and have difficulty tolerating the feelings that come with loss, then it will be a challenge for them to keep the goals of maintaining and restoring health foremost in their minds.

In a study of severely mentally ill patients, for whom learning to tolerate distress so that it does not amplify the illness is a major challenge, secure therapists were likely to avoid making emotionally provocative interventions with patients who had more attachment anxiety. Preoccupied therapists did the opposite: the more anxious attachment the patient presented, the deeper the therapists went in eliciting emotion – a case of being drawn towards the expression of intense emotions rather than the benefits of modulating those feelings. Similarly, therapists with higher levels of attachment anxiety tended to be less empathic with their patients, especially patients who were more avoidant.[18,19]

CONCLUSION

Health care takes place within the context of relationships. When a patient goes to the doctor or speaks to another health care provider, they are typically distressed by their symptom and the threat it poses. At such times their personal history of relationships, in particular their developmental experience, serves as a 'map' of what challenges and obstacles they will face, as well as what shelters or solace they may find along the way. Their beliefs about the extent to which they will be valued and helped or shunned and devalued play into how much capacity they have to present themselves straightforwardly, trust health care workers, follow advice, and accept vulnerability. Attachment theory is a useful, pragmatic approach that subsumes these interactive relational patterns and can help the health care provider appreciate their patient and shape their responses thoughtfully to maximize the odds of a successful interaction.

REFERENCES

1   Bowlby J. *Attachment and Loss: vol 1. Attachment.* New York: Basic Books; 1969.

2   Bowlby J. *Attachment and Loss: vol 2. Separation: anxiety and anger.* New York: Basic Books; 1973.

3   Bowlby J. *Attachment and Loss: vol 3. Loss: sadness and depression.* New York: Basic Books; 1980.

4   Mikulincer M, Shaver PR. *Attachment in Adulthood: structure, dynamics, and change.* New York: Guilford; 2007.

5   Cassidy J. The nature of the child's ties. In: Cassidy J, Shaver PR, editors. *Handbook of Attachment: theory, research and clinical applications.* New York: Guilford Press; 1999. pp.3–20.

6   Holmes J. Disorganized attachment and borderline personality disorder: a clinical perspective. *Attach Hum Dev.* 2004; **6**(2): 181–90.

7   Allen JG, Fonagy P. *The Development of Mentalizing and Its Role in Psychopathology and Psychotherapy.* Technical Report 02-0048. Topeka, KS: Menninger Clinic; 2002.

8   Dozier M, Stovall KC, Albus KE. Attachment and psychopathology in adulthood. In: Cassidy J, Shaver PR, editors. *Handbook of Attachment: theory, research, and clinical applications.* New York: Guilford Press; 1999. pp.497–519.

9   Demers RY, Altamore R, Mustin H, *et al.* An exploration of the dimensions of illness behavior. *J Fam Pract.* 1980; **11**(7): 1085–92.

10 Ciechanowski P, Russo J, Katon W, *et al.* Where is the patient? The association of psychosocial factors and missed primary care appointments in patients with diabetes. *Gen Hosp Psychiatry.* 2006; **28**(1): 9–17.

11 Kiesler DJ. An interpersonal communication analysis of relationship in psychotherapy. *Psychiatry.* 1979; **42**: 299–311.

12 Ravitz P, Maunder R, McBride C. Attachment, contemporary interpersonal theory and IPT: an integration of theoretical, clinical and empirical perspectives. *J Contemp Psychother.* 2008; **38**: 11–21.

13 Ciechanowski PS, Katon WJ, Russo JE, *et al.* The relationship of depressive symptoms to symptom reporting, self-care and glucose control in diabetes. *Gen Hosp Psychiatry.* 2003; **25**(4): 246–52.

14 Ciechanowski PS, Hirsch IB, Katon WJ. Interpersonal predictors of HbA(1c) in patients with type 1 diabetes. *Diabetes Care.* 2002; **25**(4): 731–6.

15 Ciechanowski PS, Katon WJ, Russo JE, *et al.* The patient–provider relationship: attachment theory and adherence to treatment in diabetes. *Am J Psychiatry.* 2001; **158**(1): 29–35.

16 Ciechanowski P, Russo J, Katon W, *et al.* Influence of patient attachment style on self-care and outcomes in diabetes. *Psychosom Med.* 2004; **66**(5): 720–8.

17 Maunder RG, Panzer A, Viljoen M, *et al.* Physicians' difficulty with emergency department patients is related to patients' attachment style. *Soc Sci Med.* 2006; **63**(2): 552–62.

18 Dozier M, Cue KL, Barnett L. Clinicians as caregivers: role of attachment organization in treatment. *J Consult Clin Psychol.* 1994; **62**(4): 793–800.

19 Rubino G, Barker C, Roth T, Fearon P. Therapist empathy and depth of interaction in response to potential alliance ruptures: the role of therapist and patient attachment styles. *Psychother Res.* 2000; **10**(4): 408–20.

CHAPTER 10

The Antisocial Patient in the Hospital

Anne Skomorowsky

Individuals with antisocial dispositions are frequently hospitalized for medical or psychiatric problems. Psychopathic behavior can encompass anything from petty crime to serial murder but in a non-forensic setting, the clinician is most likely to encounter the patient who is a nuisance. Angry, defiant, manipulative, demanding, and threatening, the antisocial patient creates chaos in the controlled environment of the hospital. These patients may inspire fear in doctors, nurses, and other staff; many staff members come to despise them.

The psychiatrist may be consulted to help manage the difficult patient. Often, management of staff countertransference becomes a priority. No one in medicine wants to harm a patient or allow him or her to harm others, so sometimes we must protect antisocial patients from our own anger. To that end, it is helpful to understand the biological and psychosocial settings that lead to antisocial behavior. It may not make the patient any more lovable, but it does seem to reduce countertransference.

In this chapter, I will introduce three patients with antisocial personality disorder who presented to our northern Manhattan general hospital. Though they are actual patients, each also represents a facet of the disorder. The first patient, Mr G, embodies the biologically predisposed sociopath – a cold, emotionally stunted hating machine. The second, Mr Q, is a demanding bully who attempts to squeeze material and emotional 'supplies' from the hospital. And last, Mr W is a gentleman with antisocial tendencies and some hope for relatedness. This by no means encompasses the scope of the disorder; however, these are typical patients whom everyone in our hospital would recognize.

CASE PRESENTATION 1

Mr G, a 42-year-old man with a history of hypertension and several admissions for cocaine-induced chest pain, was admitted for another episode. The patient asked to be transferred to psychiatry. He wanted to restart his psychiatric medications. On approach, he was a poor historian. He was vague about his complaints, saying only that he had been 'running wild in the streets' and accusing the psychiatrist of using 'a smart mouth' when pressed for more information. He did eventually say he was hearing voices and not sleeping. As soon as he and the psychiatrist began speaking, he was antagonistic and accused her of not helping him, demanded to be transferred to another hospital, threatened to 'be very aggressive as long as I am here' and to 'be like a terrorist.' He also threatened to find and kill everyone from the emergency room, and said that he would leave the hospital if discharged and flag down an ambulance. It was impossible to have any alliance with him due to his threats and his contradictory demands. He refused to take any medication because he said that if he did, 'they would say I was treated and discharge me.' When reminded that he had signed out of the psychiatric unit a month earlier, he said they shouldn't have let him sign out because he wasn't in his right mind, and 'it was their fault they didn't notice.'

Due to his being uninsured and having burned his bridges at those few psychiatric hospitals that might have accepted him, his transfer to psychiatry was delayed by nearly a week. During that time, he repeatedly intimidated staff and required security presence for staff safety. His elderly room-mate was transferred to another room in the middle of the night because Mr G threatened to 'kick his old ass' for playing his TV too loudly. A tall, thin, and very muscular man, who built himself up by lifting weights in jail, Mr G ate double portions and wandered around the unit glaring at staff and patients. He was dysphoric and appeared to derive no satisfaction from his intimidating stance on the unit. During daily visits with the psychiatrist, he continued to be both confrontational and vague, demanding admission for psychiatric treatment.

After being admitted to psychiatry some days later, Mr G continued to be disruptive on the unit. He had altercations with both male and female patients, bullied others into watching his choice of TV programs during the hours in which Spanish language TV was customarily watched, and was described as condescending and irritable by staff. The patients' lounge was closed due to the escalating tension around the TV on the unit. He refused to be discharged and threatened to sue the hospital because he did not want to spend his own money on renting a room, preferring to wait on the unit until his outpatient team could get him his own apartment. He was administratively discharged but lunged at his psychiatrist on the way out the door; he was prevented from assaulting the psychiatrist by four security guards and removed from the premises.

Mr G illustrates the 'A' criteria of the *Diagnostic and Statistical Manual of Mental Disorders* (DSM)-IV definition of antisocial personality disorder, below.[1] There is a pervasive pattern of disregard for and violation of the rights of others occurring since age 15 years, as indicated by three (or more) of the following:

➤ failure to conform to social norms with respect to lawful behaviors as indicated by repeatedly performing acts that are grounds for arrest

➤ deceitfulness, as indicated by repeated lying, use of aliases or conning others for personal profit or pleasure

➤ impulsivity or failure to plan ahead

➤ irritability and aggressiveness, as indicated by repeated physical fights or assaults

➤ reckless disregard for safety of self or others

➤ consistent irresponsibility, as indicated by repeated failure to sustain consistent work behavior or honor financial obligations

➤ lack of remorse, as indicated by being indifferent to or rationalizing having hurt, mistreated or stolen from another.

Mr G does all of the above, often in the same hour.

The question arises: why? At times it seems as though Mr G is largely motivated by expedience; he wants to get what he wants and he doesn't want to wait. Looked at in this way, his behavior may seem logical. There is a body of literature that views antisocial behavior as one way in which a predisposed individual can accomplish his goals.

For some patients antisocial behavior makes sense as a problem-solving strategy. Intimidating others has a lot to offer a person who has little and needs much, such as Mr G. The implication is that the subject tries out antisocial behavior and finds it rewarding, setting the stage for a pattern of escalating bad behavior. As Mr G's social circumstances become more stressful, for example, he is ill, homeless, lonely, recently released from jail, his need to coerce others increases.

The idea that the sociopath experiments with bad behavior and sticks with what works is borne out by studies which show that childhood aggression is predicted by body size. In one study of over 1100 children, large body size at the age of three predicted aggressive behavior at age 11, regardless of size at age 11.[2] Presumably the bigger three year olds learned that they could achieve their goals through physical intimidation, and continued to do so as they grew up. Even when no longer large for their ages, these children functioned as they had as three year olds, by pushing others around.

A number of studies have looked at biological antecedents of the antisocial personality disorder. This disorder presents early in life. Observed at the age of three, children described as 'undercontrolled' – impulsive, restless and distractible – were three times as likely as others to be diagnosed with antisocial personality disorder and 4.5 times as likely to be convicted of a violent crime. They were twice as likely to be alcohol dependent and 17 times as likely to attempt suicide.[3]

There are physiological differences associated with antisocial personality disorder. It is well established that low resting heart rate is a hallmark of the antisocial personality. This 'underarousal' may be connected to the lack of fear and the sensation-seeking tendencies of antisocial individuals. Polygraph or 'lie detector' tests are famously defeated by sociopaths. The polygraph measures the level of arousal – heart rate and skin conductance – of the subject in response to questions. When a normal person lies, his or her general arousal increases due to the discomfort and excitement generated by lying. The sociopath does not respond in the same way – his level of arousal remains the same whether he lies or tells the truth.

Sensation seeking is a stable aspect of temperament, which may be genetically mediated.[4] Daily experience shows us that some people enjoy taking chances and others seek stability. Some 'sensation seekers' may find life's ordinary routines boring. They feel empty and flat without an external source of excitement. The antisocial individual may experience his natural low arousal as unpleasant, leading him to seek out situations which will be corrective, providing excitement.[5] His natural fearlessness allows him to pursue satisfaction relentlessly, as though no danger existed.

This model for antisocial personality disorder in some ways neglects the personality behind the disorder. It is a model in which a cold-hearted logic dictates the behavior of a person who is defective due to his physical make-up and temperament. There isn't much personality there, just a shell. Isn't there a person in there somewhere?

CASE PRESENTATION 2

Mr Q is a 51-year-old man admitted for cocaine-related chest pain. His chest pain was atypical and felt to be non-cardiac in origin. Psychiatry evaluated the patient for agitation when he began throwing things in his room because he was given a cardiac breakfast tray rather than the food he wanted. He reported a history of schizophrenia. He reported greater than 30 psychiatric hospitalizations and multiple suicide attempts. He reported hearing voices and said that someone he called 'Tommy' told him to throw things. During the interview the patient elaborated on his psychiatric symptoms and by the end of the interview was claiming that he wanted to kill himself and was afraid of hurting others. He refused psychiatric medication, saying that what he really needed was admission to psychiatry for a few weeks, to get away from the street. The psychiatrist's impression was that he was malingering, as was his primary physician's.

However, when confronted with the lack of need for admission, the patient became irate and accused the doctor of 'triggering' him. He scratched himself on the arm and cheek with the plug from his IV pole. He said he would sue the hospital if discharged and would go right to the emergency room. He called the psychiatrist a 'fucking bitch slut' and when told to stop this behavior, said he didn't care what anyone said or thought, he'd been committed a hundred times and that's exactly what he wanted. He remained loud and devaluing.

The patient was known as a malingerer but had also stabbed himself with a pencil in triage and wrapped a phone cord around his neck in the emergency room. He was admitted to psychiatry. He was incensed when not given a private room. Of the psychiatry resident who was called to redirect him, he said 'I will kill that bitch.' From his double room, he called 911 to report that 'A black man is going to kill the president.' Secret Service officers visited the unit where the patient denied having made the call, though he had boasted of it to other patients.

Again one wonders, why? On the surface Mr Q is very similar to Mr G. Both are middle-aged men admitted for cocaine use and chest pain. Both became agitated and threatened the examiner when confronted about their possibly bogus symptoms. Both demanded special food and private rooms. But threatening harm to the president is not the behavior of a person who is only trying to get what he wants, motivated only by his unusual physiological make-up. It is behavior which elicits an intense response from others.

The relationship between the antisocial individual and the other is at the heart of the disorder. Mr G, the first patient, can be understood as someone with impoverished interpersonal relationships. He had no meaningful interactions with staff while on the ward. Other than fear, he inspired no emotional response from others. One was struck by his emptiness and the neutral, impersonal style of his aggression.

In the case of Mr Q, however, it was personal. His utterances were sexually aggressive and racist, intended to humiliate the listener. The term 'bitch slut' captures the disdain for women the patient meant to convey. When he called 911 to report 'a black man' plotting to kill the president, he not only threatened the president but all the African-American men on the unit and, really, everywhere, who were subject to investigation by the Secret Service.

When Mr Q threatened the president because he wanted a private room, he took his angry bluster to a new level. One could be excused for laughing at the sheer outrageousness of doing such a thing. The sober response of the Secret Service was a reminder of how explosive this kind of person can be.

In an early psychoanalytic paper titled 'Primary affect hunger,' the author describes the psychopath's insatiable appetite for care. The psychopath needs constant proof of the other's love. The relentless demands express bottomless need and hatred simultaneously.[6] Mr Q's endless requests, always wrapped up with rage, allow him to squeeze a little more juice out of the hospital and his health care providers. He needs, he demands, and he exacts revenge on those who have what he wants.

The demanding patient may be the most difficult for the clinician to tolerate. It is exhausting and there seems to be little hope of actually meeting the patient's needs – for the little things he or she requests or, in the larger sense, for the patient's health. But the patient who incites anger may have more going for him or her than the patient who merely provokes fear.

The sociopath who engages the caregiver in a struggle, as in the example of Mr Q, expresses his hope of engagement with a loving object. The child analyst D.W. Winnicott wrote that this child is one who has not given up on 'the mother over whom he or she has rights.'[7] For Winnicott, the 'nuisance value' of the sociopath is a sign of his salvageability. In this view, Mr Q is actually healthier than Mr G, who is unable to have any relationships at all.

CASE PRESENTATION 3

Mr W is a 60-year-old man with a history of diabetes, strokes, and falls due to stroke-related neurological impairments. He was admitted for treatment of infected pressure ulcers on his buttocks. Psychiatry was asked to see the patient for his vague reports of suicidal ideation.

He was cagey about his actual suicidality but it seemed he felt hopeless in many ways and had thoughts of 'going away.' He would not commit suicide *per se* but had fantasies of obtaining thousands of dollars, going to a crack house, and smoking crack until he died. He felt this would be a heroic way to go and that it would spare his wife from finding his body. When pressed, he said he didn't think he would really have the courage to do it, but did feel despondent about his poor health and dependence on his wife. Other stressors included his inadequate housing – a room in a walk-up apartment – and feeling preyed upon by various acquaintances who were aware he had expensive electronics at home and would steal from him.

The patient had never seen a psychiatrist outside the hospital but had a significant criminal history, including homicide. During a previous hospitalization he had been evaluated by the on-call psychiatrist as he was attempting to leave against medical advice. That crisis was resolved when he was allowed to air his complaints, a family meeting was arranged, and he was provided with pen and paper to record his feelings. Being given a voice allowed him to stay in the hospital.

During the present hospitalization, speaking with him was a challenge because of his circuitous, narcissistic manner and inability to state anything simply. In response to any question, he told a self-serving anecdote. His manner was condescending and he found it amusing that the psychiatrist had trouble following him. He was focused on complaints of mistreatment by doctors in other hospitals and on dramatic descriptions of medical malpractice. If asked to clarify a point, he would sigh and say he knew the psychiatrist couldn't understand him.

He did become tearful at times during the interview when speaking of his helplessness, falls, and need for help with hygiene. He spoke tangentially about 'the black community' and what he perceived as its emphasis on manliness, wealth, and power. 'In our community, sex is everything,' he said while describing his sense of loss from erectile dysfunction. His depressed mood seemed genuine but when the psychiatrist brought up the idea of treatment, he became vaguely threatening, speaking of murders, having a devoted network of friends and family who would appear at a moment's notice to 'get me out' (of the hospital), and 'bolting.' He asked, 'How would psychiatric treatment help Superman?' By which he meant, help someone who had survived everything he had survived.

Because Mr W was admitted for an antibiotic-resistant infection, he was placed in a special single room in a part of the hospital usually occupied by the hospital's wealthier clientele. His room was extra-large, had a flat-screen TV and excellent food, and as is the policy on that unit, his wife was able to stay with him on a cot set up at their request. At the time of the interview, she was sleeping comfortably on a just-made bed, all their things were hung up in the closet, and nurses poked their heads in periodically to inquire if they needed anything. When the infection cleared, Mr W was moved to a regular floor where family members were not able to stay beyond visiting hours. He had a roommate and was served the usual bad hospital food. He had lost his special status. Naturally he was angry and let the staff know it.

He verbally abused several doctors and nurses who tried to speak with him about the transfer and to reinforce the hospital rule against overnight visiting by spouses. His wife was ultimately escorted from the hospital by security. He demanded narcotic pain medications repeatedly, switching from one request to the next when told that what he had asked for would not be given. When his wife was removed from his room, he threw a cup of chocolate milk on the floor and demanded it be cleaned up immediately. Staff were afraid of him and humbly cleaned up the mess.

Though Mr W is also a 'difficult' patient, there are suggestions that he has a better prognosis than Mr Q or Mr G. Mr W is a good example of a patient whose 'nuisance value' is evidence of the potential for healthy relatedness. It is clear from his history that his psychopathology is related to loss. On a small scale, the room transfer recreated what, one speculates, he experienced throughout his life. He had something good and it was taken from him.

Over the years this patient had lost his youth, his health and his sexual potency. In his view, he was no longer sufficiently manly. His friends were thieves who preyed upon him. He could no longer care for himself and was dependent on his wife. When institutional rules required them to separate, it was intolerable for him. It is easy to imagine that his mother abandoned or abused him.

Two points are noteworthy in terms of this patient's psychological health. First, the patient has a history of at least one long-standing, loving interpersonal relationship. Second, during his previous admission, the patient permitted himself to be helped by the psychiatrist. During that admission, when the patient threatened to leave the hospital against medical advice, the psychiatrist encouraged him to express his feelings and allowed Mr W's wife to get involved in his care. By hearing him out and urging him to record his feelings in a journal, the psychiatrist gratified Mr W's need for admiration. This had the effect of bolstering his healthier defenses, defusing his sense of humiliation. With his wife in the picture, the patient felt less alone. He was able to remain in the hospital to complete his course of treatment.

As Winnicott wrote, 'At the basis of the antisocial tendency is a good experience that has been lost.' The fact that there was once something worth having is the basis for interpersonal relatedness. Mr W has the inner resources – the psychological possession of something good, even if he doesn't remember it – one needs to have a relationship with someone else, including a doctor, nurse or other health care provider.

What this means is that working with Mr W is not just a matter of containing him but of caring for him. With Mr G, the challenge was protecting oneself, other patients, and the staff from his behavior. With Mr Q, it was fending him off without retaliating. But with Mr W there is a relationship to be nurtured. If the relationship succeeds, he will be able to get the medical and psychological treatment that he needs.

CONCLUSION

Hospitalization is stressful for all patients. Consider the blatant unfairness of the elite room versus the rooms for everyone else, the horrid 'cardiac diet,' the deaf elderly room-mates with blaring TVs, the distressing separation from loved ones. Hospitals could do much to decrease acting out by, for example, providing better food in larger portions, private rooms, and a comfortable chair for family members to sleep in. This may not always be possible but it is a reasonable goal. Cases of 'iatrogenic psychopathy,' i.e. antisocial behavior attributed to medical treatment, would be fewer if patients' basic needs were met.

Nonetheless, there will always be antisocial patients. Managing them in the hospital is a matter of limit setting, bargaining, and understanding. Coping with one's own countertransference is essential. The antisocial patient exists in relationship to others and in this case, the other is the health care provider. Whenever possible, the patient's sources of strength must be discovered and exploited for his or her benefit.

REFERENCES

1   American Psychiatric Association. *Diagnostic and Statistical Manual of Mental Disorders IV*. Washington, DC: American Psychiatric Association; 1994.

2 Raine A, Reynolds C, Venables PH, *et al.* Fearlessness, stimulation-seeking, and large body size at age 3 years as early predispositions to childood aggression at age 11 years. *Arch Gen Psychiatry.* 1999; **56**(3): 283–4.

3 Caspi A, Moffitt T, Newman D, Silva P. Behavioral observations at age 3 years predict adult psychiatric disorders. *Arch Gen Psychiatry.* 1996; **53**: 1033–9.

4 Koopman JR, Boomsma DI, Heath AC, *et al.* A multivariate genetic analysis of sensation-seeking. *Behav Genet.* 1995; **25**(4): 349–56.

5 Raine A. Antisocial behavior and psychophysiology: a biosocial perspective and a prefrontal dysfunction hypothesis. In: Stoff DM, Breiling J, Maser JD, editors. *Handbook of Antisocial Behavior.* Hoboken, NJ: John Wiley and Sons; 1997. pp.289–304.

6 Levy D. Primary affect hunger. *Am J Psychiatry.* 1937; **94**: 643–52.

7 Winnicott DW. The antisocial tendency. In: *Through Pediatrics to Psychoanalysis.* New York: Basic Books; 1958.

CHAPTER 11

Assisted Suicide

Suzanne Garfinkle and Philip R. Muskin

Physician-assisted suicide brings up vexing legal and ethical questions. Here, we will focus instead on the psychological dimensions of patients' request for assisted suicide. Specifically, we will clarify some of the psychodynamic factors that inform the patient's appeal for death. We contend that the request to die should invariably be scrutinized.

Assisted suicide is legal in five places: Switzerland, The Netherlands, Belgium, Luxembourg and, in the United States, Oregon and Washington.[1] Other countries, including the UK, Spain, France, Colombia, and Australia, are entertaining legalization.[2] In 1994, Oregon passed the Death with Dignity Act,[3] legalizing physicians' aid in dying for terminally ill patients. The law authorizes physicians to prescribe lethal doses of short-acting barbiturates for patients to self-administer. Only terminally ill patients are eligible, although indications are expanding to include psychological suffering as well.[4,5]

Legal safeguards exist to protect patients, including requirements that the condition is hopeless, the decision is informed, voluntary and well considered, and the physician's action is sanctioned by a colleague.[2] Still, the safeguards have proven imperfect. The majority of patients who have died this way have not been evaluated by a mental health professional.[6] Physician-related factors have been found to lead to misuses of assisted suicide.[7] Legalization has occurred without implementing even these flawed protections.[8]

It is curious that the use of psychiatric evaluation and treatment appears to be so limited. Most people, even those who suffer due to serious illness, do not opt for hastened death. As Hendin notes, 'Strikingly, the overwhelming majority of those who are terminally ill fight for life to the end.'[4] According to Chochinov *et al*, only 9% of terminally ill patients have a 'serious and pervasive wish to die.'[9] A significant proportion of patients who request assisted death are suffering psychologically. The desire for death correlates with pain, poor social supports, and distress,[9-12,14] including loss of dignity.[15,16] The most significant correlation is with depression,[9-12] and its successful treatment dramatically decreases the wish to die.[13]

PSYCHODYNAMICS AND ASSISTED DEATH

Given the irreversible nature of death, and the multiplicity of factors that can influence its appeal to patients, we assert that in every case, a request to die should be explored in depth by the primary physician. While this idea appears benign, in practice it is difficult to accomplish. As Breitbart writes, 'We as a society make a grave error in taking the request as a minimally examined, simple request of a competent terminally ill adult.'[8]

In order to respond with sensitivity and wisdom, physicians must be curious about their patients' deeper motivations. For this reason, a psychodynamic approach is helpful. Psychodynamic work involves exploring the meaning within patients' experiences. Psychoanalysis – psychodynamic treatment in its original form – seeks to reveal a patient's underlying motivations so that he might understand himself better and make more satisfying choices. It is the aim of any psychodynamically minded clinician to listen for material that a patient does not readily express. Psychodynamics is the art of hearing what is not spoken.[15]

There are many reasons why patients suffer but it almost always involves distancing themselves and others from their most authentic feelings. People attempt to banish the feelings that they experience as embarrassing, terrifying, taboo or incongruous with other parts of themselves. The feelings may be relegated to the unconscious or they may be consciously minimized, ignored or disavowed.

When patients are very ill, many if not all of their basic psychological needs are intensified. The request for assisted suicide, in any scenario, involves the individual patient's psychological dynamics. This does not mean that the request is born of psychopathology but rather, that it has a meaning or variety of meanings to the patient that exceed what may at first be apparent to the doctor. In the next section, we will explore some of the more common underlying reasons why patients ask for hastened death.

Before doing so, let us specify the group of patients we consider. First, we draw a distinction between our group and those who are more generally inclined toward suicide. Requesting physician aid in dying is not the same as being suicidal. Suicidality is considered a form of psychopathology, whereas the request for hastened death is not.[16] Moreover, the patient who asks for hastened death is engaging another human being in his struggle. In saying 'Would you help me die?' the patient expects an interaction with the doctor, wonders about how the doctor will respond, and how their relationship will evolve. It is a communication of the most intimate nature. A patient who commits suicide and leaves behind a note communicates only after death, operating outside a social network.[16]

Second, we do not include patients asking for withdrawal or withholding of life-sustaining treatments. This is different from asking a doctor to actively cause death, as in the first case the patient dies of illness, while the latter introduces a new pathology.[17] The following apparent contradiction emerges: we do not consider the request for hastened death to indicate psychopathology, but we require psychological exploration before responding to such a request. Although moral speculation lies outside the scope of this chapter, we do believe that physicians are obligated to act in the service of life rather than death. As most physicians would agree, facilitating death should remain a last resort.

UNDERLYING PATIENT MOTIVATIONS

In certain cases, understanding the request for death does not require much psychological imagination. These cases primarily include uncontrolled pain and major depression.[18]

Pain is a physical experience that creates emotional suffering. It includes all varieties of physical discomfort, such as nausea and shortness of breath. Uncontrolled pain may create rage, sadness, and hopelessness, and may contribute to the development of depression. Inadequate pain control often results from poor physician education or moralistic views regarding narcotics. Pain should be treated aggressively, thoroughly and creatively using narcotics, nonsteroidal anti-inflammatory drugs (NSAIDs), antidepressants, anticonvulsants, and other adjuvants. In cases where pain does not respond adequately to treatment or where treatment may render the patient delirious or unconscious, patients may choose to risk death for the sake of relief. This is different from asking to die, and it is important to clarify this distinction with patients.

Major depression is distinct from the sadness or grief that is expected in the setting of physical illness. Clinical depression is never a 'normal' reaction to any life event. Physicians know that they have difficulty identifying depression in patients with physical illnesses[19-21] and often miss this diagnosis,[22-24] even though it is effective to simply ask, 'Are you depressed?'[25] When assessing a patient's request for aid in dying, it is thus prudent to consult a physician skilled in making this diagnosis.[6] That said, remission may not come easily or quickly. While many pharmacological and non-pharmacological treatments for depression have proven helpful, it may take months to find the treatment that will relieve a given patient. Psychiatric hospitalization and electroconvulsive therapy (ECT) may be appropriate steps in the care of patients with treatment-refractory depression. When depressed patients have lost hope, it is all the more incumbent on doctors to maintain belief in science, psychotherapy and time, to remove the influence of depression from this irreversible clinical decision.

The request to die as a communication

If a patient is suffering from uncontrolled pain or untreated depression, the request for death may be readily reversed with routine care, either restorative or palliative. Cases lacking these factors provide a greater challenge.

It is our general contention that in many cases, patients who ask for death do not 'really' want to die. Why would this happen? In some cases, patients may consciously wish for something else from their doctor but feel unable to bring it up. In many more cases, the wish may be unconscious, i.e. the patient does not recognize it as such and really believes what he or she wants most from their doctor is death. If the reason is truly unconscious, this is because the patient has not allowed it into conscious awareness. This may be because the idea brings up too much shame, anxiety or conflict. Whatever the patient is feeling has caused him to lose a basic sense of security, either in himself or in the world. Perhaps in his ill state he feels dirty, unappealing, burdensome to others or generally lacking in the attributes that once made him valuable as a human being. Moreover, he might feel embarrassed about asking his doctor, 'Does anyone care enough to talk me out of this or to want me to be alive?' He might want to know if others, including the doctor, believe his life is worth living and are still willing to be part of it.[8]

If what the patient wants is to feel valued by others, why does the physician become such an important representative? This depends on the patient but in general, physicians are powerful objects of transference. One has only to witness the kissing of a child's small injury to perceive the child's belief in the parent's omnipotence to heal. These powerful fantasies are reactivated in the presence of a physician, though this is often unknown to the patient. The patient may consciously have a 'realistic' view of the doctor as a trained professional with human imperfections but unconsciously may imbue the doctor with 'parental' qualities, such as the ability to provide love, protection, self-esteem, and reassurance. A very ill patient may see the physician as healthy and vigorous, a symbol of the world of the living, and may want to hear that he is still welcome there despite his infirmity. The physician might also be viewed as the moral authority upholding or condemning the worth of a patient's life.

Whatever the dynamic, a tactful physician begins by acknowledging it without stating it overtly. Making a direct 'interpretation' such as, 'Perhaps you are asking to die because you want to know that people will miss you' runs the risk of making the patient feel exposed, defensive, and angry. The physician can use his understanding to make a statement such as, 'I want to do everything I can to provide you with the best care I can offer. If you die, you will be greatly missed; how can we understand together why you want to die right now?'

Demoralization

Demoralization, easily confused with depression, is a common reaction to any adverse life event including, but not limited to, medical illness.[26] Like depression, it can include neurovegetative symptoms and suicidal ideation but unlike depression, it resolves readily with good news. Demoralization does not respond to antidepressant treatment. Treatment for demoralization includes removing the stressor and strengthening a patient's resilience through 'brief psychotherapy at the bedside'.[26]

A patient with lymphoma and uncontrolled pain asks for death. The psychiatrist listens to her mass of concerns which she produces readily but in a haphazard way. He reflects the issues back to her and asks her to prioritize them, and then transcribes this more ordered list. By the end of the interview, she appears less anxious and says, 'I can think more clearly. Now I have a plan' and ultimately chooses to continue living. A psychiatrist is not necessarily required for such an intervention but a physician must be prepared to consider the idea of demoralization and, further, its features in this specific patient. The physician must then embrace the task of challenging the demoralized part of the patient by showing her that a capacity to be assertive remains.[26]

Grief

In 1993, Dr Boudewijn Chabot, a Dutch psychiatrist, was acquitted for assisting in the suicide of a woman with no medical illness who had recently lost her two sons and divorced her husband.[4] This set a legal precedent for assisted suicide in cases of psychological suffering without medical illness. The patient had turned to her GP, a psychologist, and a social worker, all of whom refused to assist in her death. Finally, she found Dr Chabot, who believed her odds of responding to bereavement therapy were slim, likening her to a cancer patient refusing an experimental chemotherapy treatment. He consulted with several colleagues expert in medical ethics, most of whom agreed with him, and he ultimately acceded to the patient's request. After he provided the prescription, she took a lethal dose of medication while positioned on her son's bed. As she died, Chabot sat by her and coaxed, 'Think of your boys.'

Chabot did not believe his patient was clinically depressed, as she did not appear sad, just determined to die. Critics of Chabot have argued that the patient was likely depressed, that her psychological difficulties preceded the loss of her sons, and that his joining in her view prevented any chance of treating her grief.

Although normal grief is not considered a psychiatric illness by the DSM IV-TR, it is a painful psychological syndrome for which there are pathways to recovery, such as the Kübler-Ross stages of mourning. For bereavement-related depression, there is evidence to support treatments similar to those for major depressive disorder.[27] For complicated grief, a diagnosis that could fit this patient, treatments emphasizing exposure therapy through imagined conversations with the deceased and narratives of the death have proven effective.[27] In the absence of a mental health professional, a primary doctor might suggest to such a patient something like: 'Your hopelessness about psychotherapy is only natural given the intensity of your suffering. But time, and perhaps some professional help, will likely ease your pain.'

Rage, revenge, and resentment

Patients who are ill may have various experiences of rage: at themselves, at their doctors, at the world or at God for their illness and suffering. Rage is a psychological state that transcends anger and may include wishes to take revenge or to kill. Despite how understandable this feeling may be, most people who are enraged are frightened by being in that state. Part of this has to do with society's general intolerance of strong negative affects and violent impulses, although most individuals are affected by these forces. Instead of taking conscious ownership of the feeling, people defend against it; one common way is to select oneself as the target. It has been postulated that some suicidal patients are suicidal because they have unconsciously murdered the true object of their rage and are atoning for the murder through suicide. Other, often psychologically sicker patients will consciously endorse a wish to hurt significant others by killing themselves.

When confronted with such a patient, the clinician might start by pointing out the patient's anger. Statements as simple as 'You seem very angry' can allow the patient to accept this difficult emotion, which can provide some relief in itself. It can also be helpful to confront the patient's fantasy that their death will exact revenge on the doctor, family member or significant other. These patients can be helped through reality testing: 'You seem to want to harm me by dying, and although I would miss you, all that would happen is that you would be dead.' A successful intervention can help the patient realize that no revenge will ensue from their death. Further, the clinician might focus on the patient's difficulty in experiencing gratitude, which leads them away from the resentment that might be fueling their request to die.[26]

Control

'It is always consoling to think of suicide: in that way one gets through many a bad night.'[28] Nietzsche's comment suggests that a patient's request to die may be an effort to take control of life, even if this control is illusory and paradoxical. Many patients may achieve this sense of control by hoarding a lethal dose of medication, even if they never use it. The benefit of this 'psychological insurance' is one of the central arguments raised by proponents of legalizing assisted suicide.[29]

Patients may seek control through this means to varying degrees. For some, the intellectual sense of empowerment may be enough to efface any expression of a wish to die. Other patients may also want a prescription in hand. A banker with HIV, complicated by pneumonia, asked for a prescription for a lethal dose of medication for use at some point in the future. He was intelligent and without any signs of psychiatric illness other than some mild depressive symptoms that did not seem out of proportion to his medical situation. His doctor sensed that the need for control, present in many areas of his life, seemed to be driving the request for death. He wanted to reassure the patient that the ability to control his destiny could be maintained without requesting to die. He thus opened a discussion of some concrete possibilities, including drafting a detailed advance directive, and this helped the patient to feel less desperate.

In such a case, however, a primary care intervention might not be sufficient; psychotherapy could be particularly useful in helping the patient to accept loss of control in certain areas, such as exactly when and how he would die, while regaining a feeling of control over other aspects of his life. A psychoanalytical perspective would see this patient as primarily anxious about the unknown, which is imbued with danger. One of the goals of a psychodynamic treatment would be to help him recognize this fear as such rather than as a wish for death. An internist who is sensitive to this anxiety, which plagues many ill patients, might open a discussion with: 'Everyone on this planet is going to die at some point, in a way that is unknown to them. For you, right now, what is so intolerable about that uncertainty?'

Trauma

The first question to ask oneself when a patient requests aid in dying is, 'Who is this person and what shaped them?' One might think differently about someone who had a traumatic early life and now has cancer, versus a patient who had a basically happy life and now has cancer. In doing so, it is necessary to take into account the patient's view of his or her life, rather than the objective facts alone. When a patient requests aid in dying, on some level, it is safe to assume that living has become more painful or traumatic for the person than dying. It is a physician's job to understand what is so unbearable about life that makes death seem desirable.

Ms R is a 41-year-old woman with no medical problems. Her parents both died in a car accident when she was five and she was raised after that in several foster homes. She works as a pediatric social worker in a hospital and recently got married for the first time. She presents to a new physician, Dr M, for her annual physical. As Dr M is taking a social history, she describes feeling deeply fulfilled by her husband, whom she feels is her 'soul mate.' 'I was orphaned as a child,' she states, 'and if anything ever happened to Brian I would not want to go on living. I know this sounds crazy, but I need to ask – would you be able to help me die comfortably under those circumstances?'

At first Dr M wonders if Ms R suffers from a psychiatric illness that would lead her to ask about this on their first visit. 'Before we get to that, let me try to learn some more about you,' he says. After making further inquiries about her life, he finds her to be convincingly happy and functioning well in all respects. At this point, Dr M is at a loss. He feels irritated by the question, seeing it as bizarre (*Why is she so focused on her husband dying?*), unhealthy (*Why would that mean her life ought to end?*), and out of place for a routine encounter with a young, healthy patient (*I have many patients who are old and seriously ill who do not ask me about hastening their death; what is different about this person?*). He knows he cannot say any of this out loud to her and asks the patient to make another appointment soon so that they can discuss the issue in more detail, meanwhile buying himself some time to consult with a psychiatrist colleague.

A psychodynamically oriented psychiatrist would recognize the link between the patient's traumatic loss of her parents and her current preoccupation with losing her husband. A traumatic neurosis can produce efforts to master the trauma, often through repetition. One might imagine that this patient is stuck in a pattern of reliving the early loss of her parents in the fantasy of losing her husband. This repetition does not bring about the desired effect; rather, in its failure to do so, her early feeling of overwhelming loss regenerates itself. Although she is happy in her current life, on the level of unconscious fantasy, she remains stuck in the emotional state of her childhood – the worst experience she has ever had and could ever imagine, an experience whose recurrence would be, quite literally, a fate worse than death.

A patient like this requires more than a curious and empathic primary care physician, because due to the deep, unconscious nature of her motivation, she will not be able to examine her request sufficiently without psychotherapy. However, the primary care physician plays an important role in several ways. First, he must manage his own reactions to her (his countertransference) and continue to behave in a sympathetic and professional manner despite feeling annoyed, confused or overwhelmed. Second, he must begin the exploration in his office by opening a discussion rather than providing a knee-jerk response. Finally, he must recognize that the patient requires a mental health evaluation by a practitioner versed in psychodynamic work. He could use his next appointment with the patient to inquire about why she feels she would choose death in these circumstances. His main task would be to interest her in continuing the conversation with a mental health expert, not to pathologize her feelings but to emphasize that he could not participate in helping her die without both of them understanding her motivations more completely.

Split in the experience of the self

It is not uncommon for medically ill patients requesting assisted death to wish to kill the 'sick part' of themselves, leaving the healthy part to survive. They may make comments such as, 'I don't recognize myself any more' and 'this is not who I used to be.' They may feel their 'normal' personality is out of reach, taken over by their immense medical needs. If a patient is fully aware of this wish, the yearning for hastened death may be less pronounced but if the 'split' in the self is largely unconscious, i.e. if they feel consciously that the ill part is all of them, a speedy death can seem like the only option.

Ms E is a 63-year-old divorced woman who lives alone. She used to work as a librarian but has been retired on disability since she was diagnosed with multiple sclerosis 10 years ago. Her multiple sclerosis initially had an indolent course, with mild sporadic symptoms. Recently, she has begun to notice blurring of her vision when she looks to the side. At her next neuro-logical follow-up appointment, her doctor diagnoses her with intranuclear opththalmoplegia, a complication of multiple sclerosis affecting her ability to move both eyes together. To her neurologist's surprise, upon hearing the diagnosis, Ms E becomes tearful and says: 'Doctor, I seem to be getting sicker and sicker. Nothing is getting better, only worse. I think I would rather die than have to continue suffering like this. Would you be able to help me die comfortably?'

Doctor N is taken aback. He has patients with more advanced MS who strive to preserve their lives despite how grave their prognosis has become. Ms E is a relatively mild case; she is not wheelchair bound and has minimal pain. She does not appear depressed, except for crying during this conversation. Dr N racks his brain for clarity on the ethical and legal issues involved in physician-assisted suicide. He is concerned about alienating his patient by denying her request but knows it is not legal in his state. After pausing to overcome his initial reaction, he returns to considering the patient. 'Tell me about your old self,' he says.

The patient goes on to describe her 'best' years, when she was married, working, and raising her daughter. She recalls enjoying literature, movies, and socializing. 'Now I can't see, can't drive, can't even sit and read a book any more; I just sit around and complain. What do I have left?'

Ms E is describing a new, sick version of herself that lacks all the qualities she once valued. The good qualities are split off in an image of herself she recalls but fears is no longer the real Ms E. Dr N has initiated a psychological intervention that could eventually enable her to resolve the split, creating a sense of one self who is suffering but still possesses her positive attributes. In the course of this conversation, he could make a comment such as 'It may feel at times as if you don't recognize yourself, particularly when you have a great deal of physical discomfort. But the "real" you still comes through. It's OK to complain when you have needs.'

The problem may not resolve easily. When patients resort to the defense of splitting, it is because the undesired part is seen as so toxic that it must be separated from the rest of the person. If the patient continues to experience themselves in two disparate parts, and continues to fantasize about death as a way to kill one part, a referral for psychological treatment may be required. In the course of such treatment, there would be several goals. After establishing a sense of safety and a therapeutic alliance, the therapist would help the patient to recognize the split and to gradually make it unsettling or 'ego-dystonic'. In the course of doing so, the therapist would help the patient to feel less afraid of the 'sick' self, and therefore less desperate to kill it off. A more realistic sense of the whole self emerges –a person worthy of living until death occurs naturally.

Hopelessness

A patient with long-standing hypertension and diabetes with renal involvement made an appointment with a psychiatrist to request help in dying, explaining that his medical condition had become intolerable. The patient cited frequent hospitalizations, physical restrictions, and feeling like a burden on his family. The psychiatrist was puzzled as the patient had been living in quite an ill state for many years. Why now? Upon further discussion, it became apparent that the patient had become set on dying within the past month, after his nephrologist had told him that he would likely require dialysis within the next year. He had told the patient that there was little hope for a successful transplant. The psychiatrist recognized that this patient felt hopeless, prompting his request.

Hope is an essential feature in coping effectively with medical illness.[26] The seriousness of suicidal intent correlates better with the degree of hopelessness about the future than with any other indicator of depressive severity.[30] Patients' experience of hopelessness is associated with what their doctors tell them. This patient gave up on the idea of life after hearing a one-sided, grim presentation of facts from his nephrologist. Physicians must strike a balance between 'truth dumping' and withholding information, an equally destructive approach which patients usually sense, leading to mistrust. Although the nephrologist provided correct information, it was not balanced with any basis for hope.

The psychiatrist contacted the nephrologist, with the patient's permission, to gain a better understanding of the facts. The nephrologist said the patient might have access to a transplant within the next few months, although neither the transplant nor its success could be ensured. When the nephrologist shared this information with the patient, including the uncertainties, the patient's hopelessness vanished. At his next psychiatric appointment, he relinquished the idea of a hastened death and spoke instead about the 'important things left to do with life.'

Guilt, self-punishment, and atonement

Guilt is a hallmark of depressive thinking and the wish to die. In common parlance, a person feels 'guilty' when he believes he has done something 'wrong.' Guilt as a symptom, in the psychiatric sense, is a most destructive emotion. In the context of medical illness, guilt can arise through two major pathways. First, the patient may presume he has committed bad deeds, which serves as an 'explanation' for having gotten sick, a phenomenon Susan Sontag describes in wonderful detail.[31] Second, the patient may blame himself for not having responded to a treatment. This is perpetuated by the culture of medicine, which may accuse patients of 'failing' treatments. Such a dynamic is particularly toxic given the powerful transference many patients have to their physicians; like a child bringing home a failing report card that will shame the parent, a patient can feel irrationally responsible for disappointing the doctor. In extreme cases, guilt can give way to shame, an emotion that by definition causes patients to wish to disappear, which can easily promote thoughts of hastening death. It is only fitting, in such a scenario, that the patient would ask for physician-assisted death rather than take his or her own life independently, thus giving the doctor the opportunity to carry out his fantasized hatred of the patient. Death accomplishes the twin goals of vanishing and being punished. Although this strikes the reader (and equally, the clinician) as extreme and unwarranted, such thoughts may seem logical to patients influenced by the regressive pull of illness, which includes pain, the threat of loss of bodily functions, the chaos of the hospital, and the intrusive nature of being a patient.[32]

The living dead

Some patients who request to die seem to experience themselves as already dead.[33] This may result from physical or emotional suffering, the loss of social support that often accompanies serious illness, which may be equated with the end of meaningful existence, and the impact of depression or anxiety. In the case of depression, 'deadness' is often experienced by the patient as emptiness, loss of vibrancy or the potential for pleasure in the world, and lack of motivation. In the case of anxiety, deadness can take the form of numbing, dissociation or detachment, a shutting down of affect in response to feeling overwhelmed. A patient who already feels dead not only knows he or she is going to die but sees no more life left, and thus may want to get it over with quickly. In order for a physician to make a therapeutic intervention in a case like this, the physician must see the situation differently; he must believe that some life remains worth living for this person. Beyond this basic belief, the physician must utilize tact in dealing with such a patient. He must present a realistic alternative to dying, namely, a condition in which the patient can acknowledge the seriousness of the illness with its associated losses, without feeling overwhelmed.

Transformations can occur when the patient's self-experience is reflected back, at the right time and in the right way. A psychiatric consultation was requested for a patient refusing to continue chemotherapy. She had just begun the treatments and was suffering from serious nausea and pain. Although her prognosis was poor, she was expected to live for several more months into the spring. During the course of the consultation, the patient cried continuously, referring frequently to the fact that she would never see her garden bloom again. After listening to the woman describe her suffering, the psychiatrist said, 'You act as if you are already dead.' Her response was dramatic and instantaneous: her tears dried up and she looked at the consultant and took his hand. 'You mean I have something to live for?' she asked. 'I will see my garden bloom again, won't I?' Through her difficult course and her death a year later, she never stopped feeling alive, often reiterating the importance of 'not being dead until your time comes.'

CONCLUSION

In this chapter, we have argued that no request for hastened death should be indulged or denied without a thorough exploration of the patient's motivation. We have discussed some of those possible motivations, illustrating how one might approach a patient in different scenarios. For anyone involved with such patients, we cannot overstate the importance of sharing the experience with a colleague. Mental health professionals offer the benefit of their training and experience, and consultation with them can facilitate deeper and more productive work with these patients in the primary care setting.

REFERENCES

1   www.assistedsuicide.org
2   Buiting H, van Delden J, Onwuteaka-Philpsen B, *et al.* Reporting of euthanasia and physician-assisted suicide in the Netherlands: descriptive study. *BMC Med Ethics.* 2009; **10**(18).
3   2009 Summary of Oregon's Death with Dignity Act. www.oregon.gov/DHS/ph/pas/docs/year12.pdf
4   Hendin H. *Seduced by Death: doctors, patients and the Dutch cure.* New York: W.W. Norton; 1997.
5   Sheldon T. Dutch politicians are under pressure to hold 'time to die' debate. *BMJ.* 2010; **340**: c1045.
6   Ganzini L, Goy ER, Dobscha SK. Prevalence of depression and anxiety in patients requesting physicians' aid in dying: cross sectional survey. *BMJ.* 2008; **337**; a1682.
7   Hsiao-Rei Hicks MH. Physician-assisted suicide: a review of the literature concerning practical and clinical implications for UK doctors. *BMC Fam Pract.* 2006; 7(39).
8   Breitbart W. Physician-assisted suicide ruling in Montana: struggling with care of the dying, responsibility, and freedom in Big Sky Country. *Palliat Support Care.* 2010; 8(1): 1–6.
9   Chochinov HM, Wilson KG, Enns M, *et al.* Desire for death in the terminally ill. *Am J Psychiatry.* 1995; **152**(8): 1185–91.
10 Breitbart W, Rosenfeld BD, Passik SD. Interest in physician-assisted suicide among ambulatory HIV-infected patients. *Am J Psychiatry.* 1996; **153**(2): 238–42.
11 Breitbart W. Cancer pain and suicide. In: Foley K, editor. *Advances in Pain Research.* New York: Raven Press; 1999. pp.399–412.

12 Helig S. The San Francisco Medical Society euthanasia survey: results and analysis. *San Francisco Med.* 1988; **61**: 24–34.

13 Meier DE, Emmons C, Litke A, *et al.* Characteristics of patients requesting and receiving physician-assisted death. *Arch Intern Med.* 2003; **163**(13): 1537–42.

14 Breitbart W, Rosenfeld B, Gibson C, *et al.* Impact of treatment for depression on desire for hastened death in patients with advanced AIDS. *Psychosomatics.* 2010; **51**(2): 98–105.

15 Pine F. Theories of motivation in psychoanalysis. In: Person ES, Cooper AM, Gabbard GO, editors. *The American Psychiatric Publishing Textbook of Psychoanalysis.* Arlington, VA: American Psychiatric Publishing; 2005. pp.3–19.

16 Bostwick JM, Cohen LM. Differentiating suicide from life-ending acts and end-of-life decisions: a model based on chronic kidney disease and dialysis. *Psychosomatics.* 2009; **50**(1): 1–7.

17 Mueller PS, Swetz KM, Freeman MR, *et al.* Ethical analysis of withdrawing assist device support. *Mayo Clin Proc* 2010; **85**(9): 791–7.

18 Quill T. Initiating end-of-life discussions with seriously ill patients: addressing the 'elephant in the room.' *JAMA.* 2005; **284**(19): 2502–6.

19 Cavanaugh S. The diagnosis and treatment of depression in the medically ill. In: Guggenheim F, Weiner MF, editors. *Manual of Psychiatric Consultation and Emergency Care.* New York: Jason Aronson; 1984. pp.211–22.

20 Ormel J, van den Brink W, Koeter MWJ, *et al.* Recognition, management and outcome of psychological disorders in primary care: a naturalistic follow-up study. *Psychol Med.* 1990; **20**(4): 909–23.

21 Sherbourne CD, Wells KB, Hays RD, *et al.* Subthreshold depression and depressive disorder: clinical characteristics of general medical and mental health specialty outpatients. *Am J Psychiatry.* 1994; **151**(12): 1777–84.

22 Schulberg HC, Saul M, McCelland M, *et al.* Assessing depression in primary medical and psychiatric practices. *Arch Gen Psychiatry.* 1985; **42**(12): 1164–70.

23 Eisenberg L. Treating depression and anxiety in primary care: closing the gap between knowledge and practice. *N Engl J Med.* 1992; **326**(16): 1080–4.

24 Badger LW, deGruy FV, Hartman J, *et al.* Patient presentation, interview content, and the detection of depression by primary care physicians. *Psychosomat Med.* 1994; **56**(2): 128–35.

25 Chochinov HM, Wilson KG, Enns M, Lander S. 'Are you depressed?' Screening for depression in the terminally ill. *Am J Psychiatry.* 1997; **154**(5): 674–6.

26 Griffith JL, Gaby L. Brief psychotherapy at the bedside: countering demoralization from medical illness. *Psychosomatics.* 2005; **46**(2): 109–16.

27 Zhang B, El-Hawahri A, Prigerson HG. Update on bereavement research: evidence-based guidelines for the diagnosis and treatment of complicated bereavement. *J Palliat Med.* 2006; **9**(5): 1188–203.

28 Nietzsche F. Beyond good and evil (1886). Quoted in: *The Columbia Dictionary of Quotations.* New York: Columbia University Press; 1993.

29 Breitbart W, Rosenfeld B. Physician-assisted suicide: the influence of psychosocial issues. www.hospicecare.com/Ethics/physician-assisted-suicide.htm

30 Beck AT, Steer RA, Kovacs M, *et al.* Hopelessness and eventual suicide: a 10-year prospective study of patients hospitalized with suicidal ideation. *Am J Psychiatry.* 1985; **142**(5): 559–63.

31 Sontag S. *Illness as Metaphor*. New York: Farrar, Straus and Giroux; 1978.

32 Muskin PR. The medical hospital. In: Schwartz HJ, Bleiberg E, Weissman SH, editors. *Psychodynamic Concepts in General Psychiatry*. Washington, DC: American Psychiatric Press; 1995. pp.69–88.

33 Muskin PR. The request to die: role for a psychodynamic perspective on physician-assisted suicide. *JAMA*. 1998; **279**: 323–8.

CHAPTER 12

Balint Group Process: Optimizing the Doctor–Patient Relationship

Jeffrey L. Sternlieb, C. Paul Scott, Albert Lichtenstein, Donald E. Nease, and John R. Freedy

A family medicine resident told the following story with a dilemma.

> A 60-year-old male patient of mine came in for an annual visit. He had been my patient for over two years and wasn't much of a complainer. During the visit he admitted having some acute, relatively severe back pain. He thought the pain was coming from having lifted a crib he had been putting together for his first grand-child. I agreed that the pain was probably from a muscle strain but just to be sure I sent him for an x-ray. The patient didn't seem too concerned and neither was I. I gave him some ibuprofen, some exercises, and told him the pain should resolve within a week or two. I got the results of the blood work back and his PSA, which we've been following, which was borderline in the past, is now markedly elevated. The x-ray findings were consistent with metastatic disease around L4. What I'm trying to figure out is: Do I call urology and find out what the next steps are so I can tell him, or do I get him in right away and let him know the results?

Of course, this is a serious situation medically, and we could think of what the correct course of action should be. However, we might also think about what it felt like for the resident to carry the worry about this new grandfather and the prior (well intended, but false) reassurance. Or we could empathize with what it would be like to be the patient hearing the news and how difficult it would be for the doctor to manage such an emotional situation. Maybe it wasn't the right course of action that had this resident stuck but the intense emotional difficulty of the situation.

It so happens that this story was told in the context of a Balint group. A Balint group is a structured, small group experience designed to help physicians explore and better understand the unsettled feelings doctors sometimes get in the process of providing medical care to their patients. Under optimal circumstances, the relationships that doctors have with their patients are a crucial ingredient in the care they provide. When physicians struggle for any one of a wide variety of reasons with what their patients are presenting, it can affect the care they provide. Balint groups are an opportunity to get help from colleagues whom we trust and who can provide alternative ways of seeing and hearing what patients bring with them into the exam room.

After being presented with this case, the group began to explore this medical situation from the two standpoints of the doctor and of the patient. Some of the group members validated the doctor's initial desire to give reassurance based on what she knew at the time. They thought about what it would be like to tell a new grandfather that he had metastatic cancer, what that would mean for the family and, more importantly, what it would be like to try and support him through this situation. They struggled with what the role of the family doctor should be and what the patient would need from his doctor. They talked about how difficult it would be to tolerate the emotional ups and downs and how they could possibly be helpful. They wondered what it would have been like for the patient if his pain worsened enough to come in through the emergency department and hear the news from someone he had not met before.

There were many other places that the resident might have received supervision about what to do medically in this situation. However, the Balint group was unique in providing her with a safe, connected and professional environment in which to deal with the issues that had the capacity to haunt her. She had validation from peers who could understand the logic and emotion of the original reassurance. The group named the 'Oh no' feeling after getting the blood work and x-ray findings, and then went on to discuss the awful feeling of having to share bad news. There were some in the group who also talked about anticipating and dreading the possibilities of the patient's emotional reaction – crying, anger or even being frozen in shock.

The guidance or supervision this doctor received from her Balint group went beyond the typical direction outlining the proper medical procedures to follow. Medical protocol is about the symptoms or the illness. What she received was guidance about the relationship between herself and her patient. It was an acknowledgment of and support for the normalcy of the wide range of emotional responses any healer would have about their patients when faced with life-changing circumstances. Further, the guidance was not prescriptive; it was not a road map about what to say or how to react. Rather, this group's discussion was filled with permission to enter into the emotional realm of the patient's illness experience along with support for the healer's role to walk that path with their patient.

ORIGIN AND SCOPE OF BALINT WORK

Michael Balint understood that his ideas were 'bold' and would require a 'reform' of medical education. His opportunity to put these ideas into practice would wait 20 years when in 1950 he placed an advertisement in *The Lancet* offering a 'group discussion seminar on questions related to medical practice.' By this time, Balint had emigrated from Hungary to the United Kingdom and was working at the Tavistock Clinic in London. At the Tavistock, he was exposed to the group process theory of Wilfred Bion and became engaged to his future wife, Enid Albu-Eichholz, who was active in the training of social workers. Together they held casework seminars with the social work trainees and honed the techniques that would form the basis of their future work with general practitioners. This work, which Balint envisioned from the beginning as 'training cum research,' led to the publication in 1957 of *The Doctor, His Patient, and the Illness.*[1]

It is difficult to overestimate the influence of Michael and Enid Balint on contemporary medicine. Beyond the innovation of the Balint group, a group meeting regularly devoted to ongoing, case-based exploration of clinician–patient relationships, they coined the term 'patient-centered medicine'[2] and influenced much of the case-based teaching now common in medical schools. Today, Balint groups are active in many countries, attended by physicians in practice as well as in training. An International Balint Federation (www.balintinternational.com) along with 22 affiliated national societies exists to further the concepts and methods pioneered by Michael and Enid Balint. In the United States, where in the late 1960s and early 1970s the role of the general practitioner was being reinvented as family medicine, Balint's ideas found a very receptive audience. As a result, Balint groups were a feature of many of the newly created family medicine residency training programs, and continue to be a part of half or more programs.[3]

WHEN DOCTOR AND PATIENT MEET

The transaction between doctor and patient may seem like it should be a simple, straightforward one; however, it is usually anything but. Every relationship has inherent in it a contract, often implicit but a contract nonetheless. A crucial part of any contract is expectations but these expectations are typically unconscious or unrecognized, and often unnamed. They are taken for granted: 'Of course my meeting with the (*chose one*) doctor/patient will go just as I expect!'

When patients make and keep an appointment with a physician, they have a specific intention, often to receive a diagnosis and treatment recommendations for some disease, ailment or set of symptoms. Patients are also looking for reassurance that their diagnosis is not serious and that it is known and generally responds to the recommended treatment. Physicians also have expectations of their patients. They expect patients to keep their appointment, arrive on time, be able to describe all their symptoms along with providing a detailed history of the onset of these symptoms, identify any fears, worries or concerns they may have as well as the origin of these emotions, and add very little extraneous information. Neither doctors nor patients could name all these expectations. Yet, if any one of these pieces of the puzzle is missing, it may change the transaction between doctor and patient from a simple acute chief complaint to a complex and chronic relationship challenge. The result could be a dissatisfied patient and a frustrated, annoyed and puzzled physician. What went wrong? Why couldn't we connect? I wonder if she will return for another appointment. Part of me hopes she does, but part of me doesn't!

There are a number of aspects of these troublesome doctor–patient interactions that have lingering effects on both parties. When there are repeated disconnects between doctor and patient, patients begin to lose faith in their doctor and eventually in the medical system. They typically project their dissatisfaction onto their doctors. Rather than hold their frustrations and dissatisfaction in, they will share their part of the story with anyone who will listen. In a similar psychological fashion, doctors will project their negative emotions – frustration, puzzlement and annoyance – onto the patient. They often have some short-term relief when the patient leaves because they can focus on another patient whose symptoms they can diagnose or whose medical situation is one that is easily resolved. However, these feelings of inadequacy creep back into consciousness when the 'heart sink' patient appears on another day's schedule.

A DOCTOR'S DILEMMA

These patient interactions can be thought of as Balint cases: cases where the interaction with the patient caused some sort of discomfort in the physician. Every doctor has Balint cases; that is, patients who stay on our minds for one reason or another.

When the relationship is a difficult one, a typical but not natural course is to experience a gradually increasing disconnection rather than the development of a more personal and meaningful relationship between healer and patient. Each participant will defend themselves and seek support for their 'position,' feeling that they are the wronged party. The patient may look around for a different healer; the physician may do some introspection but will have difficulty fully letting go of his sense of not being good enough for this patient. An accumulation of these experiences may lead the physician to question his choice of profession.

Sometimes, a patient is on a physician's mind because their situation is very sad or tragic or it reminds the doctor of a personal situation, and the physician has some difficulty separating his own feelings from those of the patient. Another kind of 'Balint case' is the patient who relies too much on the doctor, trusting everything the doctor says and recommends without using their own sense of what will work for them. This can feel like an excess burden because the patient places the doctor on a pedestal.

The dilemmas most physicians deem worthy of consultation are not typically 'Balint cases.' They are cases that involve diagnostic or treatment complexities. Rarely do physicians decide to ask a colleague to help to understand the conflict in a relationship with a patient. One exception is when a legal issue is involved, and then the consultant is an attorney and the goal is not a better relationship but rather to minimize the negative consequence to the physician.

Despite the awareness that a placebo effect can improve the outcome, very little attention is paid to the relationship between healer and patient, either in training or in ongoing practice. The mindset of much medical education seems to be an acceptance that a number of patients will struggle to receive adequate care because of their difficulty in forming a therapeutic relationship with their physician. One of the ironies of this primary, almost exclusive focus on the biomedical aspect of training is that much of the current medical knowledge will be out of date with the continued advancement of medical science. However, the basics of developing therapeutic, healing relationships never change.

THE UNIQUE OPPORTUNITY OF A BALINT GROUP

Nearly every patient on our schedule evokes some kind of reaction. Even no reaction or recall says something about the nature of the relationship we have or don't have with a patient. However, some patients stay on our minds long after their appointment – we worry about them, we like (or don't like) them, we wish we could help them more, we don't know how to help them, we feel sad, bad or mad about our last interaction, etc., etc. When we look at our schedule for the next day, our mood, thought process and mindset could be significantly affected by a single name. We may be experiencing significant frustration or we may know that we will have to spend a significant amount of emotional energy, or we 'know' at some level that there are significant as yet unrevealed traumas that could surface at any moment. In some cases, we capture, disguise or deal with our emotional reactions by referring to the patient by some pejorative label, like 'drug seeking' or 'non-compliant,' or some psychiatric diagnosis. Instead of identifying and acknowledging our thoughts, feelings and struggles in our work with certain patients, we at times unintentionally project those feelings onto the patient. There is something about some patients that is difficult to let go of, and the problem is not primarily one of diagnosis or treatment uncertainty.

Now, imagine for a moment that you dedicate a brief time (one hour every week or every other week) when you and a small group of colleagues create an opportunity to explore what it is about a particular patient that touches you in certain ways. You begin by presenting this patient and the dilemma(s) that you experience in providing health care to them. The group gets a chance to ask clarifying questions – not about your diagnostic or treatment decisions but information to help them get a better picture of this patient and how you see him or her. And then, you are asked to sit back and listen to the group generate a wide range of possible thoughts, feelings and ways of experiencing and understanding what is going on between you and your patient. There are no case notes in the presentation; it is the impact the patient has made on you that you are presenting, and the group is asked to take in the case at an emotional level and relate and share the feelings that have welled up inside them as they listened to your presentation.

The well-trained and prepared group leader makes sure you are not unduly questioned or challenged about treatment issues. In fact, the inherent assumption in the group is that all members are competent physicians. The issue is not what you did wrong but how the relationship might be improved. The leader is also prepared to make sure the group explores what it's like to be the physician who is treating this patient as well as what it might be like to be the patient. Finally, the leader challenges the group to explore what their thoughts are about the kind of doctor this patient needs. You get a totally different perspective about the nature of your patient's relationship with you, the kind of a doctor this patient needs, and the challenges you have had in trying to be helpful. You leave this week's group relieved and renewed about your dilemma because you learn to re-examine and redefine your role with this challenging patient through the eyes and ears and hearts of your colleagues. Inevitably, the issues discussed relate to other members of the group, and they too leave with added insights.

BALINT GROUP SUBTLETIES

The Balint group experience is an organic process that evolves, develops and is subject to all the vicissitudes of any group's set of interactions and multiple relationships over time. That is, there are the typical stages of group development that are monitored and managed by the leaders who are trained in fulfilling this role. The Balint group experience begins with a number of explicit and mutually understood guidelines. Group members are requested to maintain confidentiality, speak honestly and for themselves, and respect everyone's contribution to the group discussion. They have made a commitment to meet for a predetermined amount of time (often one hour), a predetermined frequency (often every one to two weeks), and they understand that their group facilitators have received specific training in Balint group leadership. It is the unique structure of each individual's role in the group that allows for a different type of educational experience.

The role of group members is twofold. First, participants are asked to volunteer a case for the group to consider. The case should be a patient they are likely to see again in their office, and it should be a patient who stays on their mind after the appointment is completed. The presentation includes basic demographics about the patient and especially the reason why this patient stays on the doctor's mind. Once the case is presented and any clarifying questions from the group are answered, the presenter's task is to sit back and listen to the discussion. The presenter has the very unusual opportunity to present a case and then be required to listen, despite the frequently observed impulse to add information they forgot to provide or to correct impressions that evolve from the group discussion. It is precisely this temporary separation from the group that allows the presenter to hear perspectives s/he may not have considered in the past. The new perspectives may include an awareness of background information they do not have about the patient or wondering about the significance of what they did not share in the initial presentation.

The second or alternative role is for the group members who have not presented the case; they are asked to contribute to the discussion by speculating on what it might be like to be the doctor or to be the patient in the case that is presented. There is some natural give and take as the group manages to share the floor, react and respond to each other's ideas and respond to the group leaders' direction. The non-presenting participants also have an unusual opportunity that is not typically available in educational settings. Their role is explicitly not to fix or solve the presenter's dilemma, despite their often automatic impulse to do so. Rather, they are asked to speculate about the doctor's and patient's personal experiences in being with each other, and then to explore the nature of their relationship and what might be needed to make it a therapeutic one. The freedom to purely speculate is rare, especially in the healing professions. The opportunity to explore the interpersonal realm in healers' conversations about illness opens a window to look through that participants may not have fully considered as a significant factor in their work.

The role of the group leaders is to create and maintain an emotionally safe environment that can free the group members from their usual interpersonal vigilance and allow a deeper exploration of the challenges embedded in the case that is presented. The leaders do this in several ways. Initially, there is a parallel to the doctor–patient relationship that Michael Balint described as the doctor's apostolic function. Briefly, Balint asserted that it is the doctor's responsibility to teach the patient how to be the kind of patient they would like them to be. Essentially, this task has to do with establishing guidelines. In the Balint group, the leaders' role is similar; they are intervening primarily to reinforce and direct group members to speculate and explore the feelings that get stirred up in them from the case that is presented. Leaders tend to be more active in the beginning of the group's formation and its evolution by reinforcing guidelines and gently redirecting the group members – keeping the focus on the case that has been presented, encouraging speculation without regard for certainty, inviting diverse views and possibilities, and directing the group's discussion so there is a balance of considering both the doctor's and the patient's perspective.

Balint group leadership has some additional considerations. The typical model is to have two co-leaders: a physician and a mental health professional. The leaders sometimes balance their roles, with one focused on time management and the content of the discussion. Sometimes, the other leader will pay more attention to process-oriented issues, helping to insure safety from an additional perspective. Leaders are also attentive to seating arrangements to insure that one or the other can literally see every group member.

The typical flow of a Balint group begins with the assembling of the group, the leaders' invitation of a case ('Who has a case?'), a quiet time when group members consider the possibilities of presenting one of their patients, the offering and presentation of a case, an opportunity for clarifying questions, and the handing over of the case to the group. The group's discussion takes the bulk of the time and the presenter then rejoins the group, both literally (if they pushed back) or figuratively, with the freedom to participate but with no obligation to respond to anything the group offered. The leaders identify the time to end, usually thanking the presenter and the group for their participation.

There are some core elements of Balint group process that produce an important unique effect. After the presenter presents the case and the group has the chance to ask some clarifying questions, the group owns the responsibility for the discussion. This is accomplished in one of two ways. The group leader can metaphorically push the presenter back from the group, in effect putting the presenter in a Plexiglas bubble where the presenter can hear group discussion but is asked to not participate. Or the group leader can allow the presenter to remain part of the group but not permit the group to question the presenter further. Instead, the leaders redirect questions that might put the presenter on the spot back to the group as a whole.

In either case, the safety of the presenter is paramount. When we speak of safety, we are referring to safety from what might feel like an attack or criticism. This feature differentiates Balint groups from other, ordinary, teaching conferences and rounds familiar to medical trainees and teachers. In a Balint group there are no 'right answers.' The very nature of the exercise is focused on expanding the field of inquiry, even to fantasy and metaphor and play, rather than narrowing the discourse to the 'correct' diagnosis and prescription.

The concept of safety refers also to the inner world of the presenter. The forced silence and immunity from interrogation and correction allow the presenter to listen differently, to be more open to points of view and emotions against which he or she had erected defenses. As the group gains confidence that these boundaries will be enforced by the leaders, members gain courage to present cases of greater emotional vulnerability and power, which in turn enriches the group discussions.

Once the presenter is finished describing the situation, the group is responsible for discussing the case from the standpoint of both doctor and patient. Ideally, the group participants begin to imagine themselves in the role of doctor and at times, various group members voice the role of patient. In psychodynamic terms, the group examines both the transference and countertransference in the relationship. The language used is ideally in the first person: 'If I were the patient I would be feeling …' or 'If I were the doctor I would want to…' In that way the presenter and their approach or behavior in the case are not questioned or scrutinized. As stated above, the core assumption is that the presenter, and all group members for that matter, are competent and skillful. It is not the presenter's skill or decision making that is in question. Rather, the elements of a particular relationship situation are to be understood.

What is unique to the Balint process is the group's consideration of the elements in a particular relationship situation, both the transference and countertransference and what might be generating these feelings. Group members' behavior and personal dynamics are not examined for personal insights, as might be the case in group therapy. Insights develop as the other group members articulate their own feelings and viewpoints. Differing approaches to the patient might be learned but not by pointing out what mistakes were made or what the correct answer is, as in medical case presentations in supervision groups. This learning takes place when the voice of the patient is represented and possible approaches become clearer. In this unique way, the Balint process holds the physician harmless and keeps the responsibility clearly with the group to investigate how the relationship situation holds the potential for learning.

Thus, the presentation of a case and subsequent discussion are at the heart of a Balint group. Consideration of the doctor, the patient, and their relationship is the 'manifest content' of the session. Of particular interest to psychoanalysts is the parallel process, which is rarely discussed or even acknowledged openly in the group, yet the parallel process provides the group with its compelling force and interest at the deepest levels.

In a well-functioning group, the case invariably reflects one or more of the following: personal issues and conflicts of the presenter, active conflicts in the setting, relationship between presenter or members and leader. As the discussion of the case proceeds, members of the group take on aspects of the personae and feelings of the doctor and the patient, often playing out in real-time drama the interaction between the two. It is this unspoken 'latent content' that results in what Michael Balint referred to as 'a considerable, though limited, change in personality.'

Because the leaders' contract with the members precludes personal discussion of individual dynamics in order to protect the members and to assure the exercise is true to its claim as an educational one, these currents are not explored openly. However, everyone is listening and resonating personally, and an effect at multiple levels is inevitable.

Even though the direct focus is not on the group members or the group's dynamics, the unfolding parallel process informs the leadership of the group. Leaders may intervene to influence the re-enactment of the interpersonal or intrapsychic themes at play. The leaders' intervention hopefully models a different, more effective process or helps uncover deeper underlying emotional aspects of a case. The leader may simply allow the tension to build, rarely pointing to the parallels between the case and the dynamics of the discussion. Pointing out the parallels, when used sparingly, can provoke an 'aha' moment for the members, like seeing oneself in a dream.

Direct evidence of the benefit or impact of the Balint group experience is not obvious in the way one might identify the learning of how to manage a medical condition. However, it is not unusual to observe in a group's discussion the evolution of an instructive metaphor or the naming of a tension inherent in some treatment decisions, or even the sharing of a relevant personal experience affecting the case. In more established groups, pointing out parallels to the case in the group's process may be a technique more frequently used by the leader.

CONCLUSION

It has been more than 60 years since Michael and Enid Balint conceived of a group process method of studying the doctor–patient relationship and its deeper meanings. Generations of medical practitioners, psychoanalysts, and behavioral scientists have continued this study, utilizing the Balint method much as originally described and affecting its spread in the United States and around the world. An emotionally meaningful case is presented and taken up by the group. The leaders, by carefully observing boundaries, confidentiality, respect, and honesty in themselves and the members, enable the group to explore the case and its manifold levels of meaning. The physicians grow in their confidence and comfort in caring for their most difficult and challenging patients. The endless fascination and rewards of participating in a Balint group can only be appreciated by participation, and we humbly encourage all readers to look for such an opportunity.

REFERENCES

1   Balint M. *The Doctor, His Patient, and The Illness*. New York: International Universities Press; 1957.
2   Balint E. The possibilities of patient-centered medicine. *J R Coll Gen Pract*. 1969; **17**(82): 269–76.
3   Johnson AH, Brock CD, Hamadeh G, Stock R. The current status of Balint groups in US family practice residencies: a 10-year follow-up study, 1990–2000. *Family Med*. 2001; **33**(9): 672–7.

CHAPTER 13

Until Death Us Do Part: Secrets at the End of Life

Janet Plotkin-Bornstein

Judah, a 60-year-old man dying of an AIDS-related condition, discloses to his therapist just hours before he takes his final breath of life that the man whom he has referred to as his brother throughout his long hospitalization and to his entire treatment team is, in fact, not his brother but rather his lover, his partner of 20 years, the man with whom he has shared the most intimate parts of his life and himself, and to whom he must now say his last good-bye.

Francesca, a 50-year-old woman with a chronic medical condition, had been preparing for an organ transplant, which she and her family were told by her medical team was the only hope, at this time, of prolonging Francesca's life. After countless sleepless nights, and many painstaking and honest talks with her trusted physician of 15 years, she disclosed to him that, despite what she believed to be her family's wishes for her to have the life-saving transplant, she could not bear having a stranger's organ transplanted into her already frail body, a body which she could, nonetheless, still claim as fully her own. Through the years, Francesca had conveyed to her doctor, a soft-spoken, humble and caring man, how vitally important it was for her to feel as in control of her life as possible, despite her inhabiting a fragile body. When she finally shared with him that she could not tolerate carrying the organ of a stranger within her own body, and could not surrender to the experience of having a transplant, he understood and honored her wishes, despite his own sense of impending loss of a deeply valued patient. And when, in her desire to protect her family from feeling that she was betraying their wishes for her to have the transplant, and to protect them from an even deeper and more prolonged suffering, she asked her doctor not to disclose to them her decision to refuse the transplant, he again understood and honored her wishes to keep her decision a secret from her beloved family. Several days before the scheduled transplant was to have taken place, Francesca went into cardiac arrest and died, leaving her husband and adult children, in their most profound grief, haunted by the thought that Francesca had endured a deepest aloneness in what were her final hours, with a secret and unspoken knowledge that she was, in fact, dying, while they were bathed in an illusion of hope.

As a psychoanalyst, I find myself continually moved by what feels to be the sacred nature of the relationships I have with my patients, as they entrust me with their care, their deepest secrets, and those parts of the self that have felt too shameful, forbidden or unsafe to have shared with anyone else. And yet, I remain always mindful of that which is left unsaid, that which still seems to be unspeakable in the space between us. While I am invited into the most private parts of my patients' inner experiences, I am also constantly reminded of the paradoxical position of my being simultaneously an insider and an outsider, as each patient struggles, in varying degrees and in differing ways, with the desire to be known, on the one hand, and the fear of truly being seen and vulnerable, on the other. As I listen to patients tell me the narratives of their lives, I consider not just what is said in the words spoken but also the silences, the pauses, the hesitations in speaking, the breaks of eye contact, that suggest the presence of some shameful, deeply burdensome secret that still feels too fraught with danger to speak in my presence.

In my desire to empathize with my patients carrying secrets which still feel too frightening to share, and which remain hidden from me, I think about my own history of secrets about myself. I am reminded of those secrets I have eventually shared with trusted loved ones, only to feel a great sense of freedom upon sharing those secrets, as well as those that I still keep protected within myself. And, while thinking about my patients, I am compelled to wonder what secrets they may fantasize that I carry within myself, secrets about how I see them, secrets about who I really am and what my life is like outside the protected therapeutic space, secrets about my own state of health, relationships or life's struggles, or secrets about how I view the therapeutic work itself.

The complexities involved in the keeping or unfolding of secrets have been put into particularly sharp focus for me during the course of my work with people with HIV/AIDS when I was the co-ordinator of an HIV mental health program in an urban hospital. My patients shared with me their heart-breaking struggles regarding decisions about whether or not they could disclose their HIV status, and if so to whom, and under what conditions, the conditions under which they had contracted the virus, and for some, the fact of their having AIDS. They conveyed to me the courage it would take for them to finally disclose to others these facts of their lives. In significant ways, this work helped shape my focused attention on the ever-present role of secrets in all clinical matters. On a more personal note, having lost a parent early in life, I have given much consideration to issues of loss, grief and mourning, and those factors that potentially facilitate saying good-bye to all that is precious in one's life, in the most authentic, meaningful way possible.

The issue of secrets about the self becomes all the more poignant as one faces the end of one's life. As a health care professional, I believe that we who work closely with people in the final period of their lives have a vital role to play at such times. In our trusted role in working with those who are dying, we have the opportunity to help create a safe space for them to give careful consideration to that which has been privately guarded about the self but which may now feel too burdensome to keep as a secret. They can, in our empathic and respectful presence, explore the possible implications, both for themselves and their loved ones, of disclosing some long held but deeply painful secret, and consider to whom, if anyone at all, and under what conditions the secret may be safely disclosed. We also have the chance to help our patients reflect upon, and for us to honor, what secrets they feel are most meaningfully and safely kept within themselves, as well as what secrets, if any, are to be shared solely with us, the health care professional, until death do us part.

THE MANY FACES OF SECRETS

Secrets exist in many forms and in many contexts.[1,2] That which may feel too shameful or forbidden to talk about in one context may be a source of pride or healthy selfhood in another. Given the larger context within which secrets exist, several writers have described the many developmental and adaptive, as well as more problematic, functions secrets may serve.[1-4] Keeping a secret about oneself may represent a healthy attempt to assert one's individuality, sense of potency and autonomy. Such may be the case, for instance, when people keep within themselves secrets about their deepest longings, hopes and fantasies, protected from what they fear may be the intrusive and inhibiting influence of others. The making, holding onto, and sharing of secrets are intricately linked to a sense of trust and intimacy within relationships, as well as to the creation of boundaries within one's interpersonal world.

However, it is under conditions of feared, threatened or actual assault upon one's physical or psychological being that many secrets are born. The keeping of a secret may become a matter of preservation of the self in such circumstances. Such is the case, for example, when people feel the need to keep hidden from others essential aspects of themselves. Unbearable feelings of shame, and efforts to contain these feelings, become the breeding ground within which many secrets are born and maintained. And so, the facts surrounding one's illness, whether a specific psychiatric, substance abuse or medical condition, may become a tightly guarded secret, leaving one feeling like an outcast who is untouchable. I am continually reminded that many still feel the need to keep secret their living with an illness, such as depression, schizophrenia, cancer or

AIDS, due to the anticipated or feared repercussions of disclosing this secret to others. And as many secrets are born out of a desire to protect others from emotional pain, the fact that one has a terminal illness, and is dying, may itself become the most unspeakable, burdensome secret of all.[5]

Secrets born out of a sense of shame can leave one in a state of psychological imprisonment. As the keeper of a secret organizes life around who knows the secret and from whom the secret must be kept at all costs, there is the constriction of the self and one's interpersonal and emotional lives.[1] A sense of invisibility and lack of authenticity prevails, as essential parts of the self are kept in hiding.[6,7] Feelings of shame, profound loneliness and isolation, anxiety, guilt and perceived badness about the self continue to grow, as painfully destructive secrets about the self remain tightly sequestered within the soul.

While the issue of having and holding onto secrets about oneself is important throughout all stages of life, this issue takes on particular meaning as the end of life approaches. Unspoken secrets can affect who is involved in critical end-of-life treatment choices and decisions, as well as who is present at or painfully excluded from the dying person's bedside during the most intimate moments just prior to the person's passing.[6] Additionally, for the person who is dying, the presence of a tormenting secret can distort the mourning process.[8] One cannot openly mourn that which has been kept secret. The holding onto or sharing of deeply held secrets by the dying person affects the mourning process not only of the dying person but also of all those who will come to mourn the deceased. The keeping or disclosing of such secrets can shape who is invited to participate in the mourning rituals, how those rituals will honor the deceased, and what will be remembered about the deceased.[8]

For Judah, the sharing with his therapist, just prior to his death, the true nature of his romantic love for the man he had until then referred to as his 'brother' enabled him and his lover to take leave of and mourn one another in a more open, authentic manner. For the first time ever, Judah was able to experience the freedom to openly cry in the presence of a person other than his lover, as he was about to say his final good-bye to the man whom he had spent 20 precious years of his life tenderly loving. With Judah's having revealed to his therapist his tightly guarded, painful secret, I would like to believe that he was able to die with the comfort that comes with being more genuinely known by a trusted other, his therapist, with the burden of shame which he had carried for so long lifted, and with a sense of peace and wholeness, even if ever so slightly and only for the final hours of his life.

Francesca's family, years after her death, remain deeply anguished in their mourning, as they continue to wonder what she may have held secretly within herself in those final moments, hours, perhaps weeks of her life, as they waited in hopeful anticipation of her having what they believed would be a life-saving organ transplant. Did they come to realize that Francesca, in her love for her family and her unfaltering efforts to try to protect them from any sadness on her behalf, dare not speak to them of her secret wish not to have a stranger's organ transplanted into her weakened, yet still beautiful body? And as Francesca died so suddenly and seemingly unexpectedly to those who loved her most dearly, there was little chance to say that heart-wrenching but most precious final good-bye.

THE PRIVILEGED POSITION OF THE HEALTH CARE PROFESSIONAL

As I think about the very different stories of Francesca's and Judah's final hours, I am again reminded of the privileged role that health care practitioners working with those facing death may come to play. It is a role that speaks to the essential humanity shared between patient and clinician, one which transcends area of specialization. Mindful of the fact that the making and keeping of secrets is an ever-present part of life, we as health care professionals may be in a unique position to listen for the presence of long-held, painful secrets, palpable within the pauses and silences as our patients speak. In our non-intrusive, non-judgmental presence, those facing death can be given the opportunity to consider whether such secrets should remain forever unspoken, particularly as the unfolding of a secret may echo through every layer of one's interpersonal world, and impending death may leave little time for the healing of wounds opened with the secret.[1,2] Alternatively, if there is a secret about the self that feels too tormenting to carry to death, our gentle presence enables those facing the end of their lives to consider with whom that secret may be most meaningfully shared. Or perhaps, at the end of the day, they will come to feel that some tightly guarded secret, now ready to be delicately shared with another, can be safely received and held only by us, the professional bearers of others' secrets. Such is the nature of the trust placed in us.

The special role we may come to play for those facing the end of their lives, as they grapple with issues of long-held secrets about the self, comes with a great responsibility and words of caution. As we come to receive others' secrets, we are often faced with complex clinical, legal and ethical considerations.[1,2] Are there some secrets, now disclosed to us, which we as health care professionals may be legally mandated to disclose to others who may have been unknowingly placed in danger by the presence of this secret? Consider the complexities involved, for instance, in secrets involving HIV/AIDS and the possibility of transmission of the virus to unsuspecting partners.[9]

Additionally, as those in our care place their faith in us, we may carry a power to influence in unintended, subtle and possibly detrimental ways. We, too, may have our own blind spots, based on our unique histories of loss and trauma, relational histories or personal experiences with secrets. It is essential that we try to remain as aware as possible of the potential impact of these on ourselves and those we work with, so that in our thoughtful attention to our patients' secrets, we do not inadvertently position ourselves in any way that can cause harm, despite our best intentions.

Finally, I remain wondering how Francesca's last hours of life, and her family's grief and mourning, would have taken shape had Francesca been helped to convey to her family her wish not to have an organ transplant. Had Francesca been able to tell this secret to her family, rather than having been surrounded by cold and frightening machines during the final moments of her life, perhaps Francesca would have been held, as she lay dying, within the tender embrace of her loving family. These are the thoughts that plague Francesca's daughter, as she continues to mourn in my presence, with a grief which itself can feel unspeakable.

REFERENCES

1 Imber-Black E. Secrets in families and family therapy: an overview. In: Imber-Black E, editor. *Secrets in Families and Family Therapy.* New York: W.W. Norton; 1993. pp.3–28.

2 Imber-Black E. *The Secret Life of Families: truth-telling, privacy, and reconciliation in a tell-all society.* New York: Bantam Books; 1998.

3 Kahn MMR. Secret as potential space. In: Grolnick SA, Barkin L, Muensterberger W, editors. *Between Reality and Fantasy.* New Jersey: Jason Aronson; 1978. pp.259–70.

4 Skolnick NJ, Davies JM. Secrets in clinical work: a relational point of view. In: Skolnick NJ, Warshaw SJ, editors. *Relational Perspectives in Psychoanalysis.* New Jersey: Analytic Press; 1992. pp.217–38.

5 Wright LM, Nagy J. Death: the most troublesome family secret of all. In: Imber-Black E, editor. *Secrets in Families and Family Therapy.* New York: W.W. Norton; 1993. pp.121–37.

6 Compassion and Choices Magazine. Special resource issue in: The Good to Go Resource Guide, 2011. www.compassionandchoices.org

7 Sanders GL. The love that dares to speak its name: from secrecy to openness in gay and lesbian affiliations. In: Imber-Black E, editor. *Secrets in Families and Family Therapy.* New York: W.W. Norton; 1993. pp.215–42.

8 Black LW. AIDS and secrets. In: Imber-Black E, editor. *Secrets in Families and Family Therapy.* New York: W.W. Norton; 1993. pp.355–69.

9 Burris S. Clinical decision making in the shadow of law. In: Anderson JR, Barret B, editors. *Ethics in HIV-Related Psychotherapy: clinical decision making in complex cases.* Washington, DC: American Psychological Association; 2001. pp.99–129.

SECTION IV
Relationships Born of Technology

CHAPTER 14

The Process of Acquiring and Keeping an Organ Transplant

Peter Shapiro

Note: for the sake of convenience and grammatical propriety, in this chapter I refer to the individual transplant patient as male and the physician and other medical staff as female, except in situations when gender-specific issues dictate.

In order to put into context the object relationships unique to the transplant patient, it may be helpful to first describe the experience of the patient approaching and following a transplant procedure.

Most patients who require organ transplants have life-threatening end-stage disease. (Renal transplant patients have disease that requires renal replacement therapy; this threatens *quality* of life but may not be immediately life threatening.) Most of these conditions are chronic illnesses and, in many cases, lifestyle factors and the patient's behaviors (for example, smoking, alcohol and substance abuse, poor diet, non-adherence to therapy) have played a role in the development of the illness (Table 14.1). Alternative treatment options have been or may soon be exhausted. These patients are drowning in the ocean and

Table 14.1 Common indications for solid organ transplantation

Organ	Common indications
Liver	Cirrhosis secondary to alcohol; hepatitis C; hepatitis B; hepatocellular cancer
Lung	Emphysema; cystic fibrosis; interstitial lung disease; primary pulmonary hypertension
Heart	Coronary heart disease; idiopathic and other dilated cardiomyopathies; restrictive heart disease; congenital anomalies
Kidney	Renal failure secondary to hypertension, autoimmune diseases, infections, substance abuse

a transplant is the only lifeboat. They tend, therefore, to be concerned about being given an opportunity to receive a transplant. Occasional patients have sudden catastrophic illnesses (for example, fulminant hepatitis, acute myocarditis or massive acute myocardial infarction) and may not have time to give much thought to transplantation or to learn about it before being swept up in the experience. Acetaminophen overdoses may result in acute liver failure, and people who attempt suicide in this way may awaken from coma only after having had a liver transplant, totally unprepared and possibly unmotivated for what will follow.

Transplantable organs are scarce. According to the United States Department of Health and Human Services, 2011 waiting lists for solid organ transplants included 1353 patients waiting for pancreas transplants, 1769 for lung transplants, 3185 for heart transplants, 16,240 for liver transplants, and over 89,000 for renal transplants. Several thousand additional patients are waiting for multiorgan transplants. Median waiting times are over two years for renal transplants, over one year for liver transplants, over two years for pancreas transplants, over six months for heart transplants and over six months for lung transplants. Some patients wait more than five years for a suitable match, and many patients die, or are consigned to years of hemodialysis, while awaiting a transplant.[1] Lung transplants have increased in number in recent years, from 1172 in 2004 to 1770 in 2010, but the number of transplants for other organs has not increased in many years, leveling off at about 2300 per year for heart transplants, 16,000 per year for renal transplants, and 6300 per year for liver transplants.[1] The scarcity of transplantable organs imposes a societal pressure on organ transplant programs to be selective in accepting candidates for surgery. This pressure is reified in federal regulations that set minimum threshold levels for one-year survival, under threat of withdrawal of reimbursement through federally funded insurance programs (Medicare and Medicaid). All transplant programs examine potential recipients to identify medical and psychosocial factors that could preclude successful transplantation or that will require special management to reduce the risk of transplant failure and early mortality. They may propose palliative alternatives to transplantation or recommend delaying transplantation until or unless a contraindicating condition can be rectified.

Consequently, would-be transplant candidates tend to be anxious about 'passing' the evaluation process. To the extent that the evaluation depends on the patient's self-report, it is subject to his understandable tendency to attempt to put his best foot forward and minimize problems or pathologies that might make him seem unappealing to the program. Of course, objective findings from physical examination and laboratory tests are harder to falsify than information derived from self-report. The transplant physician must factor this self-report pathology-minimizing bias into her assessment of the patient.

Once accepted onto the transplant wait list, the patient has, for the most part, no control over the time of receiving a transplant and he is in a passive position. A transplant must be an adequate immunological match and, for some organs, an appropriate size for a given patient. A renal or liver transplant candidate may be able to help organize an electively scheduled transplantation with a living donor, if a suitable donor can be identified. Heart and lung transplant recipients, on the other hand, depend on cadaver donors, as do most renal and liver transplant candidates. A patient in this position may experience frustration and depression at his helplessness to control the situation, and guilt when he experiences wishes for others to die in order to provide an organ for his transplant. 'I hear a siren passing, and think, "maybe that's a good match for me" and then I feel like some kind of a vampire.' It is also common for a patient both to fear that he will die if the transplant does not arrive in time ('the sword of Damocles') and to believe that if only a transplant does happen, then all his problems will be over ('the pot of gold at the end of the rainbow'). In this setting, transplant candidates often make prayerful promises about how they intend to reform their lives if only they survive. There are no atheists in foxholes, and very few on pretransplant wait lists.

After organ explantation from the donor, organ implantation must be completed within a few hours (up to 24 hours for kidneys) to maintain organ viability. As a consequence, the patient awaiting a cadaveric donor transplant must be quickly available when called. He may be informed that other patients are also being considered as candidates for the same organ, and be kept on 'stand-by.' The intended recipient is prepared and taken to the operating room, begins immunosuppressant treatment even before the implant of the graft, and hopes for the best. Because the transplant surgeons may be performing the final stages of organ explantation simultaneously with preparation of the recipient, final evaluation of the suitability of the organ for implantation may not occur until after the patient has been taken to the operating room and sedated. Occasionally, patients are awakened to learn that surgery was canceled due to problems with the organ identified at the last possible moment. In these situations the patient is exposed to extremes of hopeful anticipation followed by marked disappointment.

Euphoria is an archetypal initial reaction upon awakening after transplant surgery, as the patient feels he has 'made it.' This feeling may be heightened by the large doses of corticosteroids typical in the initial immunosuppressant regimen, which often exacerbate mood lability. Some patients are too sick in the early post-transplant period to enjoy this euphoric state, and even those who do are likely to find it short-lived, because the early recovery process is rarely altogether smooth and easy. Most patients encounter some complications, such as bleeding, infections, wound healing problems, side-effects of medications or graft dysfunction or rejection, in the initial stages of recovery. The transplant physician sees management of these problems as the prosaic stuff of her everyday work but for the patient, they bring a disillusioning end to the euphoric fantasy that all his problems are behind him. For most patients, the hospitalization after transplantation will be at least two weeks long, sometimes much longer, as medications are adjusted and problems resolved.

Now the patient must settle in to the work of recuperation, learning how to manage medications and how to monitor for emerging problems when he goes home, participating in physical therapy and integrating the logistical demands of following a regimen, keeping appointments, and undergoing tests with the other tasks of daily life. He may find that he attends a scheduled appointment on Monday, is called back to the hospital on Tuesday when a blood test result returns from the laboratory with an abnormal value, undergoes a follow-up test on Wednesday, and is readmitted to the hospital on Thursday. He learns that having a transplant is not the end of all problems but an opportunity to replace one set of problems – the problems of organ failure – for another – the problems of living with immunosuppression and a transplant. These new problems are closely bound up with his relationships with others and his previous and desired social roles. For a while, being a transplant recipient is his full-time job. It usually takes several months for him to achieve the beginning of a sense of stability about his health and capacity to return to a social role not entirely dominated by the transplant patient sick role.

In the longer run, regardless of the patient's relationships and social role, he is left with the stark awareness that his survival, and certainly that of his graft, depends on adherence to his immunosuppressant medication regimen. Non-adherence equals death.

THE ORGAN AND THE ORGAN'S DONOR

A psychoanalyst once described the unconscious meaning of surgery as castration, in that something is taken out of the body and lost. In 1954, when Joseph Murray performed renal transplantation between identical twins, he ushered in an era of a new kind of surgery, in which something new is put into the body. This thing is alive and grows in the patient's body, but it is not originally part of the patient. Thus, 40 years ago, another psychoanalyst, Pietro Castelnuovo-Tedesco, described the unconscious meaning of organ transplantation as akin to pregnancy, as the patient carries another life inside his or her body, or as entailing a blurring of the boundary between oneself and others, necessitating the task of responding to the 'other' within oneself.[2]

One of the challenges of transplantation is the psychological incorporation of this organ-life into one's own sense of self, that is, the ability to say, for example, 'my heart' instead of 'the donor's heart that I have inside my body', while also acknowledging that this new organ and one's newly changed self must be cared for in ways that were not previously part of the care of the pre-transplant self. The patient must take immunosuppressive medications, maintain self-surveillance for signs of graft dysfunction or rejection, and see doctors regularly. Patients who do not acquire the feeling that their new organs are a part of themselves experience anxiety, a lack of control, and a feeling of vulnerability to harm from or control by their transplanted organs.[2] There is some evidence that such patients have more feeling of being traumatized by the transplant experience and poorer survival.[2,3]

The intensity of the transplant recipient's attitudes toward the transplanted organ depends to some extent on which organ is transplanted. In our informal language, we often speak of aspects of ourselves and our behavior as embodied in one organ or another – a person who acts bravely 'has guts' or, acting brazenly, 'has balls' (i.e. testicles). In particular, the idea of the heart as the container of the soul, emotion or personality is deeply entrenched in Western culture and language. We speak of sadness as being sick at heart, of loving with all our heart and, when discouraged, of losing heart, and it does seem that heart transplant patients are more prone than other transplant patients to see their grafts as endowed with the personality and emotions of their donors, but to some extent all recipients experience receiving an organ from another person as receiving a piece of the donor's personhood.

The recipient's attitude toward the transplanted organ cannot be separated from ideas and fantasies about the donor. In the adult patient, typically these fantasies are unconscious or preconscious, and they tend to be expressed, if at all, in jokes. These jokes often include aspects of racial, ethnic or gender-based stereotyping that would be disavowed if confronted but that are present in the patient's preconscious mind. For example, a middle-aged Jewish man awaiting a heart transplant commented that he would know if he were to receive the heart of a black teenage boy, because he would find that he wanted to play basketball and listen to rap music after his transplant. One version of this kind of fantasy refers to 'molecular' or 'cellular' 'memory' carried in individual cells within the transplant, leading to phenomena such as craving or dislike for certain foods arising in the recipient after the transplant. Children are more prone to be explicit and quite conscious about their fantasies of incorporation of aspects of the personhood of the donor, and to be manifestly anxious about this process. A seven-year-old girl asked whether she would no longer speak English if she received the heart of a Chinese donor, and a five-year-old boy from a fundamentalist Christian family was concerned about whether, following his transplant, he would 'still have Jesus in my heart.' Another boy, 16 years old, with disabling congenital heart disease since infancy, normal intelligence and late onset of puberty, stated that he could not accept the idea of receiving a woman's heart because 'then I will never really be a man.'

Some patients find reassurance in language that de-emphasizes the human origin of their grafts, describing having a heart transplant, for example, as akin to replacing the fuel pump on their cars. These kinds of fantasies are also manifest in popular culture, in countless romance novels and films whose plots are variations on the theme of the beautiful young bereaved widow falling in love with the man who, unbeknownst to the widow, is the recipient of a heart transplant from her deceased husband, the recipient having incorporated into himself the qualities of the donor that made him attractive to his wife in the first place.

THE FAMILY

When a patient can receive an organ from a living related donor, the act of donation by a related donor means more than the receipt of an organ. It means that a renegotiation of family relationships must ensue. Debts may be forgiven and power relationships shift. 'Black sheep' within the family may have their reputations restored by donating. The donor takes pride in having donated and pleasure in the good outcome of the recipient, may experience a part of him- or herself living on in the recipient, and may feel a sense of ownership and entitlement to speak to the recipient about his conduct in caring for the organ or resentment that this organ-gift is not being cared for or used properly. Conversely, if a donor organ fails to function properly, the donor may be blamed, scapegoated and attacked by the family. A similar phenomenon has been observed with egg donors for infertile couples: if the use of the donated eggs fails to result in a successful pregnancy, the donor may be made to feel that this was somehow her fault.

Renal transplantation can now be performed using chains or loops of unrelated donors to maximize the number of compatible matches and therefore the number of transplants that can be performed. For example, suppose that A, B, and C are renal transplant candidates each of whom has a prospective related donor, donors A, B, and C. For patients B and C, suppose that the donors are compatible tissue matches, while prospective donor A does not tissue match with recipient A but does match with recipient B, and that donor B matches well with recipient C and donor C matches well with recipient A. If each prospective donor were to donate to his related recipient, only patients B and C could receive transplants. If donor A donates to patient B, donor B donates to patient C, and donor C donates to patient A, all three patients can receive transplants (Figure 14.1). Not surprisingly, a study of prospective donors for such a program found that the level of willingness to participate is associated with the prospective donor's level of expectation that the donation will result in at least as great a likelihood for a successful transplant for the recipient to whom the donor is related as that which would have occurred had the donor donated

Panel A

Donor A incompatible with	Recipient A (no transplant)
Donor B →	Recipient B
Donor C →	Recipient C

Panel B

Donor A →	Recipient B
Donor B →	Recipient C
Donor C →	Recipient A

Figure 14.1 Chains or loops of living donors can increase availability of transplants. Flexibility in matching potential living donors to recipients may increase the number of transplants that can be accomplished. *Panel A:* if the prospective donor to patient A is not a compatible match, patient A must await another more suitable donor. Patients B and C receive transplants from their prospective donors. *Panel B:* a chain of compatible donors enables all three patients to receive transplants.

to his own relative. In short, the prospective donors feel responsible for their related recipient's outcome.[4]

Potential donors may also have many reasons, some covert, to choose not to donate. These may include fear of being ill or complications of surgery, concern about maintaining work, anticipation that another family member may be even more in need of the donated organ in the future, and ambivalence or even antipathy toward the prospective recipient. For example, the victim of child abuse by an older relative, having maintained the abuse as a secret from his family, may maintain superficially polite and friendly relations with the abuser but not wish to donate to him. Extreme clinical tact is necessary to protect this potential donor from pressure to donate.

There are other family relationship renegotiations that occur with transplantation. Often, the transplant patient has experienced a diminution of responsibility within his family as he has taken on the sick role. As the family responds to the cumulative weight of the patient's disability, they may experience feelings of anger at the patient (for not caring for himself better, for letting the family down, for abandoning the family, etc.) and desire to escape the burden of the caregiver role; however, these reactions may be outweighed by love and concern for the patient or guilt feelings at letting the patient down when he is ill. Even partners in troubled relationships who had thoughts of leaving the relationship may feel the need to stay to care for the sick patient. In a complementary way, patients often speak of their guilt for imposing burdens on and failing to support their spouses or children, and it is common for patients to espouse the goal of 'making it up' to their families after recovery – resuming roles as the breadwinner, the parent who takes care of the children, the person who does household chores, and so on.

A paradox of transplantation is that sometimes the operation is a success but the marriage dies, just when things 'should' get better. In these instances, one often observes a partner who held on in the relationship to care for the ailing patient, but who then feels permission to leave as soon as the patient is able to care for himself. One also sees partners who have extremely unrealistic expectations about how quickly the patient should recover after transplant surgery and are unwilling to maintain a care-giving role once the patient returns home. In another not uncommon scenario, the well partner has acquired a new repertoire of skills and new social roles that she is unwilling to relinquish when the transplant patient feels ready to resume previous patterns of social role relationships. The partner who previously was a homemaker but who has learned that she enjoys working outside the home may no longer be willing to return to the homemaker role, even as her husband feels guilty for having 'forced' his wife to enter the workforce to support their family while he was ill, and hopes that she will quit outside work when he recovers. (To be clear, this pattern occurs with patients of both sexes and their spouses, not just male patients.)

The children of pre- and peritransplant patients are often left to fend for themselves as their well parent concerns himself or herself with the ill patient (in the hospital, but also at home). Siblings of pediatric patients may have the same experience. These children are forced into autonomous pseudo-adult functioning prematurely. No parent may be home to cook meals, supervise homework or maintain discipline, and the children must make do as best they can. When their parent recovers and tries to reassert authority, overt conflict and acting out behaviors on the part of the children may ensue. The child, having experienced a kind of parental abandonment and developed a kind of independence, expresses his anger by refusing to allow the parent back into a controlling parental role.

When a patient receives an organ from an unidentified deceased donor, a fantasized relationship ensues between the patient and the donor's family, whom he does not know. This relationship is sometimes actualized. The patient has a debt that cannot be repaid. He owes his opportunity for regained health or survival to the generosity of the donor (if the donor's prior statement of intent to donate has the force of law) or, more often, to the deceased donor's family (if the family must consent to donation at the time of the patient's death). Patients may have the desire to meet the donor family, with a more or less vague idea about expressing gratitude and a desire to learn more about the donor, but they may not be prepared for the expectations of the donor family or for what they find out about the donor. Organ transplant programs generally encourage anonymous expression of gratitude to the donor family, but sometimes face-to-face meetings do follow. These can be moving and joyous experiences if the recipient is doing well and is not made uncomfortable by the bittersweet quality of the donor family's experience – the reminder of personal loss along with the realization of the satisfaction of transmuting tragedy into good via the opportunity to help others. The donor family experiences the satisfaction of seeing their loved one live on through the recipient, and the recipient may have his fantasies about the hoped-for positive aspects of the donor confirmed. On the other hand, he may not and entitlement, possessiveness, disapproval or disappointment expressed by the donor family can rapidly sour the recipient's experience of the relationship. Gifts create implied obligations of reciprocity, but in this situation adequate reciprocation is impossible.

When women of child-bearing age who have received transplants desire pregnancy, special concerns ensue. Clearly, for many women, child bearing is a highly valued aspect of identity and has tremendously important meaning in their relationships with their partners and families, and their presentation of themselves to the world at large. However, a heightened level of monitoring is required through the pregnancy, due to the effects of pregnancy on the metabolism of immunosuppressant drugs, with consequences for the wellbeing of the mother, and the transplacental effects of immunosuppressant drugs, with consequences for the wellbeing of the developing fetus. As a result, pregnancy is the nexus for a complicated web of conflicting relationship issues: the patient's transplant physicians may see pregnancy as an undesirable threat to the patient's health; her obstetrician, as a desirable challenge to be managed; her partner, as both desired and feared. For the patient herself, the developing fetus may be both beloved and an enemy.

OTHER PATIENTS AND THEIR FAMILIES

From very early on in the modern era of transplantation, it has been evident that transplant patients and their families constitute a community.[5] They see each other in the clinic waiting room and in the hospital, and, especially when their clinical courses run in parallel, they are likely to have relationships that engender feelings about each other's success or problems as transplant patients. Patients and family members keep track of who is still waiting, who has received a transplant, who is back in the hospital with complications, and who has died. Another patient's success can be a source of joy and hope or engender a feeling of jealousy. Patients may not understand how the next patient to receive a transplant is chosen and wonder at being 'passed over' on the wait list. Patients and their families also provide each other with support, through informal networks and organized support groups, which may be either patient or family directed or transplant program based. These networks and groups can impart useful information, provide feedback, share solutions to problems, provide concrete help, and allay feelings of aloneness.

A particularly poignant and painful aspect of the patient's relationship to other patients stems from the sense of kinship experienced either because of undergoing a transplant at the same time or because of awareness that one has received a transplanted organ from the same donor as another patient. These patients are like siblings or combat buddies. Anxiety, 'survivor guilt', and depression may occur when one patient survives but his peer dies.

THE HOSPITAL AND MEDICAL STAFF

Having an organ transplant entails an ongoing relationship with medical providers for the rest of one's life. The medical staff expect the patient to maintain adherence to a complex regimen, including taking medication, timely follow-through for laboratory testing, being a good reporter of new symptoms, maintaining a healthy lifestyle, and keeping appointments, and that he will accept medical advice. The patient expects the providers to be reliable, expert, available, and concerned for his wellbeing. Patients often regress to a considerable extent when they are acutely ill – this regression is fostered by the hospital environment and staff.[6] The patient may be bathed and fed, his medication is handed to him, his activity schedule is no longer in his control. If all goes well, the patient will smoothly emerge from regression and dependence back to adult autonomous function as he recovers from the acute episode of illness. Sometimes either the regression or the return to adult function does not proceed smoothly – the patient is too independent or oppositional, or too needy, calls for help incessantly and expresses fear, anxiety or anger at his caregivers. These relationship characteristics are to some degree determined by predispositions of the patient toward secure versus insecure attachments, which are in turn related to early childhood experiences of being cared for.[7] Patients' views of their physicians and nurses as saviors, collaborators, taskmasters or jailers, as supportive or harsh, are based largely on their own personal histories and personality characteristics, more than on the characteristics of the physicians and nurses themselves.

WORK AND EMPLOYERS

Whether patients enter the world of organ transplantation through acute or chronic illness has implications for their relationship with the working world that play out after transplantation. Some patients have been working almost up to the time of transplantation. Their role as workers is part of their identity, and they hope to return to work as soon as possible. Will their employers hold their jobs for them? Will they be medically able to return to the work they did before? Exposure to dust and mold may be too dangerous for immunosuppressed transplant recipients, and so may preclude return to employment in construction work, plumbing, and other physical labor subject to such exposures. Recurring, frequent, and unpredictable medical appointments, testing, and hospitalizations, as well as concerns over high anticipated medical costs and effects on employer-sponsored group medical insurance costs may drive employers to wish to avoid keeping transplant patients on the payroll. Patients end up attempting to conceal medical issues from prospective employers. Some patients find that they are 'insurance disabled': they would like to work but cannot find a job with health insurance benefits, and cannot afford to accept a job with no benefits, because they will have to give up Medicare coverage that was contingent on being disabled or Medicaid coverage contingent on having inadequate income, and so will have no insurance coverage to pay for their medical care. These patients may seek 'off the books' employment while trying to maintain their official 'disabled' status, collecting disability payments and maintaining their entitlement to Medicaid or Medicare insurance.

Other patients welcome an opportunity to stop work or see their illness as marking the end of their working life. Disability pensions from public funding or private insurance along with entitlement to Medicare after a period of chronic disability support adoption of a view of oneself as not able or not having a need to work any more. However, many patients who have grown accustomed to disabled status are subject to termination of their benefits when their health status has improved after transplantation. These patients may be unpleasantly surprised and become very anxious when threatened with loss of disability income and insurance because they are no longer sick. They have ceased thinking of themselves as needing or being able to compete in the job market, and are at a loss about what to do to sustain themselves.

SOCIETY

What is the societal significance of transplantation? Transplant patients are featured on television programs about medical miracles, and in books and films in which transplant recipients' lives are heroically or romantically intertwined with the lives of their donors' loved ones.[8] Hospitals compete to have the dominant transplant program in their region, viewing such programs as trophies and as tokens of their excellence. Transplant operations are among the most highly reimbursed of all medical procedures. In short, transplant patients are objects of societal curiosity, awe, and a special kind of reverence. Perhaps more than other medical marvels, this is because they exemplify immortality and the denial of death.[9] The donor (especially the dead donor) lives on in the recipient who defies death by descending into the death-like state of anesthesia, has his body cut open, has a vital organ removed, receives a living organ, and thereby is restored to life. In *The Hero with a Thousand Faces*, Joseph Campbell recognized the critical quality of the hero, throughout many cultures, as his triumph over death.[10] Thus society venerates and rewards transplant surgeons, who hold the power of restoring life in their hands, but also regards patients, especially those whose transplanted organ comes from a deceased donor, as special and apart from the ordinary.

Yet there is also fear and resentment in American society's attitude about transplants. Congressional budget negotiations seeking to limit Medicare and Medicaid costs have identified cutbacks in coverage for organ transplantation as an opportunity for savings, as have some states.[11,12] Some states have proposed limiting access to public funding for transplants in cases of illness due to alcohol or substance abuse.[13] And shortages of organs for transplantation have created black markets for the sale of organs, especially kidneys, turning potential donors, especially the poor, into resources for commercial exploitation.

CONCLUSION

By their very nature, by virtue of their scarcity, costliness, difficulty, and especially because of their uniquely death-defying character, organ transplants introduce their recipients to a constellation of new object relationships: with their transplanted organs, donors, loved ones, the families of their donors, medical staff, and with society at large. The patient's sense of self must be altered to accommodate the transplant and his new role as a transplant patient, and his experience of others is inevitably altered as well. These changes may entail great personal difficulty. Successful outcomes after transplantation require successful adaptation to the new object relationship experiences of the transplant patient.

REFERENCES

1   United States Dept of Heath and Human Services, Health Resources and Services Administration, Organ Procurement and Transplantation Network. http://optn. transplant.hrsa.gov/latestData/rptData.asp

2   Castelnuovo-Tedesco P. Organ transplant, body image, psychosis. *Psychoanal Qtrly.* 1973: 349–63.

3   Dew MA, DiMartini AF. Psychological disorders and distress after adult cardiothoracic transplantation. *J Cardiovasc Nurs* 2005; **20**(5 Suppl): S51–66.

4   Ratner LE, Rana A, Ratner ER, *et al.* The altruistic unbalanced paired kidney exchange: proof of concept and survey of potential donor and recipient attitudes. *Transplantation.* 2010; **89**(1): 15–22.

5   Kraft IA, Vick J. The transplantation milieu, St. Luke's hospital 1968–1969. *Semin Psychiatry.* 1971; **3**: 17–25.

6   Strain JJ. Psychological reactions to medical illness and hospitalization. In: Strain JJ, Grossman S, editors. *Psychological Care of the Medically Ill.* New York: Appleton-Century-Crofts; 1975. pp.23–36.

7   Maunder RG, Hunter JJ. Attachment and psychosomatic medicine: developmental contributions to stress and disease. *Psychosom Med.* 2001; **63**(4): 556–67.

8   Connelly M. *Blood Work.* New York: Warner Books; 1998.

9   Becker E. *The Denial of Death.* New York: Free Press; 1973.

10 Campbell J. *The Hero With a Thousand Faces*. Princeton, NJ: Bollingen Foundation/ Princeton University Press; 1968.

11 Administration offers health care cuts as part of budget negotiations. *New York Times*. July 5, 2011. www.nytimes.com/2011/07/05/us/05deficit.html?scp=2&sq=July+5%2C+2011&st=nyt

12 Arizona cuts funding for transplant patients. *New York Times*. December 3, 2010. www.nytimes.com/2010/12/03/us/03transplant.html?ref=arizona

13 Oregon seeks to revive health care 'rationing' plan. *New York Times*. August 14, 1992. www.nytimes.com/1992/08/14/us/oregon-seeks-to-revive-health-care-rationing-plan.html?ref=oregon

CHAPTER 15

The 'Birth Other' in Assisted Reproduction

Diane Ehrensaft

Advances in medical science have created a major shake-up in one of the most intimate arenas of family life: baby making. Infertility is no longer a terminal diagnosis. For those whose own bodies do not work to make a baby (biological infertility) or for those missing a partner to make that baby with (social infertility), introducing an outside party into conception and birth through gamete donation, gestational carriers or surrogacy is now an increasingly sought option for creating a family. Men and women can move swiftly from the travails of biological or social infertility into the domain of assisted reproductive technology in a fertile new world. All these individuals will have one thing in common: their children will be the product of science, not sex, a science that necessitates the participation of an outsider.

As science forged ahead to find new ways to help men and women have babies of their own using assisted reproductive technology (ART), the mental health field chased behind, looking to make sense of the interlocking psychological experiences of the parents, the children, and the people who donate their gametes or offer their uteri so that a baby can be born. Over time, the gap between the two professions has closed and the field of reproductive technology is now ripe for an interdisciplinary model that encompasses both the medical and the psychological issues that emerge when men and women turn to an outside party to have a baby, be it a sperm donor, egg donor, surrogate or gestational carrier.

Searching for a singular term for all these parties, I unwittingly arrived at one while taking notes for *Mommies, Daddies, Donors, Surrogates*.[1] Omitting the 'm' in 'birth mother,' I came upon the perfect term, 'birth other': a genderless assignation referring to an individual involved in the birth process but an other rather than a parent to the child.[1-4] So I will be using the term 'birth other' to refer to donors, surrogates or gestational carriers, and the term 'birth other family' to refer to the families created with the help of one or more of those outside parties.

The intention of this chapter is to share with the medical field the discoveries of developmental and relational psychoanalysis concerning the dynamics of 'birth other' families. The underlying assumption is that reproductive specialists and medical practitioners hold a unique position in the lives of these families. Integrating these psychodynamic understandings into medical patient care will provide a holistic insurance policy in which individuals and couples turning to assisted reproductive technology to build their families will have sturdy psychological as well as medical supports in that journey. As we do this, we must always keep our eyes on the prize that so often gets overlooked – the actual baby who is made. The field of assisted reproductive technology is not just helping people conceive and gestate; it is creating a whole new generation of children who were made with the help of birth others. It is to the concerns about those children's development that this chapter is also addressed.

NEW OEDIPAL CIRCLES

As a presenter at a 2011 interdisciplinary conference on reproductive technology, I introduced the concept of the Oedipal circle.[5] The traditional Oedipal triangle that evolves from mother, father, sexual intercourse, and baby just does not apply to the birth other family. Instead, we must extend the triangle to a circle that encompasses all the combinations of the people who intended to have the baby, the people who donated gametes or allowed use of their wombs, and the baby created. During the conference, an audience member pointed out that an additional member of the circle had been overlooked: the doctor who participates in bringing the baby into being. I stand corrected.

Those opposed to assisted reproductive technology births on either moral or religious grounds often feel that the doctor is playing God in an arena that should be left to nature. Those who support reproductive technology come to realize that the doctor is no God but can easily, in the minds of his or her patients, slip into the position of Medical Mother or Fertility Father. With that said, I have extended the Oedipal circle to encompass the medical professionals who bring sex and reproduction into the lab as they facilitate an assisted reproductive technology conception or gestation; so now we have 'mommy(ies), daddy(ies), birth other(s), and the nice doctor who helped make you.' I do this with the understanding that family members can experience strong attachments to the 'nice doctors' who are allowed to enter the deepest chamber of family life – baby making. To adapt D.W. Winnicott's notion that there is no baby without a mother,[6] in assisted reproductive technology there is no baby without all the people who intended to have the baby and all the people who contributed to making that baby, including birth others and medical professionals.

HOPE AND FEAR

Assisted reproductive technology family building starts the moment someone considers the option of using a birth other to have their baby. With the decision comes a seemingly contradictory set of feelings: desire, hope, fear, and, later, fatigue. For biologically infertile people, the hope that ensues when a doctor announces 'I can help you have that baby' is a phoenix experience, a new life rising from the ashes of the death experience that surfaced as they confronted their infertility. Science will offer them a second chance. Socially infertile people have the opportunity to join the mainstream of families with children, heretofore barred to them. For them, the feelings can be both exhilarating and transcendent.

Carl Jung introduced the concept of the collective unconscious – dreams, notions, and fantasies shared by a whole culture. In Western culture we find that such fantasies about children born through fantastic means go way back in written history, phantasmagorical stories carried deep in our psyches: Athena, birthed by her father from his head[7] or Hagar, surrogate for Abraham and Sarah.[8,9]

Buoyed by such fantastic birth stories embedded deep in our collective unconscious, prospective birth other parents may initially experience, alongside hope, a rush of omnipotence, envisioning moving mountains and challenging the heavens to overcome what nature said could never happen. Yet hand in hand with hope and omnipotence comes a subtle to profound sense of fear, sometimes conscious, sometimes unconscious: angst related to medical risks, both to baby and mother; anxieties related to draining of resources, both material and emotional; queasiness that bad things will come from defying both nature and cultural or religious proscriptions; worst of all, worry that after all this effort, there still will be no baby.

A dynamic that is often overlooked in working with people who turn to ART to have a child is the puncturing of the soaring fantasies by these poignant pricks of anxiety. The fears do not form in a vacuum but rather within a larger social context that ranges from totally accepting to forthrightly antagonistic regarding people who attempt to play 'God' by using science rather than 'natural' procreation to make a baby. As a society, we all seem to be affected by a phenomenon that I have labeled 'reproductive technophobia' – collective prejudices, assumptions, and negative attitudes toward the rapidly changing terrain of birth technology. Parents may either internalize that anxiety or directly confront it from the outside as they contemplate or later go on to have their birth other baby.

It is my assessment that many modern parents grapple with both chronic parental anxiety and chronic parental hyperactivity.[10] Factor in the experience of seeking out a doctor and a birth other, and these diagnoses can quickly move from chronic to acute in the face of reproductive technophobia, medical risks, drained resources, existential anxieties about challenging the 'natural order' of life, rush to action in the face of a racing biological clock or a partner's or doctor's urging, and, lastly, the battle fatigue that can follow repeated attempts to conceive. The combination of hope, fear, and exhaustion can heat to a boiling point.

Simone was a woman in her early forties. She and her husband had been trying for five years to conceive a baby – naturally, with fertility drugs, with *in vitro* fertilization (IVF), and finally with an egg donor. Max, her husband, was still hopeful and energetic: 'Let's keep going. I know we can do it.' Simone came to therapy as if she were tripping off a battlefield. She was exhausted, angry, and financially depleted. She could not even remember why she ever wanted a baby. As soon as she was able to give herself permission to take a break, her anxiety lifted and her anger dropped. In the press to provide eggs, sperm, uteri, and then baby, careful attention needs to be paid to the potential havoc wrought on the psyches of the men and women who come to the nice doctor. We must recognize when to press the pause button or desist when fear and fatigue have decimated hope.

UNEXPECTED EROTICA

Patients suffering from biological infertility may incur significant wounding to their sexual or gendered selves. When a man faces his infertility, it is often a challenge to his 'machismo' – his virility, his masculinity, his potency, not just sexually but generalized to ego strength and vitality. When a woman faces her infertility, she faces a challenge to her 'feminisma' – her ability to carry life within her and bear a child between her own hips. Patients facing social infertility may experience either shame or sorrow that they do not have a sexual partner with whom to mate and procreate. Now imagine that we bring an outside person into the lives of these people who have been struggling with an assault on their gendered or sexual selves or are missing a sexual partner with whom to conceive. That person may be a virile man with flowing sperm, a woman bursting with robust and abundant eggs, or a woman with a womb that has successfully housed her own babies and is ready to house one (or more) for someone else. This outside person is written up in all the children's books as the 'nice' man or woman who helped us have 'you.' Regretfully, these cheerful sanitized stories do not remain so tame in the fantasy lives of the men and women who are the recipients of donors' or surrogates' services. Technology has been able to successfully take the reproduction out of sex but it is far more challenging to remove the sex from reproduction, even when none occurs.

Much to their own surprise, recipients of donor gametes can find themselves immersed in sexual fantasies about the donor. If they have a partner, that partner might feel unexpected pangs of jealousy toward the donor, indeed imagining the donor and partner 'doing it.' Maureen and Craig used an anonymous sperm donor to conceive their daughter after discovering that Craig had no viable sperm. Maureen, a strikingly attractive woman, was extremely anxious about revealing to their daughter the truth of her origins, fearful that she would accuse her mother of sexually inappropriate behavior. In fact, every time Maureen spoke of the anonymous donor, known only as a blond heart surgeon from a European country, her eyes would gloss over and she would grow dreamy and distant. As she described this man, it sounded like the most erotic of intimate rendezvous, rather than a medical procedure in a lab. Craig, sitting across from her, would visibly shrink in his seat, vacillating between anger and total deflation as he felt himself reduced to the status of 'birth nobody,' forced to witness his wife's erotic encounter with the fantasized donor.

Sexual threat is not just the purview of infertile men. An infertile woman using an egg donor described herself as the odd woman out in the process. Her college friend had been the donor. She came to realize that this meant that her friend's egg would be fertilized by her husband's sperm, while she would be relegated to the role of bystander in this union between husband and friend.[11] Boiling her feelings down to their essence, this mother feels she has been put in the position of watching her husband get together with another woman while she sits on the sidelines and even participates in their love making by carrying their child.

Sexual titillation or threat is also not just the purview of heterosexual couples. Francine, a single woman, sought out a gay man who was very happy to be the donor for her child. In the months of trying to conceive, Francine was flooded with sexual fantasies about the donor, wishing they could just do it the old-fashioned way, imagining them not just a parenting but a romantic couple, despite the reality that the donor had no interest in a sexual relationship with a woman. Jan and Doreen were an older lesbian couple who decided to have a baby. Discovering that both of their eggs were no longer viable, they turned to an egg donor, an acquaintance of theirs, with Jan becoming the gestational mother after the donor's eggs were fertilized with another friend's sperm. During the pregnancy Jan and Doreen's relationship began to falter: Doreen was riddled with disturbing, unshakeable fears that Jan was in love with the egg donor and it was their baby that had been conceived. A gay dad in another family felt like the teenage wallflower at the school dance after his partner and their chosen surrogate easily conceived following repeated failed attempts with his own sperm; he imagined his partner and the surrogate twirling across the dance floor in romantic bliss as he was forced to sit on the sidelines. Another gay man in a similar situation was shocked to discover how wounded he felt and how easily the 'macho' posturing about his own sperm strength broke to the surface.[12]

Bringing a birth other into baby making can stir up erotic bedroom scenarios, stimulating fantasies of illicit extramarital sex or *ménages a trois*. Sometimes, the doctor as facilitator of the conception gets drawn into the fantasy as well. The fantasies spill out in all directions, not just in parents' but in other people's psyches. For example, husbands of women who become surrogates are often confronted with a challenging question from friends, colleagues or family members: 'How could you let your wife get pregnant with another man?' The queries are not only judgmental; they are laden with sexual innuendoes about the man's wife having an affair right under the husband's nose, the ultimate fate of a cuckold. When it comes to intrusive sexual fantasies, no participating party is exempt from the eroticized connotations of 'procreation in the afternoon' (or very early morning, as is often scheduled).

Medical and mental health professionals can join together to lay the ground work for healthy family building by alerting recipients that these seemingly irrational X-rated fantasies or sexual jealousies, in which the birth other gets transformed into a Casanova, sex goddess or sexual predator, are not so uncommon. By normalizing the fantasies and bringing them to the surface, birth other parents will be alleviated of potential guilt, shame or resentment; the fantasies will be shrunk down to size, rather than ballooning to delusional proportions; the parents will benefit by soothing the tensions between partners and paving the way for a more realistic placement of the birth other in the family's life.

'HONEY, I SHRUNK THE DONOR' PLAYS AGAINST 'FROM THIS BEAN A PARENT DID GROW'

If the birth other takes on darkening tones in the parents' psyches, they may call on defensive strategies to eliminate the threat posed by the 'real' man or woman who has been able to provide what the parent could not: deny the personhood of the helper now morphed into interloper; do a sleight of mind and reduce the donor to a vial of sperm or an egg in a dish; or shrink the surrogate or gestational carrier to a disembodied uterus. So there is no other man, just a vial of sperm. There is no other woman, just some extracted eggs or temporary housing for the baby. The medical profession may unwittingly help this defensive strategy, by referring to donors in terms of gametes rather than people, and until policy shifted toward advocating disclosure,[13] by reassuring parents that no one ever need know that it was not their own sperm or eggs that made their baby.

Some parents call on the exact opposite defensive strategy: 'From this bean a parent did grow.' Rather than reducing people to a body part, they take a body part and fashion a person. Anonymous sperm donor #156 can be transformed in the parent's eyes into the wonderful father, brilliant, funny, musically talented, who will burst on the scene to let himself be known to his child. The parent may be engaging in a family reverie about the person who helped bring a baby to his or her life, a fine activity. Yet such reveries also put the parent at risk of creating more of a whole than actually exists. 'From this bean a parent did grow' reflects (1) a parent's anxiety about leaving the donor at the level of part-object, a vial of sperm/an egg in a dish, particularly when the birth other remains anonymous; (2) a parent's desire to construct a missing father or mother for the child and create an image of the person responsible for half the child's genetic make-up who might even be a partner in fantasy.

In the struggle to take the sex out of reproduction in assisted conception, we witness a paradox between a reduction of people to parts and an illusion of whole people where there are none. Both defensive strategies are extreme and neither is based on reality. The truth lies in the middle: birth others are people who help a family have a child. They are not body parts, they are not parents or lovers.

Shrinking birth others to body parts or fashioning them into participating family members is a way of assuaging the internal unrest that may come from shame about infertility, internal dis-ease with these scientific birth techniques, worry about people's responses, anxious anticipation regarding the children's reactions, disquiet about genetic asymmetry – that one's partner and oneself will not have the same genetic relationship to the child. Intended parents also engage in other forms of fantasy to ensure their place in the Oedipal circle, as when a mother-to-be in a two-mom family announced that she was actually the other genetic parent, because she carried the warm sperm under her arm to the doctor's office to keep it warm for the insemination in her partner's uterus. Sometimes men with very low sperm counts mix their sperm with more robust sperm from a donor or even several donors. If a successful conception occurs, they can imagine that they, rather than the donor, are the genetic fathers of their children. Gay fathers have been known to mix sperm to give each a chance to win the race to the ovum, deciding never to document who won the race. In the age of reliable DNA testing, establishing genetic paternity could be easily done. Instead, the strong desire to secure oneself as a parent precludes seeking verification of biological paternity as the fathers remain in a limbo state of fantasy and reverie – maybe I am the 'real' parent, after all.

Fantasies that disavow the actual facts of the conception are understandable defenses. They protect the parents' psyches from a torrent of feelings and anxieties about the baby they so much want to be theirs. Boiled down to their core, these defenses all qualify as forms of denial,[14] called into action to assuage the angst about parental authenticity when birth other and doctor enter the Oedipal circle as additional players in the parents' and the child's life.

BOND BREAKERS

After the baby is born, the bliss of their new arrival may be spoiled by parents' gnawing worries. Genetic asymmetry is one factor at the core of the angst.

Penelope and Marie are divorced lesbian parents of two-and-a-half-year-old twins, conceived with a known sperm donor. Penelope is the genetic mother, Marie the non-genetic mother. Both are legal parents. Marie is in a rage, accusing Penelope of breast feeding the children, in her estimation definitely too old for breast feeding, behind her back. With exploration, the root of Marie's fury is not breast feeding but envy at being denied the same genetic tie to the twins that Penelope has and fear that Penelope will trump her in parent–baby bonding by playing her biological card.

Melanie Klein[15] defined basic envy as an attack on what is perceived as good – in the beginning, the mother. The frustration of not having what the mother possesses or not getting what the mother has to offer can sometimes lead the infant to want to spoil things, to get inside and attack the good mother. With time, the infant develops the capacity for gratitude for all the mother gives, and that sense of appreciation calms the tides of envy so that the child can go on to live a healthy, loving life. Yet that primitive sense of intense envy can resurface at any time, given the proper circumstances. In a two-parent family, being a non-genetic parent relying on the other parent's gametes or womb to have a baby is just such a circumstance, tempering the gratitude toward the genetic parent with rumblings of resentment or ill feeling toward the person who was able to do what the non-genetic parent could not, either because of a body that did not work or, in same-sex couples, because, by prior agreement, it was not the non-genetic parent's turn.

Fear of birth other as kidnapper is the next core factor in the bonding angst. Becoming a parent can be accompanied by a universal fear of the kidnapper coming to take the baby away.[16] The fear emanates from strong attachments to the child, parental guilt about not taking good enough care of the baby, and realization that children are placed with parents only temporarily – they will someday go away. The parental angst is projected onto an 'evil other' – someone who will want the beloved baby as much as they do and act on their desire by stealing the baby.

For parents using ART, that 'evil other' readily takes the form of the 'birth other,' no stranger to the baby but rather connected by flesh and blood. Parents not only fear that the birth other might come to claim rights to the baby. Worries surface that the child, too, may be a bond breaker, actively seeking out that outside person as the missing or even better parent. As a result, parents may take desperate measures to keep the birth other away, by insisting on anonymity, by barring the birth other access to the child or by permanently keeping the birth other conception a secret from the child. All of these are defensive measures in face of the evil other, now transformed into the birth other coming to claim the baby that, in the parents' darkest fantasies, really belongs to him or her.

The third factor in the bonding angst involves the contradictory social messages regarding blood ties and social ties. When it comes to family, we are a culture that fundamentally privileges genetic over emotional bonds. Reproductive specialists may unwittingly speak from both sides of their mouths as they say to prospective parents: 'We will do everything to help you have a genetic child of your own'; to the non-genetic parent: 'Once the baby is born, you will completely forget the baby's genes are not yours, because you are family'; to the donor: 'Your genetic ties are of no consequence – dispense your eggs in a dish or your sperm in a jar and go home to your own lives.' These latter messages fly in the face of reality: the non-genetic parent does not forget that his or her genes do not run through the child; the donor may well have thoughts and feelings about the offspring created that do have his or her genes running through them. These experiences are not necessarily barriers to bonding but they do contribute to confusion or angst if not addressed and dealt with honestly.

A mother who is having her second baby using an egg donor and her husband's sperm, her first baby having been conceived using IVF but her own eggs, expressed worry about the connections among her husband, her children, and herself. Her children and husband would be connected by their genes and she would feel like the outsider in her own family, anxious that she would be seen as less legitimate in her second child's eyes, and worried that she would have to prove her parental status by being the perfect mother to this child. This mother is suffering from attachment angst incurred by the privileging of blood over social ties: she will have to earn her mothering stripes rather than automatically receiving them as her 'blood right.' In turn, her husband, the genetic parent, may feed into this anxiety by consciously or unconsciously positioning himself as more of a parent.

The role of the reproductive technology professional team is to facilitate the establishment of 'ours' in place of a tug of war between 'yours versus mine' and to address the bonding anxieties that confront all parents who procreate with the participation of a birth other. In that vein, it is important to understand the motivation of prospective parents who go in search of donors who bear resemblance to themselves. Resemblances are bond builders. The desire for a donor who will match the non-genetic parent's traits or resemble general family traits is not just a narcissistic endeavor to find oneself reflected in one's progeny nor a strategy to hide the donor conception from the outside world. Similarity in traits and behaviors facilitates intimacy, which in turn slackens the rope in the tug of war that might otherwise ensue in laying claim to the baby, replacing it with a family portrait of commonality and inclusion.

A CHILD IS BORN

The child, the object of all of the medical procedures, is not to be forgotten, although often it is in the flurry to move forward in conception. A birth other child faces three developmental tasks:

> sorting out ways in which he or she is unique or different as a result of being medically conceived with the participation of a birth other
> establishing a sense of belonging, factoring in all members of the Oedipal circle
> fortifying an identity that takes into account being the biological product of parent(s) and an outside party.

Tackling these issues of self-concept, attachment, and identity will be an evolving process over time. The aggregate data provided by Dr Susan Golombok and her colleagues indicate that birth other children are doing well, demonstrating healthy development in attachment, relational capacities, social behaviors, identity, and cognitive abilities.[17-19] Yet experience in the consultation room indicates that acquiring those developmental achievements necessitates working through each of these three issues.

The negotiation of the three developmental tasks is of course predicated on the child having knowledge of his or her birth other origins, which is often not the case at any one moment in time or, for some children, ever. As a proponent of full disclosure, for both medical and psychological reasons,[1] I would recommend that the questions of anonymous versus known donor, disclosure to the child, disclosure to others, and level of involvement of the birth other in the child's life be addressed well before the birth of the baby and long before the family finds itself floundering in troubled waters around these very issues. As there is no baby without all the people who intended to have the baby and all the people who participated in procreating that baby, there will be no healthy child without a full tapestry that includes the threads of each of the participants as they relate to the child and to each other. So, for example, when a child goes in search of a donor, which often occurs in adolescence or beyond, mindful attention to the family tapestry from conception forward will prepare parents for that search. It will help them realize that the accomplishment of all three developmental tasks – self-concept, belonging, and identity – may be facilitated by contact with the birth other, not as an idealized or 'real' parent but as a person responsible for either the genes or the prenatal growth of that child and as a person who may also be holding that child in mind. Inviting prospective parents to begin thinking about all these matters before their baby is even a blip on the sonogram screen may be the best insurance policy for the child's healthy development.

CONCLUSION

In psychoanalytical practice, providers strive to make the unconscious conscious and to loosen up the psychological defenses that keep anxiety and conflicts at bay but also constrict a person from living a full and vital life. The rubrics of this technique can be no more pertinent than in helping people who come to the doctor to find eggs, sperm or wombs to have a baby of their own. If medical and mental health practitioners can hitch their wagons together, reproductive medicine stands a good chance of facilitating healthy outcomes for birth other families. This will be accomplished by helping parents negotiate the tensions between hope and fear, allowing parents the psychological space to explore not just the euphoric but also the darker feelings that may surface, and, lastly, inviting parents to think forward to the developmental tasks that await their children. In those ways, the families will receive maximum support in just 'doing what comes scientifically.'

REFERENCES

1 Ehrensaft D. *Mommies, Daddies, Donors, Surrogates: answering tough questions and building strong families*. New York: Guilford Press; 2005.

2 Ehrensaft D. The stork didn't bring me, I came from a dish: psychological experiences of children conceived through assisted reproductive technology. *J Infant Child Adolesc Psychother*. 2007; **6**(2): 124–40.

3 Ehrensaft D. When baby makes three or four or more: attachment, individuation, and identity in assisted-conception families. *Psychoanal Study Child*. 2008; **63**: 3–23.

4 Ehrensaft D. Just Molly and me and baby makes three: lesbian motherhood in the age of assisted reproductive technology. *J Lesbian Stud*. 2008; **12**(2–3): 161–78.

5 Ehrensaft D. Family complexes and Oedipal circles: mothers, fathers, babies, donors, and surrogates. Symposium: 'How Did I Get Here and Where Did I Come From? Clinical and Developmental Implications of Assisted Reproductive Technology', sponsored by the Margaret Mahler Foundation and the Columbia University Masters of Science in Bioethics Program, February 5 2001, New York.

6 Winnicott DW. The theory of the infant–parent relationship. In: *The Maturational Processes and the Facilitating Environment*. Madison, CT: International Universities Press; 1965. pp.37–55.

7 Graves R. *The Greek Myths*, Vol. 1. New York: Penguin; 1986.

8 *The Holy Scriptures, Book of Genesis: 16, 17*. Philadelphia: Jewish Publication Society of America; 1959.

9 Ehrensaft D. Alternatives to the stork: fatherhood fantasies in donor insemination families. *Stud Gender Sexual*. 2000; **1**(4): 371–97.

10 Ehrensaft D. *Spoiling Childhood: how well-meaning parents are giving children too much – but not what they need*. New York: Guilford Press; 1997.

11 Cooper SL, Glazer ES. *Beyond Infertility: the new paths to parenthood*. New York: Lexington Books; 1994.

12 Byrnes S. Scenes from a surrogacy. In: Bialosky J, Schulman H, editors. *Wanting a Child*. New York: Strauss and Giroux; 1998. pp.185–94.

13 Ethics Committee of the American Society for Reproductive Medicine. Informing offspring of their conception by gamete donation. *Fertil Steril*. 2004; **81**(3): 527–31.

14 Freud A. *The Ego and the Mechanisms of Defense*. Madison, CT: International Universities Press; 1966.

15 Klein M. *Envy and Gratitude*. London: Tavistock; 1957.

16 Oxenhandler N. *The Eros of Parenthood*. New York: St Martin's Press; 2001.

17 Golombok S, Murray C, Brinsden P, *et al.* Social vs. biological parenting: family functioning and the social-emotional development of children conceived by egg or sperm donation. *J Child Psychol Psychiatry*. 1999; 40: 519–27.

18 Golombok S, MacCallum F, Goodman E. The 'test-tube' generation: parent–child relationships and the psychological well-being of in vitro fertilization children at adolescence. *Child Dev*. 2001; 72: 599–608.

19 Golombok S, MacCallum F. Practitioner review: outcomes for parents and children following non-traditional conception: what do clinicians need to know? *J Child Psychol Psychiatry*. 2003; 44: 303–15.

CHAPTER 16

Man and Machine: The Relational Aspects of Organ Replacement

Maureen O'Reilly-Landry

The cross-breeding of medicine with technology has created new species of medicalized relationships and attachments, both human to human and human to machine. Novel and radical relationships have arisen between patients, machines, and people who donate their body parts. It is now possible for a woman to bear a child that is the genetic offspring of people she has never met; a human being can depend on a machine to live and function; and an individual can possess a healthy organ that only hours earlier was keeping someone else alive. At the turn of this century, psychoanalyst Zalutsky[1] noted that the speed of technological change in the practice of medicine is outstripping our ability to process its impact on our psyches and on our lives.

This chapter examines the complex intrapsychic and relational dynamics involved in response to the replacement of failed kidneys. Here, I contend that patients may form genuine relationships, however one-sided or in fantasy, with their life-sustaining machinery, the donors of their transplanted organs and even with the transplanted organs. I will use end-stage renal disease (ESRD) as a model for this examination and describe some clinical situations that typify the novel relationships created by the organ replacement therapies of dialysis and kidney transplantation, and the ways in which these alter the experience of self and other.

With renal disease, organ replacement therapies occur in the forms of dialysis treatments or kidney transplantation. With dialysis, an artificial kidney machine removes blood from the body, cleanses it and then returns it to the body. The kidney function is now situated outside the body and is no longer experienced as part of the self, yet it performs an integral self-function. A very strong psychological connection often arises between a life-giving machine and a person dependent on it to live. As with the object of all our attachments, these machines and the relationships that develop with them can become symbolized and imbued with meaning. In other words, a transference develops.

One woman with ESRD said to me about the machine that cleanses her blood in order to keep her alive: 'This is my blood-sucking lover.' This was the first time I had heard anyone speak in this way about a dialysis machine. The unexpected image took me by surprise and I stopped to reflect on what I was hearing. Until then, my experience working with patients on chronic dialysis had led me to regard the machines and treatments in much more concrete and bleak terms. I thought about them as the necessary evil they are.

Before I met this woman, I had thought that there were essentially two ways to escape the destructive yet life-giving control this machine has over one's life and oneself. One is to be lucky enough to get a kidney transplant and to live and function with someone else's kidney. And the second way is to die. But perhaps this patient is offering a third possibility.

'That's a very creative thought,' I said. Now it was her turn to be surprised. 'You're the only person to tell me that,' she said. 'Most people just think I'm disturbed. And they tell me that I complain too much and am too negative. They say I'm lucky to be alive and should be more positive.' She is seeing me because she is 'non-adherent.' She sometimes skips treatments and complains about medical clinicians, often experiencing them as uncaring or dismissive. And she becomes upset when she feels she is not being heard or understood.

To some, her behavior can seem difficult but my job is to listen and to try to understand her. I do not have to tell her to do things she doesn't want to or cannot do. So we get along fine. My role feels easy and without conflict and I like it. But medical doctors, nurses, medical technicians and social workers, all good people who genuinely want to help, become frustrated when patients don't do what they are supposed to do. Then the medical staff cannot do their job. In the world of modern medicine, patients have a job, too, which is to make the best use possible of all that modern medicine has to offer. Yet this is a job they did not apply for and likely do not want. And this patient is right when she claims to be misunderstood. She is a single mother, responsible for two young sons. There is no one to take care of her little boys during school vacations. Unlike school, dialysis offers no vacations from its thrice weekly treatments. Her sons are too young to stay by themselves and my patient is fearful about leaving them with people she doesn't know. She is upset when the dialysis administrator refuses to let her boys stay in the unit or in the waiting room on such days. They are in the way in the dialysis room and being in the waiting room leaves them unsupervised. The staff in the dialysis center cannot take responsibility for their wellbeing and are genuinely concerned about their safety as well as about the legal liability. But they may become defensive when they are blamed for something that is not their fault. My patient cannot understand why she is blamed and regarded as difficult if she doesn't come in to treatment when her boys are at home. As she sees it, the dialysis staff are the ones who are refusing to help.

I have often contemplated the plight of dialysis patients. They spend all their time trying to stay alive in order to have lives they often don't want to be living. That this woman is even able to have a playful fantasy in this high-tech medical environment is striking to me. It doesn't seem like a place where there is much room for play. But maybe that's the point. So I wonder, is this anthropomorphizing of her life-sustaining companion an effort to salvage a bit of her humanity in this cold, mechanized environment? According to relational and interpersonal psychoanalytic theories, human beings have a primary and fundamental need to be in a relationship with other people.[2] So is this dialysis patient attempting to combat the threatened collapse of her human and emotional self, which threatens to give way to the onslaught of focus on bodies, machinery and other concrete aspects of life?

'I got the idea from a vampire movie I saw once,' she says. So, what about the content of this fantasy, I wonder? What might this vampire image represent to her? Does it reflect the way she experiences the illness itself, that her vital essence and perhaps her sexuality are being taken from her by being on dialysis? This lover that gives her life also drains it from her. It makes her tired and bloated, her legs wracked by cramps. She has less time, energy and interest to invest in her own life. On the dialysis unit, she lives among the undead. Perhaps this fantasy does reflect her experience. But having it also alters her experience and transforms it, at least a little bit. It asserts her humanness. It is her refusal to give in. In her refusal to be objectified, she symbolizes her experience and is able to play with it and master it. At some level, she perceives that she has a choice – she loses her humanity and becomes a machine or the machine becomes human, or nearly so. The capacity to symbolize, a uniquely human ability, helps her to rise above her situation to combat the fear of annihilation, however narrowly, however briefly.

Boulanger[3] describes the impact of adult experiences that threaten the mind's ability to cope. She states that some events are so extraordinary and overwhelming that they cannot be symbolized and the experience cannot be processed. They resist being assimilated, even by the mature, well-developed adult mind. When experiences cannot be processed and assimilated, they can overwhelm the psyche and induce a traumatic state, seriously disrupting one's ability to function. When annihilation anxieties, those extreme anxieties brought about by confrontation with death, can be symbolized and put into words, they become psychologically more manageable.[4,5] Is this patient's engagement in fantasy, then, an effort to carve out for herself a potential space, a safe psychological arena in between reality and fantasy in which her anxieties and fears can be played out and creatively mastered?[6,7] Symbolizing by giving words and meaning to experience enables creativity and playfulness, and can convert a sense of traumatic helplessness to one of empowerment and a better integration of that experience. When a dialysis patient is able to symbolize these potentially traumatic experiences of loss of function and confrontation with death and integrate them into a new, less overwhelming, less traumatic psychological framework, she is then able to transcend her concrete reality of dire illness, dependency and threatened death.

The quality of our early relationships continues to influence us even as adults, including our medical behavior. Transferences develop in which a patient brings feelings about those who cared for him early in life to the current situation of care giving. People with secure attachments to their caregivers early in life, for example, are more likely to follow their prescribed medical regimen than are those who are more anxious and insecure in these relationships.[8] Perhaps patients who feel closely connected emotionally to a machine on which they are dependent develop such transferences to their machines. Feelings about life-sustaining machines, then, might reflect the feelings brought about by the reality of their current situation in combination with feelings about much earlier experiences in which they were dependent on others for survival.

The anthropomorphizing of life-sustaining machinery is not an infrequent phenomenon. Patients who dialyze at home sometimes name their dialysis machines and imbue them with personalities, drawing the dialyzer into their relational matrix of close family and friends. Mr S was such a person. The husband in a 40-year marriage, father to seven children and grandfather to 14 grandchildren, and revered coach to countless high school athletes, it was a devastating blow to Mr S when the need for dialysis caused him to lose his physical robustness, energy, and independence. Fortunately for this man who valued being independent, he was able to conduct his dialysis treatments successfully using one of the home dialysis modalities, and needed to come to the dialysis center only for his monthly clinic visit. Nevertheless, at home, he was dependent on a machine and on family caregivers, especially his wife, for medical maintenance and, ultimately, for his life.

Mr S became depressed with feelings of anger and resentment over the course his life had taken since becoming ill. He tried, often unsuccessfully, to avoid displacing his anger about dialysis onto his wife and the rest of his family and taking his feelings out on them. Even in the best of moods, he regarded his dialysis machine as a nuisance and a trouble-maker. Accordingly, he named his machine Lucy, after Lucille Ball's character in the 1950s sitcom *I Love Lucy*. Mr S appeared to feel identified with Lucy's Cuban-born husband, the long-suffering Ricky Ricardo, who was constantly being frustrated and rendered powerless by his wife's childish antics. Mr S enjoyed imitating Ricky's frequent, heavily accented refrain, 'Lucy, you got a lotta "splainin" to do!' (Although this is a line commonly attributed to the character Ricky Ricardo, we were unable to find a reference for it. He did, however, say things similar to this.) Mr S said that he felt his dialysis machine was making his life very difficult and that his own Lucy had 'a lotta "splainin" to do.'

In contrast to Mr S, another man, young, perennially good-natured and optimistic, and who was also doing extremely well medically, had a more positive view of his dialysis machine. In conversations, he chose to emphasize the machine's life-saving aspect rather than the burdens and problems it caused for him. He called his home dialyzer 'Lola,' the name of a showgirl in a song he enjoyed singing whenever he heard it on the radio.

The second type of kidney replacement therapy, transplantation, places a kidney from either a cadaver or a live donor inside the recipient's body. With transplantation, the kidney function now occurs within the bounds of the physical self, yet is conducted by an organ previously owned by someone else. The boundaries between self and other are disrupted and I believe the intrapsychic and interpersonal experiences are affected as well. Relationships are also created in imagination between organ recipient and donor. 'What was this person like?' the recipient may wonder about the previous owner of the vital organ that now inhabits her body. 'How did he or she die? How will I be affected by having this particular person's kidney?'

Patrick had been on chronic dialysis for four years before receiving a kidney from a cadaver. He had so much been looking forward to the day a kidney would become available that he is surprised to find himself unable to keep at bay some disquieting fantasies about the circumstances of his kidney donor's death. As time goes on, he feels more depressed than he was when he was on dialysis, because now he is guilt-ridden over the thought that he is benefiting from someone else's misfortune and that someone else died so that he could live.

As the vignettes convey, the experience of a patient in close relationship to modern medical technology can have elements of the traumatic and even the psychotic. It is stark. It can be harsh. It can feel violent, terrifying and cold. There is exchange of body organs, a machine in control of one's life – profound breakdown of boundaries between self and other, between fantasy and reality, between what is internal and what is external. Cohen described the experience of the Holocaust survivor as one that is simultaneously psychotic and real.[9] Such may be the trauma experienced by the patient with ESRD. The patient is not psychotic but the situation and the resulting experience can be.

When the transplanted organ comes from a live donor, most often a family member, the relational dynamics in the family can be played out in this new arena. Family dynamics become evident from the beginning of the process when the patient either asks or avoids asking family members to be tested to see if they are a good match medically, or when family members do or do not step forward and volunteer to be tested. But naturally, family dynamics do not end with the surgery. Here is an example of one situation in which the transplant itself reflects the dynamics of the relationship between mother and daughter.

Julie, a woman in her twenties, had spent much of her life alternating between good health and bouts of illness. Eventually, her kidneys failed and she had to begin dialysis treatments three times each week. Although this was difficult, she did not feel overwhelmed or traumatized. She knew this would be only a temporary situation because her mother was an appropriate biological match and was planning to donate one of her own healthy kidneys to her daughter. During the weeks prior to the transplant surgery, Julie and I had been discussing many of her age-appropriate concerns not directly related to her health, including her efforts to negotiate the complexities of the separation from her mother. She and her mother were close and had a generally positive relationship, but Julie was feeling a normal desire to push away from her mother to become more independent. Julie was an only child and felt her mother was having difficulty with my patient's desire for independence. We wondered together whether her mother might experience this kidney donation as a way of holding on to Julie emotionally. Julie, a perceptive and psychologically minded woman, expressed her fears as she awaited the surgery: 'I'm afraid my body will reject it,' she said of her mother's kidney. This comment captured Julie's ideas regarding a potential somatic expression of the interpersonal dynamic between herself and her mother. Fortunately, Julie did not reject her mother's kidney and she is doing well a few years later. And though there are conflicts, their mother–daughter relationship remains a good if somewhat complicated one.

Seriously medically ill patients feel misunderstood and blamed when the traumatic impact of their illness is not recognized, and they often request support groups to address the commonality of their experience. However, when the internal, subjective and uniquely personal aspects of the experience are not provided with words and a voice, the patient may remain dissociated, confused and anxious for reasons he or she may not understand. The ability to symbolize and psychically represent aspects of their distress in imagination can help to make these overwhelming anxieties somewhat more manageable.

CONCLUSION

In summary, in a very short span of time, modern science and technology have brought the field of medicine from a period of ignorance and questionable practices to an age in which medicine has great power to affect life and death. The rapidity of this development has left little time for humankind to adjust and adapt. Modern medicine has created novel experiences of self, other, mind and body, and of the relationships between them. The sudden onset of such drastic changes can lead to confusing and unassimilated psychological experiences. Engagement in the uniquely human capacity to symbolize, fantasize and play holds potential for human beings to creatively integrate the stark, concrete

SECTION V
When a Family Member is Ill

The Ambiguous Loss of Dementia: A Relational View of Complicated Grief in Caregivers

Pauline Boss

When illness or injury takes away a family member's memory or emotions, the incongruence between being here and gone is deeply disturbing. The dementia patient, the brain injured, the stroke victim, and the autistic child can be out of reach even while present. Such ambiguity creates a complicated grief for family caregivers that is in a category of its own. The pathology is relational; it is interpersonal, not intrapsychic. That is, the abnormality lies in the caregiver's relational context, not in his or her personal deficiency. The abnormality that causes so much trouble is the ambiguity – not knowing if a person is here or not here. In the 1970s, I coined the term 'ambiguous loss' to illustrate this unique and terrible type of loss. Subsequent research validated it as a predictor of depression in dementia caregivers.[1-11]

DEFINITION

Ambiguous loss is an unclear loss and thus is without closure. It is caused by an external force (e.g. illness or injury) that prevents clarity about a loved one's status as present or absent – or as dead or alive. There are two types of ambiguous loss: physical absence (kidnapped, lost at sea, given up at birth, etc.) and psychological absence (autism, addiction, traumatic brain injury, Alzheimer's disease, etc.).[4] In this chapter, I focus on the second type of ambiguous loss, psychological absence, specifically as manifested by dementia and the complicated grief it causes for those closely attached to the patient.

EFFECTS

Why does the ambiguity surrounding dementia make people feel helpless and thus more prone to depression, anxiety, and relationship disorder? First, the ambiguity surrounding the illness keeps people confused so they don't know what to do or what decisions to make. Cognitively immobilized, many choose irrational responses that close out the ill person as if already dead or act as if nothing is wrong.

Second, the ambiguity surrounding the prognosis prevents reorganization of family processes (roles, rules, rituals). Everyone stays frozen as they were before the illness occurred because there is no proof that the loss is permanent, as with death.

Third, without official validation and the customary markers of loss, the family is not offered the usual rituals and supports for bereavement. Family members are on their own. Because the loss remains unclear, any attempt to change and move forward is often viewed as disloyal and premature. With a death in the family, people know the loss is irretrievable but with the ambiguous loss of dementia, patients often have flashes of lucidity that give false hope to family caregivers. Because the loss is so unclear, family members understandably hold on to the hope that the ill person may be coming back to the way they used to be. It becomes a rollercoaster of hope and hopelessness that can last for decades.

Fourth, the ambiguity surrounding the illness causes even the strongest individuals to question their view of the world as fair and just. Their search for meaning is blocked. Using Aaron Antonovsky's term, there is no sense of coherence in their situation.[12] Finding meaning in one's plight is necessary for hope, and thus health, but with the ambiguous loss of dementia, it becomes a Sisyphusian challenge. It requires personal contemplation of a more psychoanalytical nature. It requires discussion with peers experiencing similar ambiguous losses.

Fifth, an ambiguous loss of long duration (e.g. dementia) becomes physically and psychologically exhausting for even the healthiest family members. Caregiver symptoms may be a result of fatigue, not psychological weakness. Exhaustion is, after all, the reality of care giving.

Sixth and finally, society does not recognize human loss that is not death so family members have little social support. Well-meaning friends and even professionals may tell family members of dementia patients or brain injury survivors that they are lucky because their loved one is still alive and with them. Such statements rarely give comfort and more often increase pain because the person they once had is, in reality, gone. The fact that society and professionals do not seem to recognize a loss until it is finalized by death isolates those who need support most as they struggle with uncanny and ambiguous loss.

THE MULTIPLICITY OF PROBLEMS

Ambiguous loss causes a chronic mourning that looks like depression but is often unresolved grief that continues sometimes for years, even a lifetime if closure is impossible. Ambiguous loss is also traumatizing because the confusion of absence and presence causes immobilizing stress, anxiety, ambivalence, restlessness, and agitation. In addition, with illnesses such as dementia, the caregiver loses sleep, not because of their own pathology but because there is an ill person in the house who cannot sleep and demands their attention 24/7. Finally, ambiguous losses such as dementia isolate healthy family members from their usual social environment and activities, thus shutting them off from heretofore joyful and supportive human connections. For these multiple reasons, it is no wonder caregivers become depressed and anxious.

Regardless of its source, dementia represents relational loss – loss of meaning, identity, attachment, agency, trust, attachment, and hope.[5] The deluge of ambiguity becomes debilitating on many levels. A client told me about his experience. On any given day, he saw his mother as his parent, as his child, and as a stranger. Their relationship was always in flux now, never like it was before the dementia set in. Some days he honored her requests as a dutiful son but more and more, he had to take charge. Then the next day she would scold him for speaking to her in an imperative tone.[13]

Adult children report confused identity and attachment, as they no longer know how to relate to their elders. Spouses say they can no longer interact as they had – cognitively, emotionally, sexually, and socially. Their relationships no longer make sense, helplessness sets in, identity and attachment are disturbed, ambivalence feeds on the ambiguity and in the absence of meaning, hope fades. Understandably, rational people are reluctant to grieve before a death has occurred, so most caregivers find themselves in a painful limbo. This is the frozen grief of ambiguous loss – the bedrock of complicated grief.

AMBIGUOUS LOSS THEORY

Ambiguous loss theory provides professionals from various disciplines with a new lens through which to view their patients' symptoms in a new light. The focus is on resilience, not just pathology. The focus is on context, not just the individual's deficiency. The premise of ambiguous loss theory is that ambiguity coupled with loss creates a powerful barrier to coping and grieving. There is no validation of loss (as with death) so the mind remains confused about what is happening. The brain struggles to make sense of the ambiguity. This rupture in meaning leads to symptoms such as depression, anxiety, sleep disorders, withdrawal, guilt, hopelessness, irritability, and somatic symptoms, among others. Mortality is even affected, as caregivers for those with Alzheimer's disease, for example, die at a rate 60% higher than their same-age cohort.[14]

While individual symptoms need to be treated, family caregivers should not be unjustly labeled as abnormal when the abnormality lies in the type of loss that they must endure. As professionals, we will be less prone to see family caregivers as problematic if we are more able to see the full contextual picture of how diseases such as Alzheimer's or a condition such as traumatic brain injury can rupture close relationships. While diagnoses may focus on symptoms, treatment and intervention must focus more on context and relationship.

PSYCHOANALYTICAL ROOTS

What Freud labeled as melancholia and diagnostic manuals still label as pathology is often a normal reaction to an untenable situation of loss. With dementia, the afflicted person is paradoxically both gone and still here. Family members are confused and immobilized. Time stops. Coping is blocked, grief is frozen, and behavioral adaptations are non-existent or maladaptive as the family waits for a miracle.

Bowlby wrote that the loss of a loved person is one of the most intensely painful experiences a human can suffer.[15] Today, few would disagree. But when he wrote about the complexities of ambivalence in lost attachments and the stress that motivates despair and letting go in order to lower stress and anxiety, Bowlby did not refer to losses that remain ambiguous, such as with dementia. Nor did Freud refer to this more difficult type of loss in his 'Mourning and melancholia'[16] when he suggested that the goal of recovery after loss was to relinquish one's ties to the absent person and eventually invest in a new relationship. Historically, grief experts have not thought of losses that truly have no closure.

What happens, however, when one's spouse or parent is *both* gone and still here? The confusion can traumatize, but one cannot relinquish ties to someone who is still alive without guilt. While such attachment is disturbed, it continues. The reluctance to separate that Kübler-Ross[17] referred to regarding death is magnified with the ambiguous loss of dementia. Without the finality of death, even rational people are stymied.

I think of Carolyn Feigelson, a New York psychologist whose husband fell down an elevator shaft and suffered a traumatic brain injury. She wrote about this phenomenon as uncanny loss.

> How is it possible to lose half a person? Half is dead, half remains alive ... Unlike a fairy tale whose premise is poetic reality in which nothing can surprise the reader, the uncanny story violates the observer's trust in reality. Life may then deceive by promising substance and delivering ghosts. The *doppelganger* sits at the dinner table.[18] (p.335, reprinted with permission from Wiley-Blackwell)

Indeed, it is possible to sit with the ghostly double of someone who used to be here.

Dementia requires a psychological adaptation to the uncanny and absurd. Seymour Fisher and Rhoda Fisher wrote about the idea of absurdity in 1993, but they too might blame the chronic mourner. That is, they do not consider that obtuseness and absurdity could lie in an external situation as opposed to the individual will or psyche. They wrote: 'The concept of "reality" is obscure and slippery; and most individuals have learned to play with it according to their tastes'[19] (p.195, reprinted with permission from Taylor & Francis Group). Apparently, they had not thought of caring for a family member with dementia, where the reality is not a matter of taste or play but trying to survive a long-term ambiguous loss. In such cases, the goal of traditional grief therapies – closure – would be unreasonable. Rather, the therapeutic goal is this: to increase the family caregiver's tolerance for ambiguity and uncertainty.

To be sure, living with dementia is like a story that has no ending. It leaves family members hanging on to the mystery. The vagaries of living with someone both absent and present produce a terrible anxiety of a bizarre loss, beyond normal expectations. With our aging populations increasing, and thus dementia increasing, plus more military veterans returning from wars where the signature wound is traumatic brain injury, it is urgent for us as professionals now to consider ambiguous loss as a type of loss that causes complicated grief. The culprit is the ambiguity, not the person who must endure that kind of stress and trauma.

CURRENT IDEAS ABOUT COMPLICATED GRIEF

The effects of complicated grief versus uncomplicated grief are, according to Boelen and van den Bout,[20] high levels of anxiety, depression, fatigue, low social functioning, and perception of general health. This conceptualization implies that complicated grief is abnormal based on the DSM definition of a mental disorder as being associated with distress and disability and as distinct from normal/expected reactions to the event. However, what is the expected reaction to a loss that remains unclear?

Boelen and van den Bout[20] believe that complicated grief and uncomplicated grief are distinguishable constructs. Indeed they are. Complicated grief is a distinct and measurable condition[21] but it can also result from a relational disorder, one frozen by ambiguity. The frozen grief is a result of loss that remains ambiguous and without closure. Its source lies in the context of traumatic stress, not the family member's personal pathology. Boelen and van den Bout found in their research that complicated grief was related to concurrent distress and disability, while uncomplicated grief was not. But neither they, the DSM, nor the historical giants in grief literature address the all too common effects of loss complicated by ambiguity.

In my clinical work with family caregivers for someone who is psychologically absent but physically present, I see depression, anxiety, guilt, and psychic numbing. I also hear distressing accounts of dreams as the brain struggles to find a rational ending to the story. Symptoms reflect depression and immense stress. They are often akin to symptoms of post-traumatic stress disorder (PTSD). There are differences, however.

Whereas both PTSD and ambiguous loss represent experiences that are far beyond ordinary human expectations, PTSD is an individual disorder, medically defined, individually diagnosed and treated. The goal with PTSD is to return the individual patient to health. With ambiguous loss, however, the disorder is relational and treated with the goal of resilience in the face of no solution to the ambiguity. The goal is to help people find the resilience to live with the ambiguity. If we focus only on the individual, the family more likely is seen as a nuisance. We are less likely to see family members as a necessary link to the care of the dementia patient; we are less likely to be empathic to their workload and psychological pain; we are less likely to recognize that because ambiguous loss is a relational disorder, it needs a relational intervention.

Indeed, ambiguous loss is complex with multilayered symptoms. It inherently involves trauma because of the inability to resolve the source of pain. People feel helpless and thus hopeless because there is no end to the cascade of losses that inevitably follow the onset of dementia. Before another pathology of grief is listed in future diagnostic manuals, I urge review of what has been written in recent decades about complicated *loss* that complicates *grief*. Ambiguous loss is one example. It is a disenfranchised grief, not because of stigma[22] but because of the ongoing doubt about a loved one's absence and presence.

TREATMENT AND INTERVENTION

When we as professionals understand that the source of caregivers' pathology can be their external context, and that resilience is necessary to live with the stress of ambiguity, then the treatment approach is viewed differently. The framework becomes one of stress management – managing the stress and trauma of not being able to find meaning in the ongoing incoherence about a loved one's absence and presence. Naming the situation 'ambiguous loss' is the first step in stress management, for until people know what the problem is, they cannot cope with it. In my experience, caregivers visibly breathe a sign of relief when told that what they are experiencing is 'ambiguous loss' and that it is one of the most stressful kinds of loss because there is no closure. I quickly add, 'It is not your fault. How you feel is normal given the abnormality of your loss.' Over the years, many family members have added their own interpretation to what I say. 'Oh, you're saying the situation is crazy, not me!' Whatever words they use, knowing that the pathology lies outside themselves, knowing that the trouble is not their fault decreases guilt and shame and thus increases their resilience.

Paradoxically, the therapeutic goal is to find meaning despite meaninglessness. Victor Frankl[23] called this finding a therapeutic pathway to transform suffering into newfound strength.

THE STRUCTURE OF THERAPY

To repeat, the treatment for a caregiver's ambiguous loss needs to be relational, but how is that possible if one person in the relationship is demented? At first, before the illness or condition is too debilitating, therapy can occur with husband and wife, with partners, with parent and adult child or with an entire family. Or it can take place one to one, one concerned family member with a therapist. But first, the issues of transference and termination must be rethought to accommodate the reality of chronic ambiguity in that family member's relational life (for details on how to do this, see Boss[5]). The relationship between that person and a therapist must avoid any hint of psychological absence or partial presence because that is the clinical issue itself. A therapist must be fully present, not opening mail, nor wandering in thought or dozing off while listening to a family member struggling with ambiguous loss. Also, there must be an open door policy so that the therapy can be resumed whenever needed by the family member. There should be no termination with ambiguous loss therapy because the clinical issue has no closure. This is not patient or client resistance but rather, the resistance of the ambiguity in the context of the caregiver's real-life experience.

Finally, I always recommend that mates and family members participate in groups, ideally a psychoeducational meeting of peers who are experiencing a similar kind of loss. Here they can receive practical information to help with care giving but perhaps most important, they also receive healing from the social part of such meetings. Meeting new people who have similar losses is invaluable and often leads to new human connections that continue for years. One way or the other, the structure of therapy and meetings is designed to help the caregiver know that they are not alone.

PARADOXICAL THINKING

Because of the inherent paradox in ambiguous loss, family caregivers need to use paradoxical or 'both-and' thinking. 'My loved one is both here and gone.' This kind of thinking means holding two opposing ideas at the same time, a reality for those who care for a partially lost person. While caregivers may prefer to make up their own examples, the following suggestions will stimulate that process.

➤ The person I care for is both here and not here.
➤ I can parent my parent and still be a daughter or son to them.

➤ I am both a caregiver and a person with my own identity and needs.
➤ I can both stay attached and let go.

Paradoxical thinking helps family members fight off the urge for certainty and finding an absolute solution, e.g. thinking that the person is already dead or thinking that there is nothing wrong. Neither of those absolute conclusions will reduce the stress. Sadly, denial and false closure often lead to harmful outcomes and family conflict.

GUIDELINES FOR RESILIENCE

To provide a flexible approach for use by professionals of all disciplines, I have developed six guidelines for finding resilience in the face of ambiguous loss. They were formulated on the basis of research, clinical experience, and field testing (see references[3–5,24]). I emphasize that these guidelines are not prescribed in a linear order. Use them in a flexible manner for the type of ambiguous loss you are working with. Due to space limitations, only brief descriptions can be given here but there are full chapters on each guideline in Boss.[5] The goal of all six guidelines is caregiver health and resilience in the face of ambiguous loss.

➤ **Find meaning**: give the problem a name; despite the ambiguous loss, revise and continue family celebrations and rituals; through talking with others, discover some positive meaning in the loss.
➤ **Temper mastery**: recognize the world is not always fair, externalize the blame and regain some mastery and control despite the ongoing ambiguity.
➤ **Reconstruct identity**: learn to play new roles, reflect on who you are now, who your family is now. Know that one's identity typically shifts over time.
➤ **Normalize ambivalence**: talk with others to uncover latent negative feelings (e.g. I wish it were over; I wish he or she were dead). Once identified, learn how to manage conflicted feelings; normalize guilt and harmful feelings but not harmful actions; talk with others about conflicted feelings (e.g. love and hate, joy and anger) so they do not lead to abuse or neglect, of patient or caregiver.
➤ **Revise attachment**: grieve what you have lost and celebrate what you still have, use groups and social activities to build new human connections, create good-bye rituals for the losses along the way (no longer able to travel, no longer knows who you are, etc.), know that all human attachments are less than perfect in presence.
➤ **Discover new hope**: imagine new options; laugh at absurdity; develop more patience for unanswered questions; recognize that a new hope is more likely to be found when one becomes more comfortable with the ambiguity, and thus a faith that something good could come out of what is unknown.

These are the guidelines I recommend for therapeutic or psychoeducational work with caregivers and family members who love someone who has dementia. Using a systematic structure for therapy, these guidelines allow for the sharing of stories, of both pain and success, but most of all, the sharing deflates the idea that many caregivers have that the pain of ambiguous loss is 'my pathology, my fault, my failing.'

When caregivers and family members see that others feel as they do, that most are just doing the best they can, and that no one can be perfect, they realize that they are normal, given the terrible kind of loss they must live with. Using these guidelines flexibly and in a relational setting, resilience can grow. Ideas change; people learn they are stronger than they thought. (See Boss[5] for further details on how to undertake therapy with ambiguous loss.)

RECOMMENDATIONS FOR RESEARCH AND DIAGNOSIS

We need to rethink the idea of complicated grief as only personal pathology. In addition, timelines for normal grieving should be re-examined. If a loss remains ambiguous, as with dementia or brain injury, the process of bereavement will understandably continue for years or even a lifetime. In such cases, existing timelines for resolution and closure are unreasonable. When a loss remains unclear, rather than closure or cure, the therapeutic goal is to help people live with the lack of clarity. Tolerating ambiguity and the lack of informational clarity is an atypical goal, but essential if we are to acknowledge the prolonged grief of family caregivers. In the interest of diagnostic fairness and validity, complicated grief or prolonged grief disorder from ambiguous loss must be considered for inclusion in future diagnostic manuals.

Clearly, professionals need to take a closer look at the nuances of complicated loss and grief and the irresolvability that causes them. Researchers could study this complex dynamic further with caregivers who live with loved ones who are psychologically or physically missing. Either group could provide research samples to test the idea further that complicated *loss* predicts complicated *grief*. The ambiguity surrounding the loss is the culprit, not the individual.

In addition, neuroimaging could, I hypothesize, document the terrible distress suffered by people experiencing ambiguous loss. It could also document the effect of a family member's gradual acceptance of the ambiguity as a way to stay healthy and resilient. Surely, with our epidemic of dementia and the concomitant rise in number of family caregivers, the premise that the ambiguity surrounding one's loss can cause complicated grief warrants further discussion and study.

PERSON OF THE THERAPIST

Finally, I have found that many clinicians and professionals have a hard time accepting ambiguous loss themselves. To be sure, most of us were trained to heal and when we cannot, we are distressed. When there is ambiguous loss, however, we must ourselves develop a higher tolerance for ambiguity. If we do not, our empathy and understanding of depressed caregivers and anxious family members will be insufficient. We all have had some kind of ambiguous loss – a break up, divorce, adoption or simply our parents growing old or children leaving home. Until we acknowledge our own ambiguous loss, we will not be able to see it and work with it professionally. Until we develop more comfort with ambiguity in absence and presence, we will not be able to help others live with their relational incompleteness. Resilience in this case means increasing our own tolerance and comfort with ambiguity, an essential resource for professionals working in an aging society where relational imperfections become the norm.

CONCLUSION

I have presented a more psychosocial view of complicated grief, one that takes into account a person's relational context and environment. While all losses have some degree of ambiguity for survivors, dementia is particularly painful because there is no finality or closure, at least not until death occurs which may be decades later. In this chapter, I have written that when a loss has no closure, an illness has no cure or an injury has no fix, professionals must help people find resilience. There is no other choice. When a loved one is cognitively impaired and no longer as they used to be, such loss sets the stage for an uncanny relationship that leads to complicated grief, *but it is not the caregiver's deficiency that causes the symptoms*. This more relational view of unresolved loss and grief suggests that we pay more attention to caregivers' relational contexts – their ambiguous loss and the pain that it causes. When a person loves someone who has dementia, that complicated loss understandably can lead to a complicated grief. The situation is the problem, not the individual.

REFERENCES

1   Boss P. A clarification of the concept of psychological father presence in families experiencing ambiguity of boundary. *J Marriage Fam.* 1977; **39**(1): 141–51.
2   Boss P. Normative family stress: family boundary changes across the lifespan. *Fam Relat.* 1980; **29**: 445–50.
3   Boss P. *Ambiguous Loss.* Cambridge, MA: Harvard University Press; 1999/2000.
4   Boss P. Ambiguous loss research, theory, and practice: reflections after 9/11. *J Marriage Fam.* 2004; **66**(3): 551–66.
5   Boss P. *Loss, Trauma, and Resilience: therapeutic work with ambiguous loss.* New York: Norton; 2006.
6   Boss P (editor). Special issue: Ambiguous loss. *Fam Relat.* 2007; **56**(2).

7 Boss P. Ambiguous loss theory: challenges for scholars and practitioners. *Fam Relat.* 2007; **56**(2): 105–11.

8 Boss P. *Loving Someone Who Has Dementia.* San Francisco, CA: Jossey-Bass; 2011.

9 Boss P, Caron W, Horbal J, *et al.* Predictors of depression in caregivers of dementia patients: boundary ambiguity and mastery. *Fam Process.* 1990; **29**: 245–54.

10 Boss P, Greenberg J. Family boundary ambiguity: a new variable in family stress theory. *Fam Process.* 1984; **23**(4): 535–46.

11 Caron W, Boss P, Mortimer J. Family boundary ambiguity predicts Alzheimer's outcomes. *Psychiatry.* 1999; **62**(4): 347–56.

12 Antonovsky A. *Health, Stress, and Coping: new perspectives on mental and physical well-being.* San Francisco, CA: Jossey-Bass; 1979.

13 Boss P, Couden B. Ambiguous loss from chronic physical illness: clinical interventions with individuals, couples, and families. *J Clin Psychol.* 2002; **58**(11): 1351–60.

14 Schulz R, Beach S. Caregiving as a risk factor for mortality: the caregiver health effects study. *JAMA.* 1999; **282**(23): 2215–19.

15 Bowlby J. *Attachment and Loss: vol. 3. Loss: sadness and depression.* New York: Basic Books; 1980.

16 Freud S. Mourning and melancholia. In: Strackey J, editor. *The Standard Edition of the Complete Psychological Works of Sigmund Freud.* New York: Norton; 1917/1957. pp.237–58.

17 Kübler-Ross E. *On Death and Dying.* New York: Macmillan; 1969.

18 Feigelson C. Personality death, object loss, and the uncanny. *Int J Psychoanal.* 1993; **74**(2): 331–45.

19 Fisher S, Fisher RL. *The Psychology of Adaptation to Absurdity.* Hillsdale, NJ: Erlbaum; 1993.

20 Boelen PA, van den Bout J. Complicated grief and uncomplicated grief are distinguishable constructs. *Psychiatry Res.* 2008; **157**: 311–14.

21 Prigerson HG, Maciejewski PK, Reynolds CF, *et al.* Inventory of complicated grief: a scale to measure maladaptive symptoms of loss. *Psychiatry Res.* 1995; **59**: 65–79.

22 Doka KJ, editor. *Disenfranchised Grief: recognizing hidden sorrow.* Lexington, MA: Lexington Books; 2002.

23 Frankl V. *Man's Search for Meaning: an introduction to logotherapy.* New York: Washington Square; 1963.

24 Boss P, Beaulieu L, Wieling E, *et al.* Healing loss, ambiguity, and trauma: a community-based intervention with families of union workers missing after the 9/11 attack in New York City. *J Marital Fam Ther.* 2003; **29**(4): 455–67.

CHAPTER 18

Creating Tolerance for Reflective Space: The Challenges to Thinking and Feeling in a Neonatal Intensive Care Unit

Susan Kraemer and Zina Steinberg

A neonatologist stops to show us a photo of Sam, now two, bright eyed, smiling, with his trach collar. Many had thought Sam could not survive or have any quality of life. He had fought hard for this newborn and his parents. A nurse expresses her dismay that her hair has grown in curly after her chemo treatments. Another nurse and I embrace in tears over the death of a baby who had lived 6 months on the unit with a fatal condition. In the nurses' lounge, still another nurse taking care of a critically ill 23-weeker exclaims, 'How much more can this mother take? Or the baby! She is going to be a (neurological) mess even if she makes it.' A neonatologist stops me in the hallway: 'Mrs X says she is still feeling fetal movement; I told her to talk to you!' A doctor pleads at a staff retreat: 'Can't those angry parents see I am a good person?' I ask a primary nurse as she helps the mother prepare to take her baby home after months of close relationship, 'How many of these good-byes have you had over the years?' She chokes up, this rock-solid, very calm woman, 'Oh many, yes many; and the leaving is always so bittersweet.'

As psychodynamically oriented psychologists consulting to the neonatal intensive care unit, we are reminded of Winnicott's dictum that there is no baby without a mother.[1] We work to make psychic space for the parents so that they can sustain holding their baby in mind, even when their baby cannot yet be held in their arms. But as importantly, we consistently engage doctors and nurses, helping them make psychic space for these fragile, heartbroken, trying to be hopeful parents, helping them to hold the parents in mind.[2,3]

It is both a profoundly meaningful and often harrowing privilege to come to know intimately the traumatized parents of the neonatal intensive care unit

(NICU). To be with them is to stand as witnesses to enormous dread, unbearable pain and anxiety and, at times, heart-stopping grief. We are also companions to their fragile hopes and true joys, and are fortunate to share in moments that are exquisitely ordinary – the common everyday happiness that can also exist in this unit.

Our thinking about families expands to incorporate the burden of staff who confront brutal medical and emotional realities on a daily basis. Jarring, yet necessary and inevitable, the staff and parents can move between grief and joy in just seconds. So can we.

In an environment where life and death hang in fragile balance, the need to defend against unbearable realities is a natural, even adaptive response. It is understandable that staff may busy themselves with the essential tasks of procedures and routine care and seek to avoid disorienting ambiguities and uncertainty. This is a 'culture of action,'[4] an opaque, tightly organized and highly technological medical unit; it is easy to retreat and difficult to allow time and space for reflective thought. There is much that no one wants to think about and we are sensitive both to the extreme fear, shame and guilt that so many parents carry and to the weighty responsibility carried by staff that keeps their focus on detail absolutely vital. But as we look more closely at our fears of trespassing on families' grief, of exposing them to their dread and at our own hesitation about bringing unthinkable knowledge out of the shadows, we grow alert to our own susceptibility to gaps in thinking and remembering. We have worked to understand these and to make use of our emotional responses in order to help us understand those of the medical staff. We increasingly appreciate the exquisite effort required to allow knowledge and experience to be thought about together so that present and past and future can be experienced and reflected upon in the present moment, which in the NICU often is a traumatic moment.

> Mrs X is a first-time mother of a critically ill surviving triplet. Concerned about the high risks associated with triplet pregnancies, at her doctor's urging, she reduced her pregnancy to twins. Tragically, soon after, one of the two remaining babies died. Then, at 23 weeks her water broke and she was confronted with deciding whether she should risk delivering such an extremely premature baby. During the course of many meetings at her baby's bedside she has said that she never hesitated in the face of any of these decisions, yet, in other, less circumspect moments she has confessed in a low voice, 'Perhaps I was negligent.'
>
> We meet today at her son's bedside, an arduous 6 months since his birth, 2 months past her original due date. He lies hooked up to a breathing apparatus, feeding tube, and a tangle of IVs. The specter of severe neurological impairment hovers and haunts, but remains unspoken. The young nurse (who has worked with this baby over many months) has propped up a girl baby doll next to him,

joking softly about 'his favorite girlfriend.' Mrs X says, 'Look how he looks at it! I think it reminds him of his sister!' The nurse is horrified, red with shame: 'Oh! I am so sorry! I didn't mean for you to have to think about that!' The mother quickly replies, 'It's OK. I don't think about the past; I'm just going to think about the future. We won't tell him about it. It would be too much for him to bear.'

I am unnerved, both by the nurse's upset and by the mother's efforts to reassure her. And I feel unsettled by Mrs X's intention to keep this secret. I venture, 'You know, you might feel differently about this later.' I go on: 'Children often show that they know and even have sense memories of their siblings. Maybe you will find a way to tell this story; that way you can honor your wish to not forget his sister.' Suddenly the young nurse speaks up. 'When I was a little girl, my mother was pregnant with twin boys. One of the babies died before birth. When my brother, the surviving twin, was four, he started talking about wanting to be a twin and then started insisting he was a twin. My mother told me the history but told me to keep this secret until my little brother was older. It was so hard for me; I think it was hard for my mother too.' Mrs X is silent. She slowly says, 'Maybe I will find some way to tell him. I will think about what you have said.'

I feel tremendous relief, as I have often left our conversations feeling deadened by all that I felt I couldn't say, confused by a fullness so pregnant with emptiness. As I do so often, I consider what I risk in speaking up, what I lose in staying silent. We (the authors) are always asking each other if we are containing knowledge too traumatic to be spoken about or colluding with dissociative processes around guilt or shame.

I reply, 'You are worried about giving him too much to digest, but I'm also wondering if we can think about your secrets as your effort to keep things tucked away and emotionally out of reach, and also, as your way of holding your memories, and your grief, close.' As I speak, I recognize I am also speaking to the nurse, wanting to reassure her that her playful gesture with the baby doll did not further traumatize Mrs X, but instead opened up a space within which it was now possible to begin to reflect and remember and even to anticipate the future.

Bringing a more relationship-based and contextual appreciation to an acute, intense and intensive, high-risk medical setting is an uphill struggle. The environment is structured towards keeping relationships, communication and experience fragmented and dispersed.[2,5,6] This NICU is in a large urban teaching hospital, serving a wide metropolitan area and diverse population. At any one time, there are between 65 and 80 acutely ill babies. The staff is large (more than 200 nurses, 15 attending neonatologists, fellows, residents, nurse practitioners and subspecialists of every kind) and work schedules are highly staggered, making it exceedingly difficult to keep track of a shifting cast of characters. Neonatologists are on service for three weeks and may not return for several months. Nurses typically work 13 shifts of 12 hours each every month, and they may or may not return to taking care of the same baby after their days off. Relationships begin to be built, but the inevitable comings and goings – of staff, of parents, of babies – feel like a series of losses. Parents witness others' babies turn blue, 'crash,' even die; they may say goodnight to a family whose baby is in the next isolette and return the next day to find that baby not there. Or parents see others rejoice in going home after a baby has an extended complicated hospitalization. They valiantly hold back their envy. 'When will it be our turn?'

Many premature babies live on the unit for months; others move through more quickly. Most survive and even thrive; some will die shortly after birth, others quite unexpectedly after lengthy stays. About 60 babies die each year. Babies typically progress in a two-steps-forward, one-step-back fashion. Parents may need to wait weeks or even months to first touch and then hold their babies for the first time. They are continually told that the future is uncertain, that much is unknown and will only be revealed over time. Parents ride a rollercoaster of anxiety which leaves them vulnerable and reactive. Tensions can erupt suddenly between staff members and families. When there is an ongoing relationship between the doctors, nurses, and parents, these tensions are better managed.

One of the most troubling outcomes of the lack of continuity is that it is hard to hold the parents in mind. This is complicated by the parents who tend to stay away, not only for practical real-life reasons but also because of hopelessness or fear. We are deeply concerned about these absent parents. We know that parents who are actively engaged from early on with their babies may develop stronger beliefs about their role as parents.[7] We regularly query the staff: are parents coming? Asking questions? Holding their babies? Are they learning to feed their infant? When we first began our consulting work, it was almost unbearable to see babies lying alone in their isolettes. Now, we see how easily the mother's absence slips from mind. To notice that the mother isn't there *is* to notice that there is a baby without a mother. It is so easy to keep this shadowed and out of awareness.

> Ellen, a NICU nurse for more than 20 years, is efficient, assured, and cool-headed in response to crisis. She has her own five children and many grandchildren, and relishes the connections with her large and engrossing family network. Yet she was outspokenly against new policies giving parents 24/7 access to the unit. Ellen and others who have known neonatology from the days when parents were allowed to visit their babies only at very restricted times believe that parents will burden staff members' already tense assignment, and that parents' anxiety, sadness, and grief will 'get in the way.' 'We can't do our jobs as well if they hover around, asking questions and watching us like hawks. We're the professionals. When you bring your car to the garage you leave it with the mechanic, you don't watch them fix it.'

For the past two days, Ellen has been caring for a tiny preemie who frequently 'desats' (his oxygen levels dangerously plummet) and needs to be 'bagged' (receive oxygen pumped into the lungs through a tube). Last week, Mom was touching him when he desatted; the nurse needed to rush to help. Mom has not been in the NICU since. When I ask, Ellen dismissively says, 'Maybe she's home with the other kids.' I think aloud about how Mom had been coming regularly and that Grandmother lived next door and was a great help. Could it be, I wonder, that Mom reacted to her baby turning blue while she was touching him? Ellen shrugs, all the while skillfully adjusting wires and lines connecting the baby to life-sustaining equipment. We then talk about another baby Ellen had worked with for many months whose mother was in the NICU all day, every day. I ask if it is different for her to have a mom at the bedside. Again she shrugs, but then she starts to tell me about her youngest brother, now a grown man. As a child, he was hospitalized for a significant time for undiagnosed fevers and her mom was not able to visit, as there were so many other children. When her brother finally came home, he sat huddled on his bed and wouldn't talk for what she remembers as days and days. 'I wonder if it was because no one was with him in the hospital? You know, my mother always tears up when she tells this story.'

Every nurse and doctor has a story. When we provide space for their stories, we believe it helps them gain an increased receptivity to the parents and their experience.

The NICU is a deeply shadowed place – death and damage stalk the halls and traumatic anxieties are re-evoked each day the parent steps back onto the unit and approaches his baby's bedside. Just showing up day after day is an act of faith and endurance as so many have already suffered reproductive and perinatal losses. And now their baby is one of many fragile babies born as early as 23 weeks gestation, possibly weighing less than 1 pound, or one of the babies born with severe congenital anomalies or cardiac defects that require immediate life-saving surgeries, or a baby born with fatal chromosomal defects. The neurodevelopmental future for even those who will survive is precariously uncertain. The unexpected has occurred in the most shocking of ways and, like any victim of traumatic experiences, parents are highly anxious, sometimes hypervigilant, sometimes deeply avoidant.

In the wake of dashed dreams, parents carry enormous shame and guilt. Often they try to cope by insistently questioning and second-guessing, by never leaving the bedside or by hiding out at home. Staff may bristle and feel distrusted by such questioning and vigilance, or become impatient that the 'mother can't get her act together to get here more often.' One set of behaviors may have many roots, we suggest. We try to sow seeds of curiosity. 'Maybe she is depressed, or struggling to feel she has anything good to offer,' we propose, or 'maybe we can think of the mother's vigilance as part of normal "primary maternal preoccupation"[8]; what may look like hovering is a loving "watching over," marker of attachment, perhaps.'[9] The forces ranged against such thinking require that we be persistent. Holding all this in mind is to hold close the mother and her traumatized state of mind, which can be so painful. We know full well how easy it is to move away from this pain.

> It is to be a full afternoon including meeting a visiting group of clinical psych PhD students. Before they arrive, I circle the unit and see that baby B is not there. I ask the nurse. 'Oh, he died suddenly last night, about 2 am. Mom got there just in time and she was able to hold him.' I think of Mrs B, a simple and graceful young woman with a chronic illness that made another pregnancy dangerous. This baby, now dead, was longed for, risked for. Over the weeks, as Mrs B stood vigil by her baby's bedside, she made friends with a group of other mothers and they supported one another. I look quickly around for these other moms but don't see them, and I have to meet the students. Afterwards, I hurry to the parent support group that I facilitate. The group demands my total attention. We end after about 75 minutes and as I begin to walk down the hall, three crying, agitated women approach me. 'Why didn't you tell us?' I remember what, moments before, in the press of current needs, I literally 'forgot.' And I am swamped with feeling: sadness, guilt, concern, and alarm that I had not kept in mind what I had so deeply felt.

As psychoanalysts, we can make theoretical sense of the press of dissociative forces (the 'forgetting' of traumatic experience) in the face of unbearable psychic realities. Still, the vulnerability to a 'miscarriage of thought' – the loss of one's thinking self – is disconcerting.[10] There are so many blind angles, densities, gaps, shifts, and absences of all kinds. There is also everyday familiar chitchat. 'How was your vacation?' 'Hmm, is that the Zappos website?' 'Great haircut.' Photos of a wedding are shared just steps away from an isolette where a baby is being reintubated. Life and death exist in a single moment and we can find ourselves subject to these incongruities, unexpected disruptions, and memory lapses. We try to use our own experience as we encourage the staff members' reflective capacities by serving as memory keepers and linkers and trackers of experience. Over and over again, we will say (aware that we are also speaking to ourselves): 'Remember this is a mom who ... a couple who suffered through ... try to remember this when we speak of this or that, when we react to this or that ...'

> In the weekly psychosocial rounds, the attending neonatologist, responsible for the care of severely ill baby P, a surviving twin born at 24 weeks and hospitalized now for 7 months, expressed her concern that the mother didn't know how sick her baby was. 'No one on the staff believes Mom knows what's going on,'

she worried. 'The nurses are at their wits' end with her. She goes from doctor to doctor, trying to solicit different messages of hope. Doesn't she understand her baby will probably die?'

We suggest, 'Perhaps it will help if we keep Mrs S's story in mind – the five failed IVF attempts, the death of the twin *in utero*, which precipitated P's premature birth. Remember too that Mrs S's father and grandparents have only recently died. She needs to resist knowing the tenuousness of P's situation. Denial, magical thinking, a concrete rooting in the present are her means of survival. She is confused and grief stricken, traumatized by the ways in which P is a constant reminder of his dead twin. She walks the hallways, grabbing other mothers and nurses, speaking to anyone who will listen about the "other seven frozen embryos." She holds on to this omnipotent promise. I don't think she has digested any of her losses ... we might say she is in a mindless place which leaves you and the rest of the staff carrying daily all the burden and grief of mindfulness and knowing.'

Families, of course, want answers, want certainty, want to know what will be, and at the same time, they don't want to know. These tensions are only complicated by the ways in which doctors sometimes respond to the anxious continual question of a parent: 'How's my baby doing?'

Dr C, a soft-spoken and thoughtful neonatologist, reports on a baby at a weekly interdisciplinary meeting of staff. He enumerates the multiple problems the baby is burdened with: 28 weeks gestation, respiratory distress, possible limited vision, and grade 3 brain bleed. He ends by saying, 'He's fine' and moves on to the next baby in his charge. We stop him: 'Can we go back to that first baby for a moment? With all the problems you listed, what does it mean to be "fine"?' Dr C looks up and says with earnest puzzlement, 'I don't know. I guess I mean that there's nothing acute right now.' This small moment led to a good discussion of what this may mean to parents, especially those who are numbing themselves with illusion or false hope, only to be stunned when they are then reminded at discharge of all the serious chronic problems that their baby is facing.[11,12]

We find that we need to repeatedly remind doctors and nurses about what happens when information is filtered through grief, despair, and hope. For parents in a traumatized state, information may be impossible to grasp, meanings slip, and knowledge is ephemeral. Today, at this very moment, the focus is on the decreased need for oxygen support (good news); not, for now at least, on the profound anxiety about the intracranial bleed that could have serious neurological consequences, or even the lingering worry about the prolonged high oxygen levels over the last weeks or months, and what that might portend for the neurodevelopmental future (bad news). What is said and what is heard, what is heard and what is understood need to be checked and rechecked.

Hopes, illusions, and stark realities shimmer in shadowy space and time while knowing and not knowing inevitably edge each other for attention. What are the borders, we regularly ask, between real optimism and denial? How do we help staff weather the intense interpersonal and intrapsychic demands? We move in and out of past, present, and future, looping around space and time, engaging staff at all levels, parents, grandparents, and best friends, individually, in groups, as couples. Indeed, the unit is architecturally designed as a large loop, and we circle it many times an afternoon. The work is recursive, involving a process repeated again and again – moving forward, stepping aside, keeping our eye and ear on an issue, entering in and knitting the issues into the larger framework of the unit and each family's life. It demands activity and assertion and an emotional presence, which we achieve with varying degrees of satisfaction.

At interdisciplinary rounds, the attending is concerned about Mr and Mrs L. 'They are telling the staff what to do and calling specialists on their own. They can't micro-manage the medical care of R.' We have heard these concerns before about other families. R, born full term and at first doing quite well, has now been in two different hospitals for a total of 7 months. He has been on and off life-saving equipment, near death more than once.

I met Mr and Mrs L by the bedside. While reviewing the rollercoaster they have been on, I realized how collapsed time has been for them, each event threatening to bring them directly back to the worst traumatic moments. I describe the telescoping of thought that happens when people have been traumatized previously by something similar, and remark that they have seen R so close to death – what could be more traumatic? This telescoping can be adaptive, alerting one to oncoming danger, but it can also preclude seeing distinctions. R's parents ask questions, expanding the conversation to include the mom's mother's death just months before R was born. They want to know how they can let the changing staff know what they know about R, his likes and preferences. I give them suggestions about how they can pass on these vital observations without sounding challenging, and we also talk about letting new staff know the snapshot of their experience. 'They may not be holding that in mind,' I say. 'They know what the plan of care is for today, but not what you have emotionally absorbed over these many months. Putting your comments in context will make a difference,' I assure them.

After meeting with the parents, one of their regular nurses asks to speak with me. I suggest we find a private space. Barbara says she wants 'off the case.' I ask her what happened recently to tip her like this. 'Dad somehow knows that I'm upset, and he asked if we could speak to clear the air. I don't want to do this.' 'Have you always found him difficult?' I inquire. 'No, the funny thing is I really love R – he's such an interactive, alert baby, and I like Dad. I imagine what I'd be like if R were my child and I'd be just as questioning and anxious.' 'Hmm. It is interesting that you like them so much and empathize with them. Can you find a way to let him know that he needs to back off at times, that his scrutiny can be too difficult?' 'I generally don't have a problem saying something to parents. I can be gently assertive, but I don't know why I can't do this with them.' 'Barbara, you know when I feel confused like that I try to think about what this person or situation reminds me of – what else might be on my mind.' Barbara looks up at me with wide eyes. 'I think R will die. He's like four of my last cases, and they died. I fear he's on a downhill course and I don't want to be there when that happens, and Dad saw my face today. I don't want to have a conversation with him.'

We talk about the impact of these deaths, the feelings about the grieving parents ('I don't know why they thank me when they go home with no baby'), what is provided for relatively new nurses to help them cope. So, I wonder, 'It sounds like the dad's micro-management is difficult, but the harder issue is the management of your own feelings of loss, helplessness, and ineffectiveness.' Barbara nods in agreement. I then ask how she would feel if she removed herself from the case. She says that she would feel terrible. 'I'd sneak around trying to avoid the parents.' I ask if she might find it helpful to talk regularly, to see if she could find a new way of handling her deep and caring feelings so that she can continue to be of value to the family. She likes that idea, and we exchange contact information.

Later, I write a short follow-up to the attending, who says that he met with the parents after I did and that it went well. They told him about the previous times their baby decompensated, and he responded by saying that he thought R 'would be a survivor.' He also says that he will try to support Barbara whenever she is working. I also 'loop in' one of the charge nurses who is interested to learn that the common accusation of 'parents managing' may, at times, be a way for nurses and doctors to move away from their own hopelessness, helplessness, and frustration.

Parents in the NICU suddenly find themselves in an anchorless world with hopes dashed, futures seemingly shattered, shame and guilt rampant. Staff, often unaware of the contagious impact of intense emotions, must cope with traumatized states of numbness, shock, confusion, anger and utter and complete devastated sadness. Each reacting to the other, everyone can suffer extreme emotional dysregulation. As consulting psychologists, we track and link experiences and feelings; we translate behaviors and thoughts, gently posing alternatives, hoping to spark curiosity and a more resonant narrative. This requires steady resolve. The undertow of detachment, a defense against what can often feel intolerable, is seductive indeed. As we witness the beginnings of life *in extremis*, we seek out and engage those moments that might expand tolerance for reflective space, always aware that to hold the baby in mind necessitates holding the parents as well. Or as a dad recently implored, 'Don't you get it? My baby and me – we're a package deal.'

Acknowledgments

A previous version of this chapter appeared as Cultivating a culture of awareness: nurturing reflective practices in the NICU. *Zero to Three*. 2010; **31**(2). It is reprinted here with permission of the copyright holders.

We would like to express our appreciation to the Psychoanalytic Society of the Postdoctoral Program in Psychotherapy and Psychoanalysis for awarding us a Scholar's Grant and to the Covington Foundation for generously providing the initial funding for this project

REFERENCES

1   Winnicott DW. The theory of the parent–infant relationship. In: *The Maturational Processes and the Facilitating Environment*. London: Hogarth Press/Institute of Psycho-Analysis; 1965. pp.37–55.

2   Kraemer S. So the cradle won't fall: holding the staff who hold the parents in the NICU. *Psychoanal Dialogues*. 2006; **16**(2): 149–64.

3   Cohen M. *Sent Before My time*. London: Karnac; 2003.

4   Gilkerson A. Reflective supervision in infant-family programs: adding clinical process to non-clinical settings. *Inf Mental Hlth J*. 2004; **25**(5): 424–39.

5   Kraemer S, Steinberg Z. It's rarely cold in the NICU: the permeability of psychic space. *Psychoanal Dialogues*. 2006; **16**(2):165–79.

6   Menzies IEP. The functions of social systems as a defence against anxiety: a report on a study of the nursing service of a general hospital. *Hum Relat*. 1960; **13**: 95–121.

7   Melnyk BM, Feinstein NF, Alpert-Gillis L, *et al*. Reducing premature infants' length of stay and improving parents' mental health outcomes with the Creating Opportunities for Parent Empowerment (COPE) neonatal intensive care unit program: a randomized, controlled trial. *Pediatrics*. 2006; **118**(5): e1414–27.

8   Winnicott DW. Primary maternal preoccupation. In: *Collected Papers: through paediatrics to psychoanalysis*. New York: Basic Books; 1975. pp.300–5.

9   Steinberg Z. (2004) Remembering Pandora: families and staff surviving and thriving in the NICU. Keynote address delivered at Morgan-Stanley Children's Hospital, New York-Presbyterian NICU staff retreat, Harriman, NY.

10 Kraemer S. Haunting preoccupations: remembering and forgetting in a NICU. Presented at the IARPP Conference, June 2009, Tel Aviv, Israel.

11 Groopman J. *The Anatomy of Hope: how people prevail in the face of illness*. New York: Random House; 2004.

12 Steinberg Z. Pandora meets the NICU parent, or whither hope? *Psychoanal Dialogues*. 2006; **16**(2): 133–47.

CHAPTER 19

When the Patient is Gay: Psychodynamic Reflections on Navigating the Medical System

Shara Sand

Awareness of conscious and unconscious psychological processes and the ways in which they influence behavior can make the difference between alienation and collaborative partnership between patient and medical clinician. A psychodynamic examination of the subtle and not so subtle aspects of interpersonal interactions involving gay, lesbian, bisexual, transgender or queer (GLBTQ) persons can be informative and useful for all participants in the medical encounter. Further, navigating the health care system while facing the death of a same-sex partner poses its own challenges. When working with GLBTQ individuals and families, two important questions should be kept in mind. Are the caregivers and families of GLBTQ households fundamentally different from their heterosexual counterparts? What issues exist for GLBTQ families beyond the more commonly known stressors for caregivers of terminally ill loved ones? Understanding the dynamics that confront GLBTQ people can help to identify issues that may need to be addressed in order to provide the best possible care to GLBTQ patients.

GAY, LESBIAN, BISEXUAL, TRANSGENDER OR QUEER IDENTITY, HEALTH CARE AND MICROAGGRESSIONS

The AIDS crisis that began in 1981 created a greater awareness of the presence of gay men as patients and caregivers in doctors' offices and hospitals, as many started dying of rare and incurable diseases. In a less dramatic way, the increase in breast cancer rates and the identification of childlessness as a risk factor in developing breast cancer has resulted in greater awareness of the disease in the lesbian community and an increase in the utilization of services related to breast health. The greater availability of hormonal treatments has brought increased numbers of transgender patients into endocrinologists' offices. Nevertheless, this population remains reluctant to address issues of genital and reproductive health with their doctors. Additionally, and contrary to the popular belief that GLBTQ people are all childless, studies report that 22–44% of GLBTQ couples are parents.[1] The number of children growing up in GLBTQ-headed households will continue to increase as alternative means of creating families grow and become available.

Unfortunately, health care professionals and their staff have had to rely on on-the-job training to learn about the unique issues that can arise when working with GLBTQ populations. There is a paucity of information available to those working with sexual minority populations in health care settings, and it is hoped that this chapter can add to the growing body of literature on this subject.

Obvious and overt acts of prejudice and discrimination still occur but as greater numbers of minority groups have voiced concern and protest regarding such treatment, a more subtle and insidious type of bias has developed, in the form of microaggressions. Sue and Capodilupo[2] state that sexual minorities must confront subtle and not so subtle defamation related to sexual orientation, which can be termed sexual orientation microaggressions. Microaggressions can be conscious but most are unconscious articulations by those who consider themselves to be accepting and egalitarian in their attitudes regarding GLBTQ people. They can take the form of obliviousness to the indirect insults that are often unknowingly lobbed, which serve to perpetuate sexual stigmas. Common examples reflect the use of heterosexist language, the assumption of universality in the GLBTQ experience and verbal devaluations.[3] The result can be that GLBTQ people feel uncomfortable around those whose language is peppered with microaggressions, which can result in feeling demeaned and rejected.

The following examples are taken from accounts related by both patients and colleagues. The oncologist discussing a stage 4 cancer diagnosis and caretaking issues who asks the middle-aged gay or lesbian couple who self-identify as domestic partners, 'So do you boys/girls live together?' The use of 'boys and girls' is both distancing and demeaning, and the question is not likely to be asked of a heterosexual couple who indicate they are married. Similarly, the physician who says to a gay male couple, 'I'm assuming your relationship is non-monogamous, at least that's what I hear on TV' and in the belief that this is a way of expressing openness and acceptance. Or the gynecologist who tells a lesbian with endometrial cancer, 'I'll just do a hysterectomy; it's clear you're not using your uterus for anything.' Such comments are made with little awareness of how they sting, offend and assault the dignity of the GLBTQ person's identity. While intending to convey acceptance, they are actually unconscious projections reflecting unresolved negative feelings surrounding minority sexual and gender orientations.

On a systemic level, it is standard practice in our health care system to give non-menopausal women a pregnancy test when they seek emergency room (ER) services; this includes lesbians. No amount of protestation that there has been no heterosexual activity can dissuade ER personnel from insisting on a urine sample. I have heard many lesbian patients describe this scenario, and have been subject to it myself on several occasions. Refusals to comply have been met with such statements as, 'What's the big deal?' 'Why should you care?' 'If you say you're not pregnant, why are you so afraid?' There is no awareness that these questions and the test itself reflect a denial of a lesbian's identity as well as a presumption of heterosexuality. It is a practice that is infantilizing, insulting and far from cost-effective. Similarly, hospital visiting policies privilege 'immediate family', which ignores the fact that the majority of gays and lesbians still cannot get married, though they view their partners as immediate family. The result is that GLBTQ patients and their caregivers' needs are potentially less likely to be met as a result of unconscious subtle disparagements that can result in mistrust.[3] In these cases medical personnel are simply following hospital rules, which is why such issues need to be addressed at a systemic level. Hospital policies and medical protocols must first recognize and then address differences in sexual orientation procedural manuals. This is similar to the need for medical research to address gender differences in disease processes and treatments. Until that occurs, the recognition by staff that 'business as usual' sometimes does not apply to GLBTQ people would reflect an empathic response that would likely facilitate trust, co-operation and compliance.

DEATH AND DYING

The process of dying is perhaps the most difficult task of living. It is a time of great emotional stress, one in which some of the most primitive fears and anxieties are generated. For those who are terminally ill, there is the desire to live life to the end in the way they choose. Maintaining some degree of control over one's circumstances is often the most vital concern among those facing death.[4-7] Coping with dying often revolves around several recurrent themes. Loss of control, loss of body integrity, helplessness and dependency are all prominent when working with the terminally ill. These are universal issues that appear in all analytic work; however, they are often the primary focus in working with the dying patient. The leading causes of death in the US are heart disease, cancer, and stroke. Rates vary by race, ethnicity and culture, with GLBTQ people cutting across these categories.

Like all people, GLBTQ get sick and die each year. They die suddenly or slowly, old or young, just like their heterosexual counterparts. And just like their heterosexual peers, they access the medical and mental health systems through both private and public insurance systems. Generally, more than 80% of deaths occur with at least several weeks warning,[4] which means that caregivers, patients and health care professionals have a significant amount of time in which they interact in a triadic constellation, navigating the rocky terrain of dying. Understanding the dying process from a psychoanalytic perspective will lay the foundation for exploring issues of sexual orientation that can become more prominent in end-of-life contexts.

The patient's medical condition, regardless of sexual or gender identities, becomes a powerful emotional factor, an unwanted intruder. Often days and weeks are spent undergoing tests to determine the cause of symptoms, which are often uncomfortable, debilitating and life threatening. The patient must often struggle with daily pain, discomfort and a decreasing ability to care for themselves. There is often a need to adapt to a chronic and unstable medical condition, which is an arduous process involving the integration of cognitive and affective states.[8] Friends, family and even medical staff can be reluctant to acknowledge the patient's terminal condition and may discourage the patient from talking about their experience and feelings about dying. However, providing an opportunity to talk about dying may allow for the resolution and consolidation of life's unfinished business, which can lessen anxiety and increase feelings of control. All of this takes place in the context of the person's character style and defensive structure, along with their reactions to the disease process, and interactions with family, friends, and hospital staff. Now into this complicated stew of illness, fear of death, unresolved conflicts and complex relational issues, add sexual orientation. There is no evidence to suggest that GLBTQ people will respond any differently to illness and dying. The fundamental difference occurs when considering sexual identity and gender identity, along with the impact that racial, ethnic and religious identity issues have on the assumptions of self that are made by others.

LOVING AND HATING: DOES SEXUAL ORIENTATION MATTER?

Both clinician and caregiver need to be aware of potential secrets surrounding sexuality, tensions and hostility regarding sexual orientation between the GLBTQ family and the family of origin, and discomfort or bias among hospital staff. The answers to several important questions can be helpful in guiding the work with GLBTQ patients. As health care provider, are you aware of your patient's sexual orientation? Do you know whether they are 'out' in their personal life and/or in their professional life? Are you aware of issues specific to GLBTQ patients and the ways in which sexual minority status can affect physical and mental health? GLBTQ people must live in a society frequently hostile to their existence, one replete with laws that prevent them achieving full equality with their heterosexual peers. There is a lack of recognition of the legitimacy of GLBTQ relationships and stigma has been shown to negatively affect physical and emotional health.[9,10] Many states will not permit gays and lesbians to become foster parents or to adopt children, or permit second parent adoptions for the partner of a biological parent. There can also be a lack of familial and religious support that can leave the GLBTQ person feeling alone and isolated while attempting to navigate a stigmatized identity.

These experiences make it important to understand the mechanisms of hatred and disgust that are often incorporated into the GLBTQ person's identity. Additionally, understanding the conscious choices involved in coming out and being out as a GLBTQ person is best described in this way: coming out is a decision to articulate one's identity and being out is living that identity in a genuine way.[11] Identity disclosure takes place on a variety of levels: to oneself, friends, family, co-workers, and the broader public. It is not a one-time-only occurrence, nor a singular process. It is a series of life-long actions that help to maintain the integrity of the self.

A study examining factors that would best prepare therapists for working with GLBTQ patients found that being open-minded and open to diversity, as well as being aware of one's own comfort level with homosexuality, were factors that sexual minority patients considered most important. Additionally, it was found that fear of homophobic treatment was the most common concern and, unsurprisingly, a desire for the therapist to recognize that homosexuality was not a 'lifestyle choice.' There is no reason to believe that these results would not apply to physicians and other health care professionals.[3] It is important to understand that being out involves a relational process in which there is enormous potential for the loss of interpersonal connections and relationships with important people in the individual's world. The revelation of an unacceptable identity can lead to painful experiences of regret and profound feelings of humiliation, shame, and disappointment. It can also lead to rejection and relational losses, both fantasized and real. For some, these losses may precipitate a need to grieve the loss of the heterosexual self and the schema that had previously organized their lives, including their dreams for the future. Confronting such feelings can often lead to further feelings of loss, shame, and unworthiness, resulting in a devalued sense of self.[12]

The patient who is confronting terminal illness with a reprehensible self-identity will likely experience greater distress and alienation from those who are responsible for their care. The potential for the patient to project their self-loathing onto medical personnel may result in the staff disliking the patient, which can then potentially be interpreted by the patient as a homophobic response. It is important to understand that these projections represent the anxiety that surges when being hated is feared. Those who are hated for their sexual orientation are seen as repellant, inferior, and perverted, deserving of any shameful feelings that result from their same-sex desire. When an identity is inherently defined as existing outside normative standards, then others see those who embrace that identity as guilty of having violated these standards; thus GLBTQ people become a repository for the projection of others' hated selves, in this instance, disavowed homoerotic feelings. The degree of hatred and disavowal projected is dependent on many sociocultural factors. Homosexuality has existed at all times in both history and place. It is behavior that has been understood differently depending on the society and on that society's cultural expectations. Some societies do not label homosexuality as something negative, an illness or a problematic deviation from the norm, while others impose harsh penalties for homosexual behavior.[13]

It is extremely important to keep in mind that GLBTQ culture has often been defined by white, middle-class standards, which are clearly not the norms for all races, ethnicities, and cultures. African-American, Latino and Asian cultures often have more insulated family systems, which can be more highly valued by GLBTQ people, resulting in lesser degrees of openness regarding matters of sexual orientation. These are also communities that may place higher values on religious affiliations, which also can determine how out or in the closet sexual minorities may be.[14] It is always important to be mindful of these issues and not assume that white values and attitudes will apply to all GLBTQ people. There are many ways in which microaggressions are expressed towards ethnic and racial minority cultures as well as sexual orientation minorities. Being aware of double and triple minority status and the attendant stressors that can affect physical and mental health is important for all health care professionals. The self develops in relation to others and the projection of hatred can become internalized, containing both hatred and fear of the self as a reviled being. It is in this way that disgust also becomes incorporated into self-identity. It is a powerful affective component of hatred and reflects offended sensibilities and values. Multiple minority status frequently results in multiple stressors and types of oppression.

Many GLBTQ people anecdotally report that the manner and tone, as well as the physical touch of physicians, changed after the revelation of sexual or gender minority status. They report that their doctors no longer smile; their language becomes more formal and their sentences staccato and clipped. They feel roughly handled, especially by same-sex practitioners, and can feel the physician's fear that their touch will be sexually interpreted. Thus, the projective process of hatred unfolds. A lack of empathy for behavior that feels personally repulsive and unthinkable results in an internal process whereby the feelings of disgust get projected onto the GLBTQ person in the form of: 'You are a disgusting, revolting person.' This mindset is what Kevin Cathcart, a prominent gay rights lawyer, refers to as the 'ick factor.'[15] It is in this way that the GLBTQ person becomes the hated other, targeted as a perpetrator of unspeakable acts. The mirror held up to many GLBTQ people does not reflect acceptance; thus the need to anticipate and confront disparaging comments and potentially shameful feelings in the most mundane or intimate situations, including at the doctor's office. Hatred may not be so obvious and pronounced, but it can occur in much subtler conscious and unconscious ways.

DANIEL AND MIKE

I met Daniel when he was in crisis. He was uncertain whether or not he should end his relationship with his boyfriend, Mike, his very first with a man. Daniel was a 39-year-old, buttoned-up and completely closeted accountant whose neat-as-a-pin, starched shirts matched his precise and careful manner of moving through the world. He was the most closeted person I had met in my many years of practicing in New York City. No one knew about his sexual orientation, not even his younger brother, whom he suspected was also gay. Daniel worked for a conservative banking organization and publicly dated women. He was a practicing Catholic and while he didn't disapprove of sex prior to marriage, he used this as the reason for avoiding sexual activity in his heterosexual relationships, which all ended after a short period of time.

Daniel was 37 when he began his first relationship with an older man whom he met shortly after being transferred to London. Mike, 20 years older, was equally as closeted and religious; the two enjoyed biking, dining, and going to church together. Daniel had recently returned to New York and the plan was for Mike to join him. He was concerned about Mike's fidelity, and uncertain whether he wanted to remain in the relationship. He also came to me because there was no other place in his life he could be gay. Daniel uttered the words 'I am gay' for the first time in my office. Shortly after we began working together, Mike was diagnosed with amyotrophic lateral sclerosis (ALS) and Daniel, instead of ending the relationship, became Mike's primary caretaker. He arranged for Mike to come to New York, moved out of his bedroom and into a two-bedroom apartment, anticipating the inevitability of Mike's need of 24-hour care, and quit his job.

Daniel and Mike suffered many indignities as they entered a world inhabited by incurable disease. When speaking with a neurologist regarding an experimental treatment, they were asked repeatedly why Mike's children, residing in Dallas, weren't more involved with his care. My patient reported that his partner had not revealed his sexual identity to his adult children, and this physician laughed and said, 'That's ridiculous, he's their father, what is there to be afraid of?' This same doctor later said, 'I'm reluctant to try this treatment without his family's knowledge,' ignoring the fact that Daniel was also his partner's family, serving as his health care proxy, power of attorney and estate executor. It is possible that this physician was concerned about the potential litigation that families of origin often resort to when a GLBTQ partner has legal rights that the family feels should be theirs. Additionally, it can sometimes be difficult for health care professionals to conceive that a patient would want to keep family members at arm's length about such matters instead of reaching out for care and support. These types of situations often call for sensitivity and inquiry. What is the basis of the patient's anxiety regarding the revelation of their sexual orientation? Is there a way in which the physician could be helpful in facilitating a patient's disclosure? Rather than dismissing concerns, an inquiry could provide details that lead to a greater understanding of the complexity of the family dynamics at work. When encountering a resistant physician, the caregiver should be prepared to provide some education about the risks of coming out and the wish to proceed in a way that will provide the best care and comfort for the patient.

These examples illustrate the need to be aware of why and when patients may be open regarding their orientation to their families of origin, or not. Accepting and inquiring as to why and how a patient moves through the world when it concerns their orientation is important. There is no one right way to be, and being out to everyone is not necessarily the best strategy for everyone. Respecting patient decisions is important and working with what feels safe and comfortable is what will facilitate the best doctor–patient relationship and the most optimal level of care. These types of responses did not encourage their reluctant emergence from the closet. Daniel felt he continually had to convince doctors and nurses that he was the primary caretaker, and he reported that many health care professionals involved in Mike's care interacted with him as though he was Mike's son, not partner.

Daniel left treatment with me after three years, when Mike became almost completely paralyzed and bedbound. He had decided Mike should be near his family as he began actively dying and was busy preparing for their move to Texas. Throughout this time, Daniel went along with Mike's wish to remain closeted to his children and sister, so continued to act the role of good friend. I did not hear from Daniel for a while, though one day, about nine months later, I happened to look at the obituaries. I recognized Mike's name; I also recognized Daniel's younger brother's name. They had each died within a day of each other, Mike from ALS and Johnny from advanced diabetes. I felt myself inhale sharply and I felt for Daniel, imagining him stoically mourning, depressed and alone in his isolated world. I got a call from Daniel shortly after the first anniversary of the deaths of the only two men he had ever loved. We agreed to meet; Daniel wanted to deal with his grief and come to terms with his identity, shedding the uncomfortable closet in which he was living.

CONCLUSION

It behooves clinicians in all specialties to develop an awareness of the dynamics of GLBTQ couples, their children, their families of choice, and their families of origin. GLBTQ patients and their caregivers are all too aware of the frequent need to educate the professionals charged with their care. While it is a step forward that these patients are comfortable with their orientations and open to educating their physicians, many are not, and feel stymied in their ability to communicate effectively. I hear about my patients' encounters with physicians on a regular basis in my practice. In fact, one of the most common complaints raised by my GLBTQ patients is that they have to educate their straight doctors about basic aspects of who they are as people. Many eventually seek out GLBTQ practitioners, with whom the basics are often known, so the focus can be on the specifics of their health needs. In this age of managed care, people want to use their precious allotment of time with their physician discussing their health concerns rather than give a *Basic Issues in Working with a GLBTQ Population* lecture. This is not to say that straight doctors cannot treat GLBTQ people; it means knowing what questions will help a patient to feel like you are trying to understand them and which questions induce a rising tide of stomach acid instead.

It is best never to assume what a person's sexual orientation is. There is no one way that gay men, lesbians, bisexuals or transgender people look, walk or talk. Some may appear in ways that seem more stereotypical, but many don't. On intake or informational forms, be inclusive. In the options for 'marital status,' include choices for 'domestic partner' and 'same-sex spouse.' Regarding gender, include identifiers such as 'transman,' transwoman,' 'transgender' or simply a category for 'other.' This communicates to the potential patient that you are able to recognize that there are sexual and gender minorities, which can facilitate the formation of trust necessary between doctor and patient. If you are uncertain how to refer to a person's sexual orientation or gender identity, rather than fumble while guessing, simply ask the patient what their preferred terminology is for themselves and their partner or spouse. It is also important to make sure your office staff are educated about and comfortable working with GLBTQ patients. I have heard many a person report that they will not go back to a physician because of homophobic comments made by nursing and/ or office staff in spite of having no complaints about the physician or quality of care received.

Physicians can help to insure that their practices are GLBTQ friendly by holding staff trainings and assessing the degree of knowledge and comfort staff have regarding GLBTQ people by asking potential employees a few interview questions regarding their awareness and comfort level with GLBTQ persons.

REFERENCES

1   National Vital Statistics Reports. 2010; **58**(19).
2   Sue DW, Capodilupo CM. Racial, gender and sexual orientation microaggressions: implications for counseling and psychotherapy. In: Sue DW, Capodilupo CM, edi-

tors. *Counseling the Culturally Diverse: theory and* practice, 5th ed. Hoboken, NJ: John Wiley; 2008. pp.105–30.

3   Nadal KL, Rivera DP, Corpus M. Sexual orientation and transgender microaggressions in everyday life: experiences of lesbians, gays, bisexuals, and transgender individuals. In: Sue DW, editor. *Microaggressions and Marginality: manifestation, dynamics, and impact.* New York: John Wiley; 2010. pp.217–40.

4   Schulz R, Schlarb J. Two decades of research on dying: what do we know about the patient? *Omega.* 1987–1988; **18**: 299–317.

5   Oberfield R. Terminal Illness: death and bereavement – toward an understanding of its nature. *Perspect Biol Med.* 1984; **28**: 140–55.

6   Cassem N. The dying patient. In: Hackett T, Cassem N, editors. *Massachusetts General Hospital Handbook of General Psychiatry.* Littleton, MA: PSG Publishing; 1987. pp.332–52.

7   Feldman A. The dying patient. *Psychiatr Clin North Am.* 1987; **10**: 101–8.

8   Groves J, Kucharski A. Brief psychotherapy. In: Hackett T, Cassem N, editors. *Massachusetts General Hospital Handbook of General Psychiatry.* Littleton, MA: PSG Publishing; 1987. pp.309–31.

9   Burn S, Kadlec K, Rexer R. Effects of subtle heterosexism on gays, lesbians and bisexuals. *J Homosexual.* 2005; **49**(2): 23–38.

10 Meyer I. Prejudice, social stress, and mental health in lesbian, gay, and bisexual populations: conceptual issues and research evidence. *Psychol Bull.* 2003; **129**(5): 674–97.

11 Barbone S, Rice L. Coming out, being out, and acts of virtue. *J Homosexual.* 1994; **27**(3/4): 91–110.

12 Kiersky S. Exiled desire: the problem of reality in psychoanalysis and lesbian experience. *Psychoanal Psychother.* 1996; **13**(2): 130–41.

13 Young-Bruehl E. Homophobias: a diagnostic and political manual. In: Moss D, editor. *Hating in the First Person Plural: psychoanalytic essays on racism, homophobia, misogyny, and terror.* New York: Other Press; 2003. pp.145–59.

14 Greene B. Ethnic minority lesbians and gay men: mental health and treatment issues. In: Greene B, editor. *Ethnic and Cultural Diversity Among Lesbians and Gay Men.* Thousand Oaks, CA: Sage; 1997. pp.216–39.

15 Anderson EA. *Out of the Closets and into the Courts: legal opportunity, structure and gay rights litigation.* Ann Arbor, MI: University of Michigan Press; 2004.

CHAPTER 20

The Psychodynamics of Elder Abuse

Tamara McClintock Greenberg

We are at an unprecedented time in the history of aging. Adults are living longer lives than ever before and a large number of these elders will receive care at home or in facilities under their children's management. Feeling aggressively towards one's parents is a normal psychological phenomenon and a normal part of child development. However, if adult children caring for an elder parent have not learned to handle their anger or have not come to terms with their aggressive feelings, this can set the stage for its expression in the form of elder abuse.

Both traditional and contemporary psychoanalytic theories recognize that aggressive feelings are part of normal, healthy development. We all have angry feelings toward our parents. As children, we can feel angry about the ways we have been left out of the closeness of our parents' relationship or that we will never achieve the success our parents have. However, angry feelings toward parents are often more pronounced in the case of child abuse, neglect or unmet emotional needs. The stresses of caring for an elder parent who is ill can simply tip the scales toward a situation in which a child feels compelled to act on unresolved feelings.

Traditional psychoanalytic approaches have tended to privilege fantasy over reality. This approach makes sense in that a lot of us have ideas about engaging in particular behaviors (usually those that are sexual or aggressive), but rarely do so. In fact, if we are in psychodynamic treatment (I use the terms psychoanalytic and psychodynamic synonymously), it is often because we are worried about acting on our feelings. These worries often serve the function of keeping us from acting on our impulses. In other words, anxiety about aggression and sexuality serves to keep us in line. Worry acts like a social conscience. We don't act out aggressively because we don't really want to hurt those we love.

Though many of us might struggle consciously or unconsciously with angry and aggressive feelings toward parents, fantasy and reality can collide when having to care for a parent who is ill. For example, when caring for a parent with dementia, even the most calm and grounded can find themselves in situations in which angry thoughts lead to aggressive actions. For clinicians working with the elderly or the adults caring for them, elder abuse or milder forms of maltreatment are frequent issues that need to be addressed. Given the record numbers of adults over the age of 65, we will all likely be confronted with the need to understand and communicate about the dynamics of elder maltreatment and conflicts elders have with caretakers.

All states have clear statutes regarding when and how to report elder abuse. This chapter will address the more complex issues of what to do and what to say when elder abuse is actively occurring or, more commonly, when it is suspected but not substantiated. Indeed, a number of 'borderline' cases can make us worry that elderly patients are not treated as well as they should be. The majority of my focus will be on adult children taking care of elder parents. Though elder abuse occurs in all caretaking situations, clinically, the most difficult situations are often related to sorting out how to intervene given the intense emotions that occur between elders and children providing care.

DEFINITION AND PREVALENCE OF ELDER ABUSE

Elder abuse can be broadly defined as psychological, physical or sexual abuse, as well as neglect and financial exploitation against an elderly adult, most frequently defined as someone over the age of 65. Abuse can involve acts of omission or commission.[1] In the United States, each state has slightly varying definitions of elder abuse and reporting requirements. Most professionals who come in contact with children are trained in appropriate reporting of suspected child abuse. Those who work with the elderly, however, are often unaware of specific reporting requirements regarding maltreatment in the elderly. For example, although physicians and nurses tend to be dissatisfied with the response of authorities in elder abuse cases, emergency room personnel tended to be unaware of the laws and reporting requirements.[2]

Elder abuse often goes undisclosed. However, it appears to be fairly common, particularly among the elderly with dementia. A fascinating fact about abuse of the elderly is that people who are in positions of caretaking the elderly consistently report having been abusive at a rate that far exceeds what elders themselves report.[3-5] Experts contend that actual rates of abuse are very high and that reported cases represent only a fraction of actual cases.[6]

The consequences of elder abuse are ominous. Research suggests that the consequences of abuse in the elderly can strongly affect mortality. For example, women aged 50–79 years who reported physical abuse or physical abuse combined with verbal abuse had a higher mortality rate than women who reported no abuse.[7] Similarly, in a study of both men and women, abuse was associated with shorter life spans.[8]

Certain elder patients have risk factors that increase the chance of abuse. The weaker they are, the more vulnerable they are to being abused. Older people who are more dependent and frail, more socially isolated or who have severe illness or cognitive impairment are most likely to be abused.[9] Additionally, another recent study found that lower age, lack of social support, unemployment, and history of a previous traumatic event in elders were strongly associated with elder maltreatment.[10]

Depressed mood, anxiety, and resentment about being in a caretaking role were associated with abusive behavior in a United Kingdom study of family members caring for elders with dementia.[11] The following case examples reflect the research findings and illustrate the disquieting nature of the clinical situation.

PSYCHODYNAMIC UNDERSTANDINGS OF ELDER ABUSE

It is not hard to imagine the many ways in which adult children may feel and act aggressively toward parents. Consider the following case example (identifying information has been disguised to protect confidentiality).

I was referred to see Albert at the request of his primary care physician. Albert, 79 years old, was living alone in an assisted living facility. He had moved across the country at the urging of his daughter when Albert's wife was still alive. The couple was reportedly agreeable to the move. However, within three months of the move, Albert's wife of 47 years died from complications of a long-standing medical condition. Albert was referred to see me when he became depressed. His daughter, Sally, who lived in the area, made the arrangements for our initial meeting. Sally held the Power of Attorney for both health care and finances for Albert and so legally, Sally was required to provide the legal consent for psychotherapy. As is common for adult children with elderly parents, Sally was present during the first meeting. During the session, she spent considerable time vetting me before letting Albert speak with me. During the second meeting and throughout the treatment, I met with Albert alone and sporadically with him and his daughter.

Though Albert's personality was quite passive, he told me during the second meeting that he did not like the West Coast city in which he resided. He missed his large home in the Midwest and acknowledged that had he known that his wife would die so soon after they moved, he would never have agreed to leave. He missed his friends and knew almost no one in his new location. Further, he tended to be shy, and had trouble making friends in his long-term care facility. Albert agreed to meet weekly with me and to have these meetings without his daughter present. As I worked with Albert, he told me he was paying for Sally's living expenses. Although there was plenty of money (from the estate of Albert's wife), Albert expressed reservations about committing so much money to Sally, but when I asked him directly if he felt that he was being unduly pressured to support Sally, he often replied by saying, 'I am happy to help Sally. She had a rough childhood and if I can give this back to her, I am happy to do so.' When Albert said this, he made little eye contact with me, a hint that he felt shameful about the way he had treated his daughter. Additionally, though he relatedly told me he fully consented to helping Sally financially, he often commented parenthetically about how much money he was giving her. I never felt convinced that Sally was not exerting pressure on Albert, nor that Albert really felt as generous as he seemed.

In this and a number of other clinical situations, I have suspected that an elder is being abused or financially exploited, only to be told by my elder patient that I am 'making too much out of something' and that 'everything is OK.' In such situations, I have been left to wonder about my motivations in suspecting maltreatment. Is my suspicion of aggression based on some difficulty I feel in treating a patient or a family? However, it eventually becomes clear that I am caught up in a situation in which someone feels guilty. In this situation, Albert seemed to feel quite guilty regarding Sally's childhood. A great deal of our time in therapy was spent discussing Sally and her siblings' childhoods. Albert expressed a lot of regret about not having been home more when his children were young and that when he was home, he paid little attention to them. Since his deceased wife was an alcoholic, Albert worried that his children were not being treated well. But instead of trying to be present more at home, he found himself spending more time at his office and eventually had a long-term affair with a co-worker.

Though Albert experienced a great deal of guilt about his children, Sally, the only child actively involved in Albert's care, expressed no guilt whatsoever about receiving money from her father, even though she was herself in middle age. When I told her that the amount of money her father was providing could be viewed by an outsider as potentially excessive, she reminded me that she had full legal control of her father's finances and that she and her father agreed that she should be compensated for her caretaking efforts.

Due to Albert's insistence over many months that he was aware of the amount of money being given to Sally and that he consented to this arrangement, I did not report this situation to legal authorities.

Equally as important as the decision regarding whether or not to report elder abuse is what we deem to be the paramount dynamics between an elder and the person(s) taking care of them. In other words, the adult children who find themselves caring for an elderly parent often have special characteristics and dynamics. In my experience, especially in situations in which psychological treatment is sought, the child who ends up providing the majority of care for an elderly parent is often the child who felt most left out of both parental and family dynamics and in which there had been parental abuse or neglect. When there are other siblings who are much less involved in parental care, they seem to have been able to 'move on' by creating their own families. Though these other siblings might be involved in parental care, the emotional valence afforded to this care is less pronounced. In other words, they often do what is needed (attend family meetings, make decisions regarding care choices, etc.) but the tone of these activities is often one of the need to complete a task. They do what is needed and then attend to their lives. The children who present for treatment when taking care of an elder parent, however, are those who are deeply worried and conflicted about their role as caretaker. On the one hand, they may feel relieved to be the 'responsible one' caring for an elderly parent, which can feel like a victory when sibling relationships have been rivalrous. However, they may also feel both unduly burdened and overly responsible for the care of a parent. Feelings of resentment can be a surprising and unintended consequence.

For many adults confronting the final years of a parent's life, there can be a great deal of pain. This pain is not only related to the eventual loss of a parent or difficulty bearing the suffering and vulnerability of someone once viewed as so powerful, but the realization that one will not get a chance to redo a difficult childhood. When a child has felt victimized, the presence of a weak parent can cause a resurgence of angry feelings. Consciously or unconsciously, there may be a feeling of wanting to hurt the parent who was once so powerful. Additionally, sadness and grief about the end of a parent's life can be overwhelming. Focusing on anger can serve as a distraction. Indeed, feeling powerful can help us all avoid sadness and loss.

Taking care of a parent in a situation in which an adult child has carried a lot of anger about how they were raised can make compartmentalization of anger and aggressive feelings difficult. When an adult caring for a parent can allow themselves to become aware of both anger and longing, we can not only prevent maltreatment but help these adult children come to terms with what they have missed out on. For example, a woman in her fifties caring for her mother with dementia told me that when she had finished taking her mother to the doctor and was on her way back to the facility her mother lived in, while stopped at a traffic signal, she turned to her mother and said, 'Mom, you realize that I am a better daughter than my sisters, right? Please tell me I was your favorite!' Her mother's dementia was severe and she had little expressive language ability, and so simply stared back at my patient in silence. My patient, mortified by her behavior, understood just how sad she was to have felt so left out by her family in her own childhood, and how angry she felt about taking care of her mother now, knowing that these earlier experiences would never be revisited and replaced.

For adult children who are now in caretaking roles, one of the main aims of therapy is to help the son or daughter become aware of possible conflicting motivations for caring for their parents. Such a goal is often indicated when children present for treatment complaining of a paucity of interpersonal relationships and the belief that caretaking responsibilities are what are keeping the adult child from being successful and happy. Children who put their lives on hold while caring for a parent are often caught up in a futile attempt to change the past. This is a very different situation than when an adult who presents for therapy has meaningful interpersonal relationships, a satisfying career, and is bereaved about a parent's medical or cognitive decline. This latter scenario often involves helping the adult child to grieve and prepare for the death and loss of the parent. Such treatments are much less complicated. Even when these children might refer parents for psychotherapy, it is often in the spirit of 'I want to do whatever I can to help mom or dad cope.' Our role in such situations is more straightforward and elder abuse or maltreatment is often less of a concern.

FAMILIES IN MEDICAL SETTINGS

Medical clinicians are often in the position of needing to decide how to intervene when dealing with families in which elder maltreatment is suspected. Given the nature of medical encounters, contact with elders and family caretakers is brief and relatively less emotional, though signs of stress in caregivers can be quite apparent. Consider the case of Joseph and his mother, Leslie.

Leslie was a woman in her early sixties who was readmitted to the hospital following back surgery due to an infection in her surgery site. Leslie was on disability due to multiple medical problems. Joseph, her son, lived with her and reportedly helped her with shopping, cooking, and taking her to medical appointments. Though Joseph initially claimed he did not mind helping his mother out, staff in the hospital saw it differently. Leslie and Joseph were heard arguing frequently with both mother and son calling each other names. Staff were concerned that Adult Protective Services should be called, as they feared that Leslie was being abused. When I interviewed Leslie and Joseph (both separately and together), their stories were consistent. Leslie admitted to financially supporting Joseph, as he was unemployed. Joseph admitted to resenting his caretaking role and added that he thought his mother was abusing both narcotic pain medications as well as benzodiazepines. It was clear that neither Leslie nor Joseph was happy with their current situation but like a couple in a bad marriage, felt trapped. We quickly came to the conclusion that the two needed a better discharge plan. The social worker got involved and helped Leslie think of who else could care for her once discharged. She agreed to live with a relative in another part of the state. Joseph, seeming freed from what he experienced as a burden, made plans to move to another state.

In dealing with cases of suspected maltreatment, whether or not the issue will be reported to authorities, it is imperative to talk openly with all parties involved about concerns. For example, I will frequently ask caretakers, 'How are you feeling about how your mom is being treated, including how you treat her?' In the best of circumstances, such a question can be an opening for a caretaker to talk about difficulties associated with taking care of a parent. Often children are so caught up in feelings of shame, guilt, and resentment, it genuinely does not occur to them to get emotional support. Frequently, hearing from an authority on how difficult their situation is creates an emotional space so that they can think more clearly about what their options are. Additionally, validating just how difficult it is to take care of a parent who is demented or medically ill relieves the child of the tremendous shame he may carry regarding his anger. Often children in this situation forget that their feelings are normal.

Although psychoanalytic literature on the issue of elder abuse is sparse, one of the best-known articles on the dynamics of aggressive feelings toward parents was written by Hans Loewald.[12] Loewald described that though we are all capable of destructive feelings toward our parents, these feelings are highly conflictual because of competing needs to be close or even merged with them. Therefore, at some point, we are all in a bind: to feel that we are entitled to be separate, successful adults requires comfort in leaving our parents behind. This symbolic eradication is not just about aggression; it is about feeling like we deserve a happy life independent of our parents. To do this, we also have to relinquish and grieve the ways in which we do not feel merged with our parents as when we were very young children. Many of us seem to navigate this tricky and complicated emotional terrain with some success. We can feel bad about the losses in our childhood and feel comfortable having a life separate from our parents. Children like Joseph, however, have trouble getting away. They are caught in both feelings of rage and the desire to feel complete with a parent. They hang on and hope that by being the perfect caretaker, they will both be invited to stay forever and be given permission to leave. Such fantasies cannot ever come true. The reality is that we don't get a second chance at having our parents repair what did not go right in childhood and parents themselves may have given the message, sometimes too often, that they do not want their children to ever grow up. Though therapy can help sort these issues out, sometimes brief interventions, such as what happened with Leslie and Joseph, can be enough. Both parties needed permission to be free of what was rapidly becoming a very destructive and potentially abusive dynamic.

Of course, not all cases end as well as it did for Leslie and Joseph. In such cases, I often recommend to medical staff that they refer both the elder and the adult child to therapy. Ideally, the two should have separate therapists.

Medical clinicians are often the front-line staff when dealing with elders and their child caretakers. Physicians and other medical staff often have superior skills when dealing with complicated family dynamics and can be extraordinarily patient. When it comes to suspected cases of elder abuse, however, physicians and other medical clinicians can feel timid. Timidity, particularly when it is out of character for the medical clinician, can often be a sign that they are trying to avoid some aggressive dynamic. This should be a sign to try to talk separately with the elder and his or her child caretaker and to try to have an honest conversation about how things really are. When children bring a parent to a physician's office, it is often expected that only medical issues will be discussed. Though medical issues are paramount, so are the extra few minutes it might take to ask about the stress affecting a caretaker and the elder. Medical clinicians often want to avoid complicated emotional conversations for a number of reasons. However, given that elder abuse can affect both quality of life and mortality, it is likely better in the long run to intervene early.

WHAT'S AHEAD: ELDERS IN THE NEXT DECADES

Though we can't give children the ideal childhoods they wish for, we can provide the understanding needed to help adult children and parents grieve the loss of a better parenting situation. By acknowledging guilt and anger, we can do our part to protect the elderly and their children who will increasingly become a part of all of our clinical practices. By being prepared to have difficult conversations, we can improve the quality of life of some of those we treat.

REFERENCES

1 Wolf RS. Introduction: the nature and scope of elder abuse. *Generations*. 2000; **24**(2): 6–12.

2 Almogue A, Weiss A, Marcus EL, *et al.* Attitudes and knowledge of medical and nursing staff toward elder abuse. *Arch Gerontol Geriatr*. 2010; **51**: 86–91.

3 Cooper C, Blanchard M, Selwood A, *et al.* Family carers' distress and abusive behavior longitudinal study. *Br J Psychiatry*. 2010; **196**: 480–5.

4 Post L, Page C, Conner T, *et al.* Elder abuse in long-term care: types, patterns, and risk factors. *Res Aging*. 2010; **32**(3): 323–48.

5 Cooper C, Selwood A, Livingston G. The prevalence of elder abuse and neglect: a systematic review. *Age Ageing*. 2008; **37**: 151–60.

6 National Center on Elder Abuse at the American Public Human Services Association in collaboration with Westat I. *The National Elder Abuse Incidence Study: Final Report*. Washington, DC: National Aging Information Center; 1998.

7 Baker MW, La Croix AZ, Wu C, *et al.* Mortality risk associated with physical and verbal abuse in women aged 50–79. *J Am Geriatr Soc*. 2009; **57**: 1799–809.

8 Lachs MS, Williams CS, O'Brien S, *et al.* The mortality of elder mistreatment. *JAMA*. 1998; **280**: 428–32.

9 Pinsker DM, McFarland K, Pachana NA. Exploitation in older adults: social vulnerability and personality factors. *J Appl Geriatr*. 2010; **29**(6): 740–61.

10 Aciemo R, Hernandez MA, Amstadter AB, *et al.* Prevalence and correlates of emotional, physical, sexual, and financial abuse and potential neglect in the United States: the National Elder Mistreatment Study. *Am J Public Health*. 2010; **100**(2): 292–7.

Index